CLARK MCGINN graduated in Philosophy at Glasgow University and then moved to London as a graduate trainee for one of the large clearing banks. Over 25 years later, he has a wide range of City experience having worked in branches and dealing rooms, for British and American institutions, in both commercial banks and investment banks in London and New York. He is currently Senior Director of an asset finance team in a large UK bank.

Professionally and philosophically, he has observed the ups and downs of the financial markets and has heard 'never again' once too often. He has watched greed and fear struggle for mastery of the financial world in a seemingly unbreakable cycle of booms and busts with each turning point coming as an apparent surprise to bankers, politicians, regulators and the public. The financial crisis we face now is only unique in its size, every other factor in its makeup has happened before – several times before – and over centuries.

Without understanding that, there will be no effective financial reform.

Clark lives in Harrow-on-the-Hill with his wife and family and in his spare time, when not commuting to the City, he writes and speaks on financial and Scottish topics. He is a renowned after dinner speaker on Robert Burns and has addressed audiences large and small – bankers and otherwise – all around the world. His *The Ultimate Burns Supper Book* and *The Ultimate Guide to Being Scottish* are also published by Luath.

D1100295

Out of Pocket How Collective Amnesia lost the world its wealth, again

CLARK McGINN

Luath Press Limited

EDINBURGH

www.luath.co.uk

First published 2010

ISBN: 978-1-906307-82-0

The paper used in this book is recyclable. It is made from
low-chlorine pulps produced in a low-energy, low-emissions
manner from renewable forests.

Printed and bound by
CPI Mackays, Chatham ME5 8TD

Typeset in 10.5 point Sabon by
3btype.com

To Ann, my own gold standard.

Greed and the lust for power are dangerous masters.
They breed impatience; for man's life is short
and he needs quick results. They breed jealousy and
disloyalty; for offices and possessions are limited and it is
impossible to satisfy every claimant.

Sir Steven Runciman, *The Crusades*

...And we know what a rip-roaring success the Crusades were (!)

'Can't repeat the past?... Why of course you can!'

F Scott Fitzgerald, *The Great Gatsby*

Contents

Acknowledgements

This is a very personal look at the mess we are in and is entirely my view, not reflecting any position held by the bank I work for, nor the others who have employed me over the last 25 years of booms and busts. There are no solutions posited, for this (or something very similar) will inevitably happen again but I hope that this book reminds people of the simple truth that in any economy where you have the chance of making money, you have the opportunity to lose it all. It has happened many times before, so the righteous indignation of some of today's commentators is hard to swallow.

My personal thanks are due to my friends and colleagues with whom I have worked and in particular those good friends who, usually over lunch, have joined in debate about the wisdom and folly of the financial centres of London and New York in particular through the cycle of bubble and inevitable correction.

I would also like to acknowledge the hard work of hundreds of thousands of ordinary men and women in banks across the world who provide a socially important function and who don't share in the mega bonus pool. Those still in work have had to pick up the papers every day and see their lives and livelihood attacked, not without cause, but without proportion.

Like the biggest banks, I owe huge debts to many people, my specific thanks to John O'Neill and Siobhan Smyth who reviewed an early draft of the Glossary, to Andrew Merrifield and Peter Firth for their thoughts, to Alan Taylor for helping daily, to Ann and my girls for their constant support, to Gavin and the Luath team who were incredibly patient with me as the markets moved faster than the manuscript and especially to Cat Vernal who edited the book.

Finally, I'd like to say thank you to the people who are saying that this will never happen again. That's the best chance I have for a second edition!

Clark McGinn
Harrow-on-the-Hill, November 2009

Introduction

How did this all happen again?

For we brought nothing into this world, and it is certain we can carry nothing out.

And having food and raiment let us be therewith content.

But they that will be rich fall into temptation and a snare, and into many foolish and hurtful lusts, which drown men in destruction and perdition.

For the love of money is the root of all evil: which while some coveted after, they have erred from the faith, and pierced themselves through with many sorrows.

I Timothy vi, 7–10

Can you remember that warm feeling of prosperity, of sound money, cash in your pocket and a comfortable life in a nice house in rising markets? Have you any idea where all that went? Here we all are on a downwardly spiralling rollercoaster with the whole world on board shrieking with financial pain and for financial retribution. This is already the greatest financial catastrophe in history – commentators bandy words like 'unique', 'unprecedented', 'the worst' and even despite the few green shoots purported to be found, we seem resigned to years of hardship ahead, in stark contrast to the happy lotus years of plenty.

And why are we all out of pocket today? For me the root of the problem is that it is *not* unique or unprecedented. This may be the biggest crash, crunch or crisis (for the time being) but it is in no way the first. By the logic of the cycle, therefore, it is certainly not going to be the final word.

The very fact that we are all surprised proves that we all have a mechanism in the human brain which shelters us from bad memories – which the Jung at heart can call Collective Amnesia. This symptom of the human condition affects us all – whether we be bankers, regulators, investors, consumers, borrowers, politicians or lawyers – you, me, the butcher, the baker and the candlestick maker are all equally affected. The excitement of the boom years, the smell of money, the ability to upscale one's business and personal wealth faster than any previous generation and, tragically, the belief that 'this time is different' combined to create a reckless disregard for the simple facts of history: Collective Amnesia trumped the simple fact that *every boom has its bust*.

All of us, our whole society across the developed world, chased the market up and up and over the top. Because we all forgot – or chose to forget – that the value of everything can go *down* as well as *up*.

How could this happen? The siren call is the easy one: it's all the fault of those bankers! The mad scientists playing with financial fire and creating toxic debt waste which would engulf us all in monetary ruin. The cigar-chomping red-braces-wearing pin-striped BMW-driving titans whose bonuses dwarfed the GDP of small African nations; who fly from meeting to conference to summer holiday on a remote atoll by a gas-guzzling corporate jet; financial geniuses who probably only paused the deal flow to grind the faces of the poor in the dust from time to time.

Those reprobate bankers who forced us consumers to consume. Those bankers who forced us to run up store card bills and then to refinance them out of home equity. Those bankers who forced us to stop saving for a rainy day and spend our savings to fly off for a sunny day's holiday on the credit card instead. JM Keynes warned us in the aftermath of the Great Depression that five shillings saved put a man out of work for a day – and certainly the long march of credit meant that in our boom £5 not borrowed would put a banker off his target! As the financial author Bill Bonner predicted in 2003:

> The entire world economy rests on the consumer; if he ever
> stops spending money he doesn't have on things he doesn't
> need – we're done for.

He sounds pretty insightful now. But in 2003 he was virtually alone with his opinion. Of course, as hindsight is a wonderful thing, more commentators are inclined to remember his prophecies. This is Collective Amnesia at its best in the creation of the boom and its relentless growth, it affected almost all of us, so that there were no little boys to laugh at the Emperor's New Clothes or challenge the conventional wisdom that we were in a long term era of prosperity where inflation and market volatility had been consigned to history.

Making money in the financial markets should be a scientific balance between risk and reward (at least that's what the city boys will tell you). In practice it's driven by two competing human instincts: greed and fear. So here we are today in the midst of a global recession which is affecting each and every one of us right slap bang in the wallet and the whole world throws up its hands and says: 'How could this have happened?' The simple fact is that it happened in exactly the same way as all the other previous financial slumps – greed outpaced fear, and confidence became folly such that in time, there was no money left to borrow from thoughtless lenders to buy bubble investments from the financial geniuses and so, naturally, the whole mechanism toppled over on itself.

It could have been easily avoided had the protagonists and their regulators (not to mention legislators, economists and journalists) only looked at history and learned from the similar mistakes made previously. The only difference this time is the scale of the losses – (and the bonuses in the last few years!). But the same errors have been made many times over many years. Whether the root was in tulips or the foundations were in property, whether investors were bamboozled (often at their own request) by structured investment vehicles or off-balance sheet entities, whether the great new asset class was in currencies or vegetable oil, exotic countries or derivatives – the rush to be faster, higher, stronger in the financial Olympics condemns banks to a cycle that demands more and more pedalling using greater and greater gearing to climb steeper and steeper hills with riskier and riskier artificial stimulants until the inevitable heart attack. Whether the crisis hits you at the top of Mont Ventoux (fuelled by cocaine) or at the peak of the economic cycle (fuelled by credit), the same happens – you lose forward momentum and fall over, leaving those standing behind you to peer down at the endless decline in front of them.

Getting out of intensive care (financial or medical) is a tricky business – staying out of it is even harder! As with heart disease, we can understand financial sclerosis only if we study the bad habits of the patient's past and set some clear best practice for future health.

Human nature means that there is no market for cashmere coats in June – sufficient is the day for the evil thereof, gather ye rosebuds while ye may and the dance to the music of time are warnings that we often fail to heed. In financial markets there have been many commentators but few prophets – in the papers Tim Congdon, Charles Goodhart, Samuel Brittan and Gillian Tett spoke out consistently against the one-way view of the market. Bubbles, booms and busts have been extensively chronicled in fiction by Dumas, Dickens, Zola and Trollope, and a host of hack writers and in thoughtful volumes by Dr Charles Mackay, Professor Charles Kindleberger (who died before he could add this one to his research) and JK Galbraith. But in the sunshine their writings were eclipsed by the wealth of boom books and articles perpetrating the drum beat of demand. In the rising markets, you'd have to really search the bookshelves to come by any volume devoted to warning of a bull market – even classics like Galbraith's *The Great Crash* were hard to find.

Some years ago I was sitting at a bar in the financial district in New York writing an article. My text was the aforementioned *The Great Crash*. It was in mid 2000 and the barman came over solemnly to ask me to put away the book as the title was scaring the customers and putting them off the CNBC broadcast. Mind you, even Galbraith had difficulty in finding his book in the 1950s – he was travelling and, like many authors, wanted to check his book was on sale in the airport bookshop. He couldn't find it, and, concerned, he asked the bookseller – she sagely observed that *The Great Crash* was not a book to sell in an airport. The message always seems to be 'don't scare the customers'.

If you look at the many times institutions have made losses, you can see how financial history repeats itself – not as Marx would have it first as tragedy, secondly as farce – just in ever growing cost. Human ingenuity can find many ways to make money, but looking back, the ways that we lose large amounts of cash are fewer in number – and if we understand those ways, then maybe we can at least alleviate the highs and lows of the cycle we are just beginning.

The biggest lie that the banks, authorities and commentators can give to the people of the world today is 'This Will Never Happen Again'.

The first part of this little exposition – this remedy for Collective Amnesia – is to look at several periods of history in which part or parts of this crisis happened before. All these histories are easily accessible in history books, academic journals and even in literature. Read, mark, learn and inwardly digest.

The second part looks at what banks are supposed to do and how they are supposed to do it. It is a look at the plumbing that underpins not just the financial world, but the whole world. It is only when one realises that the banks are the biggest borrowers in the world that this crunch starts to make sense.

Then in the third section, using historical and literary examples, and the base concepts of banking, we rehearse the basic laws of finance – and how they were all broken in the recent boom years, as they had been before and with the same horrible consequences to your pocket. As good old Edmund Burke warned us: 'Those who don't learn from the past are condemned to repeat it.'

Last of all, we take a look at the jargon and weasel words which have been used and abused by both financiers and journalists, for new and complicated words for old and forgotten mistakes helps forgetfulness.

The aim of this book is quite simple – to try and explain the big issues around banking and international finance that we are facing today without mind-bending economics, or too much accounting mumbo-jumbo and with as few banking buzzwords as possible. Because those are a few of the things that got us into this hole in the first place.

Maybe if we all try hard we can overcome Collective Amnesia and remember the inherent cyclicity of financial life. Maybe not. But surely it must be worth a try.

> To every thing there is a season, and a time to every purpose under the heaven:
> A time to be born, and a time to die; a time to plant, and a time to pluck up that which is planted;
> A time to kill, and a time to heal; a time to break down, and a time to build up;
> A time to weep, and a time to laugh; a time to mourn, and a time to dance;
> A time to cast away stones, and a time to gather stones together; a time to embrace, and a time to refrain from embracing;
> A time to get, and a time to lose; a time to keep, and a time to cast away;
> A time to rend, and a time to sew; a time to keep silence, and a time to speak;
> A time to love, and a time to hate; a time of war, and a time of peace.
>
> **That which hath been is now; and that which is to be hath already been.**
>
> Ecclesiastes iii, 1–8 and 15

Part I
Case Studies – We've Been Here Before
(And Still Haven't Learned)

If it looks too good to be true – it is

'All that glisters is not gold.'

William Shakespeare, *The Merchant of Venice*, 1596/98

The proof of Collective Amnesia is that we have lost truckloads of money in similar ways over centuries. So these case studies really permeate every other part of the thesis that every financial generation reaches a stage in its economic development where the desire for ever increasing prosperity banishes rational expectation that markets and prices do not rise forever. By failing to remember the events of previous crashes, panics and stresses we all share in creating the next one.

This section of the book is not about developing a set of scientific tests or laws but it is about reminding us how money and wealth have been lost before and in ways similar to today. Consider it more a form of sanity check.

Let's look at an example: I call it the myth of the free option. Use this simple catechism:

> QUESTION: How can this deal, investment, deposit or asset be worth more than all the others or yield more than all the others?

> ANSWER: Because there's something in this deal you haven't noticed (yet – but you sure will when it bites you).

A really simple example is bank deposits. If a particular bank is offering interest rates much higher than its rivals, it is an indication that it may want (or even need) those deposits more than its conventional rivals. Maybe it has a low deposit base with few clients wishing to commit to term deposits, or maybe it's having difficulty in raising wholesale finance. Maybe it's not covered by the same depositor guarantee?

When the Bank Of Credit And Commerce International (known in the markets as BCCI) was forcibly closed down by the Bank of England in 1991, a range of local authorities and national bodies were depositors with the failed bank – the biggest was the Western Isles Council in Scotland with a (then) whopping £24m. When the Iceland banks went pop in 2008, history repeated itself with the biggest council depositor (Kent) at risk for £50m.

Why? Because not all banks are equal. Banks who are growing too fast, or who have weaker balance sheets or are poorly regarded in the interbank markets have to offer a higher interest rate on deposits to entice depositors through the doors. Deposits are the oxygen of their life – without daily doses, the bank's balance sheet will asphyxiate. BCCI's large depositors didn't twig this at the time, but they felt that they had been wronged as they had regarded that any bank with branches in the UK – from Barclays to BCCI – that operated under a Bank of England licence was the same risk. I am not sure how they rationalised the higher rates they were receiving but they squealed with pain when it stopped. History (and stupidity) repeats itself, for the UK councils depositing their surpluses 15 years later with Icelandic banks made the same mistake. Except, of course, that they need only have remembered what happened to their colleagues at the time of BCCI. Then The Western Isles Council had the best part of half of its annual budget at risk and only got three quarters back over almost a decade. The lesson had been heeded in the '90s when the pain was fresh, but Collective Amnesia encouraged the council treasurers back into the same mistake.

All our investments are based on credit – a common English word which has evolved from the Latin *credere*, to believe. A creditor is, therefore, an investor who believes in his counterparty enough to give him cash. That is perfectly credible, but remember that the word 'credulous' comes from the same root!

The good news is that, really, there are very few ways in which you can lose money. The bad news is that the great financial minds of our age had either forgotten them (and just don't know what's about to happen) or hoped to be out of the market before the sun went down (and just don't care as they've taken their profits and left the problems in the public's hands). This short book wants to use three resources to which every single investor has access – and to encourage you to use them to your own financial safety:

> **Common sense** – we have a healthy cynicism with our political leaders ('Why is this lying b*st*rd lying to me?') but rarely do we challenge our financiers with the same distrust ('If it looks too good to be true, it is').
> **History** – investors have traditionally lost money in exactly the same ways over the centuries. Together we'll identify them in the light of examples from the history books of yesteryear and the newspapers of more recent times.
> **A good book** – the investment cycle is driven by the myriad financiers in high skyscrapers in diverse locations, but all of their motivation boils down to the balance between fear and greed. Greed was pretty big until recently. We can't dissect the brains of my fellow bankers and brokers (in many cases, a small enough scalpel probably hasn't been invented) but we can use the talents of some of the greatest writers in the

English language who examine the motivation, cause and effect of financial disaster in books, poems, plays and cinema.

Just about 20 years ago many bankers in London sat happily counting the income on loans to one of Britain's major public companies, MCC plc, or to its related private companies in the wider group controlled by a famous great entrepreneur – a household name on both sides of the Atlantic, Robert Maxwell. Banks, lawyers, advisors, accountants, investors and ordinary shareholders had, for years, supported this titan, this self-made man who bought and sold companies across the world. Robert Maxwell could even afford one of the most opulent super-yachts in the world to allow a few brief moments of relaxation from his dominance of industry.

Yet, at the dizzying height of his power, on 5 November 1991, a short Reuters message flashed over screens in London: 'Robert Maxwell feared lost at sea.' In circumstances not entirely clear to this day, Maxwell fell or jumped from the back of the MV *Lady Ghislaine* and drowned somewhere off the Canary Isles.

Some minutes later, a second headline announced to the London Stock Exchange that a major US investment house had just sold a significant percentage of the issued shares in MCC. That group of 'relationship bankers' to the Maxwell group spent an anxious Guy Fawkes' Night waiting for the fat to hit the bonfire. Within a month everyone was under water. The mess was so huge that every single major lawyer in London and New York was under instruction by one or other of the aggrieved parties – for Maxwell had blown hundreds of millions of pounds taken from the banks, general creditors and even his companies' pension funds. The subsequent investigations, trials and legislation rumbled along (as is their wont) and new laws were passed (which brought their own problems, as is their wont).

This was the first time I had been directly involved in the danger of losing money and I can remember clearly the absolute shock – watching the tape with the share price stumbling, halting, weakening, failing, falling, tumbling then finding its own last cliff to go lemming. I can also recall the puzzlement of spectators, commentators and participants, each asking: 'How in the professional mercantile field did so many directors, in so many banks, from so many countries lend so much to one crook? How could they be so wrong? How could it have been avoided?'

The answer was simple – by learning from previous transactions. Maxwell had been investigated by the UK authorities some years before and was described by the Department of Trade & Industry in a 1973 formal report as 'not, in our opinion, a person who can be relied upon to exercise proper stewardship of a publicly quoted company'. Detailed questions should have been asked – the company structure of the Maxwell group was a constant cut-and-paste job with new acquisitions inside and outside the group, disposals, transfers of businesses and various extraordinary accounting changes such that no one could have a firm view of the credit of that kaleidoscope (his bullying nature was famed as well – so any sensible query earned the questioner a lambasting). On top of that, any bank not joining in with the herd voluntarily gave up its share the money that it could make from Maxwell, hence lower bonuses and smaller dividends!

The financial district in London is still known as 'the City' (or 'the Square Mile') and in New York it is called 'Wall Street' (even though the physical buildings have moved out to Canary Wharf or drifted up to Midtown). Whatever the post/zip code, they are inhabited by men and women who share this virulent, but until now unnamed, cyclical Collective Amnesia. The wave that took Maxwell to the top was hardly the first boom in the markets. There was the South Sea Bubble, the Mississippi Scheme, the Latin American debt crisis (No! not that one – the one in 1825–30), the Railway Mania, the Gold Squeeze, the Silver Corner, the Robber Barons, the Baring Crisis, the dot com boom, and so on. In almost all of these great capital upheavals, the oversupply of bank liquidity (the victory of the marketing animal over the credit machine) led financiers into the quest for the indestructible financial god – the modern Midas.

The Maxwell downfall is immense, but not unique. His crimes and follies, his bluster and duplicity, are woven into a carpet long enough to link Lombard Street EC3 to Broad Street 10004. But it simply replaced earlier rugs. Each boom had a central figure: John Blunt, who harnessed the rapacious nobles on the board of the South Sea Company; Sir Gregor MacGregor, who sold millions in bonds in behalf of the State of Poyais (a country in Honduras whose existence was as fictional as a free lunch in the City); George Hudson, 'the Railway King' in England; or Commodore Vanderbilt in the USA; and Jabez Balfour MP of the 'Liberator' Building Society, who liberated life savings as a hobby. The list continues down to today to the household names who have surrendered their households for a leasehold in the Big House.

The late Victorian hack writer, D Morier Evans, in his book *Facts, Failures and Frauds* (L000112 in the CIOB library in London – no need to rush, it's been taken out only once since 1968), records with wistful remembrance his shock at the Victorian Values of the 1850s and '60s and the happy way in which the City aided the systematic gulling of the poor investor. We and our credit committees should have read the life of George Hudson, the 'Railway King', of whom Morier said:

> Hudson's credit was so great, that his mere word appeared to supply the place of actual resources. He well knew what he was worth in this respect; and with a close eye and a practised hand, he weighed the ever available fund represented by his reputation, against all it would bear of unchecked responsibility, licence and latitude.

Through the systematic use of equity issues based on fraudulently prepared accounts, a keen eye for bullying competitors, acquisitions which flattered profits and the sale of raw materials to his public companies from his private companies, he made £538,000 (or the best part of £40 million in today's money) before being discovered and broadly disgraced; though his constituents in York, who had participated in the success around him, erected a statue to the old crook, which still stands there today.

Hudson died in 1871, and in the following year the great novelist Anthony Trollope wrote his most bleak and bitter view of the world and the urge to make money in his novel *The Way We Live Now*, which centred on the corrupt career of Augustus Melmotte, the great and mercurial financier.

From a mysterious background in Central Europe, our antihero left Vienna after a series questionable but profitable business practices came to light to make a triumphal arrival in London in a magnificent coach pulled by four priceless horses (helicopters not having been invented). Money abounds and is highly visible and allows him to enjoy (or at least buy) the company of Cabinet Ministers, bankers and at his peak the Emperor of China (even in 1872 it was forecast to be the next great growth market). With many public projects in hand, his star rises proportionately to the manipulated stock prices by which they are funded (by his purchasing at the nominal price and selling at market value), until he stands and becomes Member of Parliament for Westminster. Trollope describes his villain's strength in an early chapter:

> In the City, Mr Melmotte's name was worth any amount of money, – though his character was perhaps worth little.

The stakes rise even higher for Melmotte, who moves from shady speculation to more blatant crime. Driven by a desire to marry his daughter into the peerage, to own a country estate and, crucially, to generate hard cash to continue to buy and inflate his worthless scrip, he forges the sale papers for a country estate (then promptly mortgages it and forgets to pay the vendor). The merry-go-round is spinning faster and the kites are flying ever higher, so he continues his calligraphic hobby until rumours also start to fly. Finally, he is tipped off by his lead banker (who wisely does a bunk before the crash) and the final act sees Melmotte go to the House of Commons, where he gets drunk (which, allegedly, still happens today), and tries to make a speech but falls over instead. After this there is nothing to do but go home, and in the dead of night all alone he poisons himself. He leaves his family and bereft creditors thicker than the clichéd leaves of Vallambrosa.

One of the remaining bankers, ruefully looking at a £60,000 loss (close to £4m today), summed up Melmotte's crash:

> His business was quite irregular, but there was very much of it, and some of it immensely profitable. He took us in completely.

Accidents happen. In the financial field, they happen repetitively. Banking should be easy – you aggregate the individual savings of a community, grouping those funds into larger loans which you give to businesses to create wealth, which flows back to you and ultimately to all the little folk too. The fact that the underlying model is easy (and I guess awfully well paid!) is why there are so many bankers in the world (like rats, you're never more than three feet away from a financier in London). Because there are too many noses at the trough, the model has to be jazzed up so that there is enough cash to pay all the bonuses. That's where things start to go wrong. That, and the fact that everyone forgets what happened before.

As these next case studies will show, too often we are happy to accept the famous Rumsfeld line: 'I would not say that the future is necessarily less predictable than the past. I think the past was not predictable when it started.' You might think these case studies are fairy tales (once upon a bank balance...) but look hard at each then read last week's papers. See the resemblance? If only bank boards, regulators, investors and politicians had, then, gosh, this book wouldn't have been written.

Nothing is free in banking – there is always a charge (direct or indirect) or a cost or a compromise. It's your own fault if you don't ask what it is.

> But, Mousie, thou art no thy lane,
> In proving foresight may be vain;
> The best-laid schemes o' mice an' men
> Gang aft agley,
> An' lea'e us nought but grief an' pain,
> For promis'd joy!

Still thou art blest, compar'd wi' me
The present only toucheth thee:
But, Och! I backward cast my e'e.
 On prospects drear!
An' forward, tho' I canna see,
 I guess an' fear!

Robert Burns, 'To a Mouse', 1785

CASE STUDY ONE

THE SOUTH SEA PARADISE:
LONDON 1719 AND COUNTLESS STOCKMARKET
BUBBLES SINCE

> The advance, by all good means, of the price of the stock was the only way to promote the good of the company.
>
> John Blunt, Governor, The South Sea Company, January 1720

> The South Sea company... had an immense capital divided among an immense number of proprietors. It was naturally to be expected, therefore, that folly, negligence, and profusion should prevail in the whole management of their affairs.
>
> Adam Smith, 1776

Blunt by name, but sharp by nature: Sir John Blunt, Britain's first great financial manipulator couldn't just stoop low, he could limbo dance under a dachshund. He was proud to be a self-made man (which relieved anyone else of the awful responsibility) having started by copying letters for 6d and then lending shillings at 33 per cent per annum (all this before credit cards). He built up enough cash to make his name in the City by the promotion of the New River Company, the dismal performance of which permitted just sufficient time to pay the directors a personal lump sum before sinking below the waves.

In early 18th-century England there were relatively few formally established companies as we would know them now, with shareholders and some form of limited liability. One of the largest, and least successful, was The South Sea Company, which had been formed to buy a limited right for Englishmen to trade (in slaves and goods) with the Spanish empire of the New World. Blunt became a director of the South Sea Company in 1711 and watched its inefficient Board fail to trade profitably with South America, partly through the machinations of Spanish bureaucracy and protectionism and partly through the regular bouts of war between His Britannic Majesty and His Most Catholic Majesty over the years. As the original business plan was not going to make anyone (especially Blunt) a fortune, our anti-hero suggested generating some income by buying up the fairly unsuccessful national lottery loan (thank heavens some things have changed), which impressed King George I, who accepted Blunt's invitation to join the Board (proving that the best kind of corporate chairman is a celebrity who can't speak English) and in 1719, looking across the Channel at the Mississippi Scheme (of which more soon...), Blunt resolved to be a Law unto himself.

His plan was clever and original. Unfortunately, the clever parts were not original while the original parts were not clever (a bit like this joke). Blunt proposed to purchase most of the UK's national debt if Parliament allowed him to create £100 of new South Sea stock for every £100 of government stock bought in. Blunt could make a handsome turn if he kept the market value of South Sea stock high. If, for example, South Sea traded at £200 and an investor offered to exchange £1,000 in Government Debt, the Company was allowed to issue ten £100 South Sea Share certificates. Ten times the face value (or 'nominal value') comes to £1,000. But at the price trading in the stockmarket each certificate could be sold for twice the nominal value. So Blunt's first avenue for making a profit was to swap £1,000 of Government Debt for £1,000 of South Sea shares at the current market price – that's five certificates. The magic was that Blunt had been allowed to print ten in total so he now had five remaining which he could sell in the market for a clear £1,000 profit or use them as free bribes to influential politicians and investors.

The scheme depended on supporters: initially to swing Parliament to approve this audacious wheeze, but secondly to buy the stock and keep the price high. Luckily, the Postmaster General, James Craggs, was a kindred spirit (he rose from being a footman by blackmailing his mistresses' lovers). His son, the joint Foreign Secretary, would also be helpful, although Craggs the Younger was only half as corrupt as his father (largely because he was only half as devious). The Craggses took Blunt to meet John Aislabie, the Chancellor of the Exchequer, the finance minister of Great Britain. These great minds decided to form their own personal Tripartite Agreement to manage the operation of this new market in shares.

Aislabie was the least effective politician since Caligula's horse, but he was broke (MPs received no formal expenses in those days) and so he promised to pilot a bill through Parliament for a percentage of the overall take. The conspirators compiled a list of the great and the greedy whose influence would be essential. In return for their public support, fictitious stock was allocated against each name (needless to say, without the boring necessity of payment). Once the bill was enacted, the non-existent stock would be 'sold' raising a 'profit' for the helper. Blunt didn't believe in skimping: the enormous sum of £1.25 million (a cool £17 billion today) was promised to the King's two mistresses (the fat one and the tall one), their nieces, the First Lord, the Secretary to the Treasury and a hundred influential backbenchers (and no doubt a handful of personal friends and relations within the Blunt clan).

The inducements were a great success, but Blunt anticipated opposition from Robert Walpole, who was cunning, ambitious and, by the admittedly low standards of the day, honest. Walpole was also aware of the fiscal and political crisis brewing in France and expected Law's inevitable collapse bringing all that country from paper money into hard currency (the 'or dur' in French). Blunt was cautiously aware of Walpole's abilities and his power in Parliament and so as an astute operator, he treated him with nervous respect. He also knew that he would be too difficult (or expensive) to buy off, so it had to be a fight on the floor of the House of Commons. Walpole could afford (literally) to have scruples – his power came from his government position as Paymaster General. This was quite a boring job, acting as cashier to HM Government, except for the fact that Parliament would vote once a year to agree the budget and that whole year's proposed expenditure would be paid into the Paymaster's personal account. Naturally it seemed only fair that he should have the right to keep the interest earned on these vast sums. Honesty pays. If the warrants authorising payment were late in coming, so much the better; or, if you could cut a deal on cheese, cloths or horses and take a commission, there was nothing to stop you. In simple terms, all you had to do was show at the end of the year a simple account of warrants in and cash out; everything else was between the Paymaster, his conscience and his bankers.

In some ways, Walpole was not sure how to jump, particularly given the King's involvement – so he and his supporters prevailed upon the Bank of England (as one of the only formally chartered companies) to raise a counterbid. The Old Lady Of Threadneedle Street sharpened her pencil and proposed more advantageous terms, but Blunt bluntly trumped them once more with a more generous South Sea offer.

The Commons vote was close – 144 to 140 in favour of the South Sea (especially considering that 100 MPs had been bought) – and was won only by the offer of a £7.5 million cash payment to the Government. Walpole retired to read his French newspapers.

Over the next six months, by rumour, extravagant forecasts, well-publicised share offers, unauthorised issue of shares, payment of subscriptions by ever-decreasing instalments and an ingenious scheme whereby the Company lent the cash raised back to the investors to permit them to buy yet more stock, Blunt managed to raise core investor demand for the shares growing and – crucially – to keep a source of liquidity available to help people exercise that demand. This pushed the market price from £128 to £1,050.

But you can't have one bubble in a bath: hundreds of imitators appeared. There were proposals to fund insurance companies, whale fisheries, hair exchanges, donkey breeding franchises and even a company to build a perpetual motion machine. While most of the list of ventures look simply barking, some of these almost make sense today (where would IKEA and MFI be without a company 'to make furniture out of sawdust'?).The most enterprising promoter issued his prospectus 'For an Undertaking of Great Advantage, But – no one to Know What It Is' (no one did find out as he raised £2,000 from enthusiastic punters and did a bunk on the same day! Gullible's Travels.) We should not laugh: in our own recent Dotcom boom, for example, equity was raised by two entrepreneurs who refused to write a business plan as the market was developing too quickly; in a very odd turn of events, the gentlemen spent the venture capital with no return to the investors.

These 'bubble companies' were more than irritating rivals to Blunt – they started starving him of the capital he needed to boost the South Sea shares. The small investments of thousands of members of the public kept the South Sea merry-go-round moving. Every time an investor wasted his money on a rival company, that was one less mug propping up Blunt's massive bubble. And he needed it propped up because he and his cronies had spent most of the capital inflow on bribes and jollies but there was a legally binding contract with the Government that needed paying in hard cash, and even oiling the wheels a bit more could only postpone the day of payment not cancel it.

He had to do something.

Typically enough he had a powerful tool. The South Sea Company was a total scam, but one indisputable fact was that it had been properly and legally created as an independent company whereas the bubble companies (good or bad) had by and large just started business without going through any costly and time consuming formalities. Technically without a Royal Charter or an Act of Parliament a bubble company had no right to trade, no corporate governance and – dangerously for the shareholders – no limited liability. If Blunt could use this to his advantage and have the Courts declare his rivals as trading without legal authority, then he would be the only game in town once more. He needed to have a monopoly of all the mugs to succeed.

After detailed legal discussion (assisted by a further round of cash and shares for the Justices), the Court agreed and popped each of the Bubbles in August. Only Royal Exchange and London Assurance escaped, as they both hurriedly stumped up the £600,000 necessary to buy the issue of a Charter. Yet in the rout, even they took a huge hit, their shares falling in a single week by 75 per cent and 86 per cent respectively as the wave of buyers became a tidal wave of sellers. Panic hit Exchange Alley, where the kerb-side market bought and bought bubble shares as fortunes were lost overnight. From Exchange Alley to Skid Row.

Poor Blunt had not forecast the effect as investors covered the losses they made in the Bubbles by selling South Sea stock! The priced lurched southwards while Blunt went east to Tunbridge Wells, leaving Craggs holding the baby. And the baby had severe colic...

The day before the legal quill popped the baby bubbles, Blunt's stock (metaphorically and numerically) flew high – the South Sea was off its peak but showed a fine £900 in market trading. With the reverse in the market it was drifting down daily – the directors (with no good reason or logic save to support the price) announced an extra dividend of 30 per cent at the year end – and an incredible guaranteed dividend of 50 per cent for each of the coming 12 years. They were perfectly aware that there was insufficient cash to look after the next 12 weeks let alone promise dividends in years ahead. A month later, with the price dropping daily, Craggs Senior knew he was against the wall. He had no choice but to speak to Walpole and the Bank of England.

Walpole brokered a deal in the wee small hours (the handwritten contract is still in the Bank of England archives) and Craggs thought he had bought time as his rivals had agreed to buy a block of stock at £400 – slightly over the day's closing price.

Craggs went to bed thinking he had succeeded in his role as financial nanny until he heard the disastrous news that the company's bankers, the Sword Blade Company, had cut and run. It had been forced into collapse after a long and bitter rivalry with the Bank of England whose political clout was just too much to overcome. The South Sea price collapsed to £190 and the Bank of England weaselled out of the agreements (largely because it was almost bust itself) and Parliament bayed for blood (especially the 451 honourable members who were investors!). But there was a problem: the directors had broken no laws. In a furious debate, a retrospective law was passed, making the transfer of stock without valuable consideration a crime.

The company secretary fled to Belgium where there was no extradition treaty. By an amazing coincidence, he also took most of the evidence incriminating the King and his mistresses and was (therefore?) never caught. This drove the Commons wild, and they expelled the six MPs who were South Sea directors, establishing a secret committee to investigate ministerial responsibility. The Lords wanted a committee, too, and imprisoned five more directors, including Blunt, who had been trying to keep his head down. As we have seen recently, when our legislators have slept all the way up the price curve, the denizens of the Palace of Westminster are all too keen to be seen to be hyperactive after the crash.

Sir John, naturally, was to be the star witness. Blunt didn't give evidence; he gave a virtuoso performance, with extensive memory loss before the Commons and a refusal to testify to the Lords (as he had already given evidence to the Commons). However, the time came to strike a bargain and Blunt grassed (and by spreading the blame, he escaped prison).

The MPs were incandescent – as ever politicians making up heat after the event rather than generating light before. Everyone on the floor of the House attempted to hold a monopoly of virtue and MP after MP trumpeted against the vices of capitalism which promoted personal gain over common good, while politely forgetting their own role in the affair. (Just like current legislators who pontificate on the crash while having squeezed their massive expenses to – and even beyond – the limits of sense, those speaking in the South Sea debate saw no irony in their new found virtue.)

Those backbench voices which had been silent in the debates to approve the plan were now the loudest in its condemnation and soon the rhetoric of denunciation shifted to a harsher tone of retribution with one vociferous backbencher refusing to support hanging the directors as it was just too good for them. His considered solution was they should each be tied in a sack with a monkey and a snake and thrown alive into the Thames. This amendment was not voted upon, whether because it was too rabble rousing or whether members felt that it was demeaning to snakes, I do not know.

Of the six cabinet ministers implicated, Aislabie (who had netted over £800,000, perhaps about £10bn today) resigned as Chancellor and ended up imprisoned in the Tower of London. The First Lord of the Treasury escaped censure thanks to Walpole's eloquent advocacy (which was necessary to stop the collapse of the Government and which 'coincidentally' establish a succession plan featuring Walpole), while the Treasury Secretary's rich relatives pulled strings to free him. Craggs the Younger died of pox before his trial (proving that his social principles weren't much better than his financial ones) but the government gave him a state funeral and he now lies in Westminster Abbey as he lied in the House. Craggs the Elder was found dead in bed on the very day he was due to testify (having died from overexertion, trying to save both faces).

Retribution was more painful than it is today: the directors' estates and personal wealth were confiscated, bringing in the best part of £2 million and allowing a £33/6/8 dividend to be paid to creditors for every £100 held. The First Lord acknowledged his debt by stepping down, allowing Walpole to become the first Prime Minister as we would recognise the office nowadays.

And Blunt? He died in comfort in 1733 in Bath with a handsome pension from his son (who had sold out his South Sea stock nice and early and was sitting on a pile of cash).

This was an early example of what we have experienced time and time again. A particular share or a specific sector looks as if it will grow and grow without setback. If there is sufficient liquidity in the market, many people can join in and while they have the cash (or can borrow) to do that, then the momentum carries on. Sometimes the support of an egotistical management team or the endorsement by stock pickers and researchers provide the adrenaline in the blood veins of the bulls. Sometimes as in the South Sea it is all based on a swindle. Unfortunately, Collective Amnesia is at work again.

In May 1720 the Archbishop of Dublin wrote: 'most who go into this matter are well aware that it will not succeed but hope to sell before the price falls'. Unfortunately, archbishops' pronouncements don't tend to help it seems. Dr Williams the current Archbishop of Canterbury recently complained that bankers were 'unrepentant' in the aftermath of this present crash having not heeded his previous warnings that they were speculating in 'idolatry', or as he described it, 'projecting of reality and substance onto things that don't have them.'

But it is not just the financiers who project a rosy glow on finance. The only reason that bubbles work is that **everyone** wants to participate. It's interesting that the English Church Commissioners lost up to £800m in 1992 on real estate investments they admitted were 'mismanaged' while their latest accounts show a year on year decline of over £1bn given the dramatic falls in equities (including the banks they invested in) and our old friend the property market.

The standard warning 'the value of your investments can go down as well as up' should in honesty be amended to 'the value of your investments WILL go down as well as going up' to remind us all. Identifying the bubble

– both in our own minds and in the regulatory sphere – must be a priority to prevent the unbridled hysteria on the way up and the wound licking witch-hunt on the day after we all fall down.

> The corruption of the market led predictably to personal corruption, to the payments of vast sums of shareholders' money to those who assisted in this matter, whether by devising or implementing the scheme, or by recruiting for it or providing the finance to put it into effect.
>
> Mr Justice Henry, *The Guinness Case*, 1990

CASE STUDY TWO

MISSISSIPPI BLUES:
PARIS (AND A BIT OF NORTH AMERICA) 1719

> As long as the credit of this [John Law's] bank subsisted,
> it appeared to the French to be perfectly solid. The bubble no
> sooner burst, than the whole nation was thrown into astonish-
> ment and consternation. Nobody could conceive from whence
> the credit had sprung; what had created such mountains of
> wealth in so short a time; and by what witchcraft and
> fascination it had been made to disappear in an instant.

> Sir James Steuart, 1770

In 1715 night fell on the Sun King and the glorious reign of Louis XIV passed into the books of the historians and the hands of the accountants. Before the royal remains sank into the earth, the economy had sunk into the mire under the extravagance and corruption of Louis's great foreign policy and even greater architectural ambition. Six feet of clay covered the aspirations of the monarch, but about three billion livres (about £32 billion today) couldn't cover the royal debts – and with government expenditure running at 95 per cent of the state's total revenue, debt service (like the old king's requiem service) was but a pious hope.

The noted *bon viveur*, Louis, Duc d'Orleans, was made Regent to the infant Louis XV to resolve the crisis. Two parties fought: one radical view calling for National Bankruptcy, the other traditional approach suggesting wholesale devaluation of the currency (essentially stealing one-fifth of each silver coin). The old school won the argument; the people lost their 20 per cent. They were as happy as a French farmer eating English lamb and the mint sauce they were offered was worse – all government payments would be made in paper, not coins. Not even the government accepted these use-less IOUs as legal tender, so it was effectively a forced loan on the taxpayer, with only the most desperate selling their 'billets' to another for cash at huge discounts to face value to raise at least a little liquidity.

Enter John Law of Lauriston, the pawky and pockmarked son of an Edin-burgh goldsmith/banker. Like so many Scots lads then and now, he'd sought his fortune in London. There he made his entry into society as a well-dressed killer gambler, which divided opinion – to half of the *beau monde* he was 'Beau Law', to his denigrators (probably the guys he fleeced at cards), he was 'Jessamy John'. But after an injudicious flirt, a fatal duel (with an ex-army captain who was possibly in a homosexual relationship with a leading government politician), a consequent murder trial, and a mysterious, last-minute escape from a British jail (whether by the agency of the dead man's lover or his enemies, we will never know), Law had established himself in exile in Paris as a preternaturally successful gambler with the engaging habit of dissipating his winnings by publishing abstruse pamphlets on banking. (At that time, combining gambling and banking seemed an unusual combination – less so nowadays.) As fate would have it, a copy of one of the Scotsman's pamphlets fell into the sober hands of M Le Duc, who recognised a good bet when he saw one. And Son Altesse had so many other cares on his mind: the opera, the dancing girls, the all-night parties and a near-incestuous love for his daughter la Duchesse de Berri meant that there were not enough hours in the day to attend to the minutiae of banking. If in doubt, delegate – particularly if you have a brainy chap who will do all the work and pass back the bulk of the profits, too.

The first good idea was the creation in May 1716 of Messrs Law et Cie, a private bank authorised by the Regent to issue paper money secured on the royal revenues and lands. Investors were pleased as the initial L6 million in capital was to be subscribed 25 per cent in gold and 75 per cent in the near-worthless government IOUs (known as 'billets') at their nominal value. But Law's stroke of genius was to guarantee to exchange his notes for gold on demand and in the weight of coin current at the note's date of issue. Now an independent bank had created both an exit for the holders of the trash paper and a certainty of value in paper money, avoiding the risk of governmental default or devaluation. The joy of this was that Law's notes could be accurately valued in ounces of refined gold and the repayment was guaranteed formally by the state on the security of its vast landed estate in France.

Freedom from devaluation was enthusiastically grasped, and the authorised note issue of L60 million was quickly disbursed. Within the year, a Law bank note of L100 traded at L115 while a similar billet fetched only L21½! Law's paper became the effective currency of the realm.

Two bad ideas followed. Flushed with success (or at least pride), Law sought and was granted exclusive trading rights to the French province of Mississippi. In those days, North America was divided into three spheres of influence: the smallest was the Spanish enclave, which covered Florida, the Mexican border and California; while the East Coast was controlled by the British from Georgia to the border of Quebec; and the French held sway in Canada and the vast tract they called the Louisiana.

This was a party bigger than Bourbon Street – for France's Louisiana domain covered not just the Big Easy, but all the land on either side of the Mississippi River – Arkansas and Missouri, Mississippi, Illinois, Iowa and Wisconsin, and the flat lands of Minnesota, too.

Today, the GDP of those US states combined would give them membership of the G8, but, at that time, the footsteps of the French explorers were newly printed in these millions of acres of wilderness, with aboriginal peoples who had not quite worked out what this new game of 'sovereignty' involved. Law and the Regent could see the value of the natural resources and living space to grow a colonial population as the British had done from Halifax to Savannah.

To accomplish this, John Law needed three things: control of the province (which was in his pocket if he could square his boss); capital to exploit the potential of the land (which, given the prestige of his bank, should be forthcoming) and colonists to tame the woods and indigenous peoples.

Regent Louis was entranced by the offer of a new capital to be built in his honour (New Orleans – a city which grew up to share in many of its god-father's vices – *laissez les bonnes temps rouler* covers both town and noble-man rather well), but he was not a fool in monetary terms. Law would be permitted to raise shares in his new Mississippi Company – which was chartered as a totally separate venture from the venerable bank – for Law estimated that a clear L100m (equal to about five per cent on top of the national debt) was needed to develop the concession to meet his scheme. The Regent, however, wanted the old billets hoovered up and so the quid pro quo was that Law could have his shares issued to the public, but the shares had to be bought by exchanging the new scrip for the old govern-ment paper. Instead of the lump sum of L100m in cash he needed upfront, Law was left with L100m in government paper so his plans were con-strained as his cash supply was limited to the annual interest on the shabby old billets foisted on him. It was a fraction of the ready money he needed to implement his *grande projet*.

The first offer of Mississippi Company stock was issued at L500, but it failed to catch the public's interest. Despite some incredible feats of puff from Law over the next months, they remained on the B list and the Mississippi shares were soon trading below L300. As a gambler, Law knew the only way out was to play high – so in May 1719, when the price was stagnant at L250, he publicly announced his intention to buy on his own account blocks of 200 shares at L500 per share in November 1719. It worked. Jean Publique couldn't believe that anyone would be stupid enough to do this without certain insider knowledge of profits – everyone began to buy and the ticker ticked up towards L1,000.

Law developed a heroic capacity for self-publicity, and his PR department worked at full steam, celebrating the joys of colonial life in the New Country, for the scheme needed willing workers as much as wodges of wonga. Law realised that the investors needed something in their hands *now*. He had resolved the financial crisis by reforming banking and he was creating a mighty new colony which would transform French society and its economy – but he needed ongoing developments to keep the investors hungry (and to bring in cash). Out of these twin needs, he persuaded the Regent to let the Mississippi Company nibble away at the other state monopolies. The Law System of Business – transparency, management and close interaction between financial and mercantile markets – was hymned daily as the New Paradigm. From goldsmith to Goldilocks.

First to be delivered into his care was the tobacco trade, which was swallowed up in a puff; then the trading rights to the Indies, to China and even into Africa were added into the Mississippi portmanteau. The share price kept turning above L1,200 as investors read daily about the growth of the company and its global prospects. In the centre of this wizardry sat John Law, happily calculating that his system could be multiplied and replicated almost without end.

And so he carried on and took the markets with him; when Law persuaded the Regent to award him the right to mint all the coins in France, the share price doubled to L2,000. In August 1720 he 'won' the franchise to collect taxes and the price jumped to L5,000. Law was now the most famous man in Europe (Orleans was happy to give Law the credit, as long as he kept the cash). Then Law fell under the illness that usually hits the Scots in the World Cup – *folie de grandeur*: the Mississippi Company made a formal offer to buy the entire French national debt of L1.5 billion, receiving an interest rate of three per cent per annum.

The Government was happy with this idea as it was (as often as it could afford) currently paying four per cent to small investors – so it now would have one compliant creditor at a cheaper rate. On the other hand, the public were overjoyed for they had nice shiny new banknotes repaying the dingy old billets in full (after a long wait) and as a bonus they had a special offer to buy the new Mississippi stock whose price could only rise. The Mississippi

Company, in turn, were happy because the Banque Royale – as Law et Cie was now called – was printing the notes that would allow them to buy the Mississippi stock (now at L10,000 on the promise of a L200 dividend for each L500 share), the proceeds of which enabled the Company to pay the Government. Happy Days! Everyone grew rich!

Law kept a tight rein on the share issuance. His close management of the shares was one of the important factors in the price rise. He knew that he had to drip new shares into the market, restricting supply so that the demand would pump up the share price in the secondary market. Once that reached its next peak, he could issue a few more in a new public offering. And so on and so on and so on. To buy new shares from the company, one had to be an existing shareholder: the original shares were known in the slang as 'Grandmothers' – one needed a granny in one's portfolio to subscribe for Filles (her 'daughters') and in time her 'Grandes Filles', which was a strong incentive to buy in the secondary market. Once the shares were widely spread through the whole population, Law maintained demand by permitting future share issues to be bought by paying 12 monthly instalments – but you received the share on the day of purchase and shared in its dividend even though you hadn't paid for it in full. It would have been rude not to have a part of this generous offer from France's saviour, for after all the public were not just enriching themselves, but enriching La France!

Law was well aware of what he was trying to achieve and how he needed to run the game. The Duc, however, was impatient and thought that it was time to have a bigger share of the tarte tatin. So the Regent's bad idea was to take over the Banque Royale and, on the old political adage of 'you can't have too much of a good thing', set the banknote printing presses to full steam ahead. Law's precept of maintaining a strict reserve of gold and silver against the value of note in issue was cast aside – which was a direct repudiation of the cornerstone of the success of the initial phase of Law's scheme. The practical underpinning of the scheme was the public's confidence in paper issued by Law's banks. Not just that the new notes issued by Law were guaranteed to be redeemed at fair value but crucially because of the linkage between the quantity of notes in issue and the real resources of the Banque Royale to redeem them if a noteholder came to the counters to exchange paper for gold. Those reserves in the Banque both guaranteed the value of the notes but crucially also restricted the number that could be issued. That was what gave the market the confidence and belief in them, and maintained their worth. Now (in a move often followed since) the argument ran that the markets had gained a confidence in the Law system in and of itself. Formal reserves may have been needed in the bad old days, but now we had a new paradigm, a period of new growth that would benefit all mankind. Issuing more notes would provide additional liquidity to stimulate additional growth (and in turn yet more notes, *ad nauseam*) and that incremental growth would be the economic cushion which replaced the requirement to keep boring old gold in a box in a bank vault.

The markets took off like a race. The street Law lived in with his wife and family, the Rue Quincampoix, became an impromptu stockmarket with the shopkeepers turning their counters over to the jobbers and where a famous hunchbacked beggar made a fortune by hiring out his back as a desk for enthusiastic speculators to sign the many transfer documents to buy and sell as quickly as they could in a rising market – and how it was rising. The word 'millionaire' was coined as Dukes and footmen, Marquises and merchants, Barons and brothel keepers jostled here for shares at L18,000, but while wheeling and dealing and making fine profits, they failed to notice the inexorable rise of the price of ordinary things. At the peak some 624,000 full shares were issued in the Mississippi Company, imputing a market capitalisation of nearly 10 times the national debt taken over three years before. The bedrock of the Law Empire's income though remained the three per cent per annum government interest, which, in context, was an insignificant L60m – not a lot of cash to pay dividends!

In January 1720, at an unbelievable market price of L20,000, a number of large holders of stock sold out (in both senses), looking to gold and jewels as safe havens, thus causing an awareness of the fragility of paper wealth. As we now know, too much money was chasing too few goods: inflation had appeared with the price of foodstuffs and ordinary goods climbing – not as fast as the share price – but fast enough to scare people. The Empire of Law founded on a golden guarantee was about to turn into the Empire of Disorder.

Some feeble attempts were made to stabilise the currency during the first half of 1720; Law was about to make his final, desperate play. Like all good Presbyterians, Law kept the Sabbath, but he wanted to keep everything else too. Something had to give. As his religion barred him from high office in the royal government, he became a Roman Catholic and, seconds later, took on the role of Comptroller General (thus effectively becoming the Prime Minister of France), merging the Banque Royal and Mississippi Company at a fixed share price of L9,000. Confidence was weak, and Law had to use his new powers to protect the bank, as the Regent's monetary policy had left it with only enough gold to redeem two per cent of the note issue. This was far too low a reserve to cover any popular move to exchange notes. A run had to be averted. Almost at all costs.

The natural first step was to make a party political broadcast to reassure the people and to ask all to share in a period of belt-tightening to save society. Edicts were issued and the Mississippi stock was legally marked-to-market at L9,000 but these were not effective steps – in fact, it rather put the wind up the market. Law was falling fast now, though neither he nor the world were yet aware of the fact: idea after idea was spun out of Quincampoix, now silent of speculators, but soon to be thronged with people wanting to tear the Scot apart. Ugly scenes followed the fateful and fatal Edict of 21 May 1720. As Law could not restore confidence by words alone he had to turn to force and he made it illegal to draw gold from the Bank. Furthermore, both Livres (gold or paper) and Mississippi stock were declared to be worth 10 per cent less each week until they reached 50 per cent of the May value. Law ran out of luck. Within the week he had lost his position, and lynch mobs waited on street corners (which goes to show that running up debts isn't bad, it's running into creditors that can hurt). The greatest Scottish financier in the world became the poster child of the crash.

The Regent did what any great statesman would do: at once he blamed Law, then he stripped the lower and middle classes (but not the nobles) of their speculative wealth. In the financial settlement to end the Mississippi Bubble, he built the ladder that would see his family and his class climb the scaffold as the whole royal fabric of France was swept away in July 1789.

Law escaped by the skin of his teeth – his windows were stoned and his name and reputation were destroyed. The Scotsman had fallen as low as he had flown so high – a financial Icarus who winged it once too often. A mock obituary circulated, for he had become the face of financial failure:

Ci gît cet Écossais célèbre,	*Here lies the famous Scot,*
Ce calculateur sans égal,	*A mathematician without equal,*
Qui par les règles d'algèbre	*Who used the rules of algebra*
À mis la France à l'hôpital!	*To put France in hospital (or workhouse!).*

At first he had access to a handsome pension (sounds familiar), but he lost his estates, investments and savings when he fled France. When the Regent finally succumbed to his last excesses, the pension died too and Law soon ran through his portable wealth and had to retire penniless to tour continental casinos until his death in Venice in 1729. There, in the Piazza San Marco, the grand tourists could see a shabby but still sharp Scot, where he had been reduced to supporting himself by betting £100 to sixpence that tourists couldn't throw six double sixes in a row.

Law had always been better at statistics than economics: the hundreds who tossed the dice couldn't win, any more than the French could pay off their debts without pain. Those who claim that ability are like the Mississippi itself, thin at the head and wide at the mouth.

Almost 50 years later, Adam Smith wrote Law's epitaph in *The Wealth of Nations*:

> The idea of the possibility of multiplying paper to almost any extent was the real foundation of what is called the Mississippi scheme, the most extravagant prospect of both banking and stock jobbing that, perhaps, the world ever saw.

Thank heavens we have all learned these hard lessons. Haven't we? Every asset, scheme or project needs paying for. That payment needs finance. Finance depends on confidence. It's no worry if you can borrow money and not have to pay it back until all your own payments have come in. But whether you are a bank, a country or a consumer, the temptation to borrow against a 'certain' result naturally leads to imprudence.

TIPTOE THROUGH THE TULIPS:
THE NETHERLANDS 1634–
THE MODEL FOR ASSET BUBBLES EVER SINCE

Consequently, and to indulge his own idea of happiness, Cornelius began to be interested in the study of plants and insects, collected and classified the Flora of all the Dutch islands, arranged the whole entomology of the province, on which he wrote a treatise, with plates drawn by his own hands; and at last, being at a loss what to do with his time, and especially with his money, which went on accumulating at a most alarming rate, he took it into his head to select for himself, from all the follies of his country and of his age, one of the most elegant and expensive, he became a tulip-fancier.

It was the time when the Dutch and the Portuguese, rivalling each other in this branch of horticulture, had begun to worship that flower, and to make more of a cult of it than ever naturalists dared to make of the human race for fear of arousing the jealousy of God.

Alexandre Dumas père, *The Black Tulip*, 1850

When you walk down your local high street on Saturday, look in the estate agent's window (assuming it's not boarded up) and compare the cost of your house with its market value. Of course we've all learned about negative equity in the past but it was a hard-learned lesson and we were all certain it couldn't happen again. While house prices are soft today, it's just a blip as a result of the Crunch, and the papers tell me that prices aren't falling that much. Are they?

The man on the Clapham Omnibus has found ways of losing his money since before either Clapham or the Omnibus were invented, as have the other international representations of the ordinary investor: La Veuve de Carpentras in France, Mrs Watanabe in Japan, The Belgian Dentist in Europe and of course Mom and Pop on Main Street USA. Yet after centuries, no one has yet analysed why normal (and generally rational) men and women such as these fall into the mania of investment, and out its back door into Queer Street. To be honest, this case study won't either, but it will tell you the cautionary tale of the great Tulip Mania.

The fondness of the Dutch for dykes and windmills is eminently sensible and explicable, their love of tulips less so. From the first sight of the tulban bulb by a rich Dutch merchant, to the wholesale importation of flowers from Constantinople (the modern Istanbul) in the 1590s, no fashionable house in Amsterdam was without its tulip bowl. Soon, specialist societies indulged in fanatical cross-breeding (of tulip bulbs) to generate stronger, more colourful blooms and these colours and fashions soon spread through the whole of society.

Demand grew throughout 1634 as people bought bulbs and blooms; chimneys were left unswept while truant boys discussed the relative merits of the 'Admiral Van der Eyck' against the 'Childer' and shops remained closed while errant shopkeepers spent a week's takings on a pair of 'Admiral Leifkins'. As the desire for perfection, novelty and perfect novelty raged, furious clamorous demand soon outstripped supply. Then a curious thing happened. As the bulbs were scarce, could be accurately valued, were portable and widely traded, people saw the traits that they were looking for in an investment. Tulips became an asset.

Demand grew! By Easter 1635 the price of a fairly average bundle of 40 roots had risen to 100,000 Florins (worth £2.3 million today). Now, one individual bulb was no longer within reach of the man in the street and so the vendors created 'shares' in each bulb. The 'perit' was a share by weight (about the size of an aspirin) and syndicates would club together to buy the most sought-after bulbs, and, I presume, to smell the flower in proportionate shares.

Demand grew as the introduction of the perit enabled small investors (or should we call them speculators now?) to aspire to more wonderful plants, including the ultimate 'Semper Augustus', a snip at 5,500 Florins for 200 perits. (That's about £3.56 million per kilogram at today's values – today gold is only trading at £2,200 per kilo!)

Demand grew! Investors scrambled to liquidate other assets, flooding the market with land, livestock and jewellery until the value of all non-floral property started to fall as fast as the tulips were rising. The crunch came in 1636 when three wonderful specimens – bulbs of Semper Augustus – came on the market. One in Haarlem was bartered for 14 acres of land, while one in Amsterdam traded for 4,600 Florins and a carriage. A third was mistaken for an onion by an English sailor and eaten for lunch – the only time in history when eating a raw onion brought tears to the eyes of the beholder.

Demand grew and the local stock exchanges, starved of deals in traditional stocks, opened tulip markets to fill the gap. Fashions change, but the dealer's nature doesn't. Dutch stock jobbers may not have worn white socks, but they knew how to fix a price and make a turn by developing horticultural arbitrage to take profits preferably, of course, without ever owning a physical plant. Contracts to buy bulbs were now forward looking – put your money down today for delivery of the bulbs in three months; in the meantime, the contract itself was tradeable too, which added volumes to the market.

Demand grew! In an unintentional parody of the Twelve Days of Christmas, one single bulb of Viceroy was bought for

8,000 lbs of wheat	2 Hogsheads of strong wine
16,000 lbs of rye	1,000 gallons of beer
4 fat oxen	500 gallons of wine
2 fat sheep	1,000 lbs of cheese
4 fat swine	a complete bed
a suit of dress clothes	and a silver drinking cup

Demand grew! Specialist lawyers (called the Tulip Notaries) drew complicated contracts to balance the quality thresholds of the societies against the greed of the investors (and make a good fee by positioning themselves as the middlemen in every deal). However, innovation was failing; the attempt to grow the ultimate Black Tulip had spilt too much red ink. Growers and jobbers had amassed sums too difficult to spend in the domestic markets and so the wall of money began to find English stocks more attractive than tulip stalks. October 1636 saw a medium-sized Viceroy bulb knocked down at 6,000 Florins, but the stuffing was knocked out of the market by rumours about capital flying to London.

Demand fell. Prices followed. The November delivery of bulbs saw a rash of defaults. Vendors lost cash flow and defaulted themselves on the November and December contracts. Writs flew. Tempers boiled. Prices still fell.

The Amsterdam Town Council stepped in amidst angry scenes in a vain attempt to be the ultimate Dutch Uncle. Unfortunately, many burghers were investors and over three unedifying weeks they fought for a dirty compromise. A law was passed (or bought) ruling that contracts entered into after November 1636 must stand, but prior contracts could be avoided by the purchaser paying 10 per cent of the contract price to the vendor, allowing the purchaser to walk away.

Prices still fell – and as the market price now stood at about eight per cent of the boom price, no one was even prepared to pay the 10 per cent to escape their outstanding contracts. Now the fertiliser hit the forcing frame as incensed speculators proved Gilmore's Law: 'In any financial change, the people who are pleased will be less pleased than the displeased are displeased.' The vendors went to court in an attempt to force completion of every contract lawfully entered into at its agreed original value.

Prices fell even more. The courts, displaying a commercial wisdom almost unheard of since, ruled that tulip contracts were, in fact, gambling debts since (with 20/20 hindsight) no one in his right commercial mind would pay so much for one flower. As a 'debt of honour' in a near universal principle of contract law, the debts were unenforceable. (Oddly enough, history is far too shy to reveal the extent of the tulip holdings of their Honours on the Bench.)

Prices couldn't fall much further, but they had a determined attempt. After nearly a year of masterly inactivity, the provincial council at The Hague finally came into agreement with the Amsterdam Town Council, and the whole saga drifted into oblivion. The cynical law of averages applied: those who made profits were allowed to keep them and those who made losses were allowed to keep *them*.

The modern moral is relatively simple. As long as everyone wants to buy something, be it houses, stocks, bonds, incredibly structured black boxes, or trust-me-this-isn't-toxic derivatives, then the price goes up. As long as there are banks to finance you, or you have other liquid assets, you can borrow and realise that liquidity and pour it into the bottomless pit of the boom. Collective Amnesia works two-fold here: firstly in forgetting the boom presages the bust, but secondly that people who voluntarily leave the bubble and cash out (like the Dutch bods who sold their tulips to move into English stocks) are the winners. The longer you stay on the Titanic, the more certain your fate.

So there is a moral here, but also a warning. Not just the obvious economics: demand – even irrational demand – increases the price of anything in limited supply but the sad thought about those tulips which made and lost families' fortunes is that the colour and smell of the Semper Augustus remains unknown.

As Oscar Wilde quipped, 'a cynic knows the price of everything and the value of nothing.'

The mercantile community will have been unusually fortunate if during the period of rising prices it has not made great mistakes. Such a period naturally excites the sanguine and the ardent; they fancy that the prosperity they see will last always, that it is only the beginning of a greater prosperity. They altogether over-estimate the demand for the article they deal in, or the work they do. They all in their degree—and the ablest and the cleverest the most—work much more than they should and trade far above their means. Every great crisis reveals the excessive speculations of many houses which no one before suspected, and which commonly indeed had not begun or had not carried very far those speculations, till they were tempted by the daily rising price and the surrounding fever.

Walter Bagehot, *Lombard Street*, 1873

SOVEREIGN'S DEBT:
LATIN AMERICA 1820S AND INTERNATIONAL DEBT
CRISES 1890S, 1970S, 1980S, 1990S

> KNOW ALL MEN by these Presents, That WE, GREGOR
> THE FIRST, Sovereign **Prince** of the Independent State of
> **Poyais** and its Dependencies, **Cazique** of the Poyer Nation, &c
> &c &c have, for the purpose of consolidating the said State,
> defraying the Expenses of the same, and promoting the
> general development of the natural Advantages of the country,
> negotiated and raised a Loan of TWO HUNDRED
> THOUSAND POUNDS STERLING.
>
> Rubric, £100 Poyais Bond (No. B11) 6 October 1823

One of the seismic financial crises was the Latin American debt crisis which started in 1982 when Mexico finally admitted it could no longer service the vast US dollar denominated debts that it had incurred. Most other 'less developed country' governments had to agree and act similarly, causing financial instability in the region and across the world's financial markets. Vast sums of US dollars generated by the oil price boom had been recirculated by lending to the sovereign South American governments on the popular opinion that 'countries don't go bust'.

A worldwide plan brokered by (and named after) the US Treasury Secretary, the Brady Plan successfully resolved the problem after several years of wrangling – and despite a further hiccup in 1994, this financial mechanism took illiquid loans off the international banks' balance sheets and turned them into tradable bonds with a fair sharing of the pain of loss between debtors and creditors. It will come as no surprise that substantial sums had been lost in previous generations too!

Gregor MacGregor was considerably more imaginative in his ambitions than his parents were in naming him. His dream of martial success led him from his Scottish roots to a military career against Napoleon and from there to the side of Simon Bolivar, the founder and liberator of Latin America. His victories against the Spanish oppressors helped free Venezuela and earned him a General's epaulettes, Bolivar's patronage and (most importantly) Bolivar's well-dowried niece as a wife.

Bolivar's men needed modern arms, and who best to visit London to raise money than Gregor, or 'Sir Gregor' as he now called himself. As one of

Wellington's heroes on his arrival home, he tasted fame, high living and, crucially, investor demand for Latin American debt. Relying on the enlightened (or not as it turned out) self-interest of the armament manufacturers, MacGregor raised loans, incurred debts and generally had a whale of a time.

His return to Caracas was less happy as he had relatively little to show for the time and money spent and we can only imagine the acrimonious conversations with Bolivar, or even worse, his niece Mrs MacGregor about Gregor's London shenanigans. MacGregor realised it was time to go on campaign and volunteered to police the northernmost borders of the new state. In fact, this operation became a series of private wars where military advantage was a consideration second to private gain. In 1821, having had two years of mindless scrapping MacGregor stumbled on the Mosquito people living on the coast of present-day Honduras.

Their king welcomed MacGregor to his camp with open arms and expressions of joy, thinking that this was a British Army. This was because an overenthusiastic trader in 1670 had annexed the whole coast on behalf of the British Empire. The locals, who had been guaranteed guns, booze and bright-red cloth stayed loyal to their absent paramount king in London, even although a century later the Foreign Office forgot to colour that particular bit pink when it replaced its map and thus absentmindedly dropped its 500 loyal subjects off the roll of imperial history.

The monarch of the Mosquito Coast, King George Frederick II, pressed MacGregor to stay (at least until the rum ran out) but increasingly ardent messages were coming from Bolivar (and his niece) to explain what was going on. Once again, Gregor had no good news to impart, and so he felt it was time to branch out on the independence front and make a bit of money for himself. MacGregor put the bite on the Mosquito King and obtained a grant of land from His Illiterate Majesty. Armed with the title deeds, he deserted Bolivar (and the niece) and, in the new and entirely self-appointed role as the King's Cazique (an ancient local title of chieftainship) he fled for London to burst on the stage as a New World statesman in the glittering world of the Court of St James.

His arrival in London in 1820 coincided with a boom in Latin American investment. These brand new states were breaking free of Colonial Spain and were looking for new partners and markets. Great Britain, the economic powerhouse of the world was the focus of these new markets to raise capital and buy into the wealth of the new economies. Not only was Gregor MacGregor a Hero, a Liberator and now apparently the Premier of one of the independent states but he also had something to sell – propertics that were in hot demand from British capitalists.

His plan was simple: the London investors had evinced a near unlimited appetite to buy bonds to build Bolivar's dream of independent democracy throughout Latin America – with a bit of luck, they would pay to satisfy MacGregor's dream of financial independence.

Firstly, as a good marketing man, he realised you couldn't sell anything with 'Mosquito Coast' in the title so rebranding King Geo Fred II and his empire of swampland was imperative – and it was probably better not to bring the old Rum King into the equation anyway, so MacGregor called his make believe country 'Poyais' and added it to the list of unfamiliar names bandied about in the City.

Secondly, MacGregor had saved enough gold from his campaigns to salt the mine. A legation opened in Dowgate Hill in the City with the opulence of gold and marble that would not be seen again until the famous refitting of the European Bank For Reconstruction And Development headquarters under Jacques Attalli (where the generous fit-out budget for its London HQ was set at £53 million but ended up at over £65 million). As soon as the highly polished doors opened, the Lord Mayor himself and all the major merchants and bankers were to call to meet the great ambassador while his staff appeared in green uniforms, to escort Gregor around the fashionable houses of London in a gilded liveried carriage accompanied by flunkies and even a military attaché. For a modest fee, copywriters produced more immodest claims for the new state than if it had been trying to host the Olympics. Before long, everyone was talking about MacGregor and wanting to share in his apparent success in this new found Garden of Eden.

With a false show of reluctance, he announced his major investment opportunity – the £200,000 Poyais Loan launched by one of the most reputable and dignified (i.e. dimmest) investment banks in the City, who underwrote the whole issue at 80, the same deal as for the recent issue for the real Republic of Columbia. After commissions this netted MacGregor the equivalent of £13 million today.

A beautiful loan document was engraved by Ackerman, the most famous publisher of his day, and it listed the security the new state would provide: customs duties (which didn't exist) would be gathered by (imaginary) officers who would store (undiscovered) gold in (unbuilt) warehouses to be shipped by (uncharted) vessels to meet payments on the (all too real) bonds. But it did look good on the pretty paper. It gave investors a good solid feeling.

Public enthusiasm was so great that people came to the legation to emigrate! (Obviously believing that it was cheaper to live beyond your means in a new country.) MacGregor described his capital city, St Joseph's, in such glowing terms – its tree-lined boulevards, its opera house, its great and noble Anglican cathedral, and, above all, its three Houses of Parliament, all guarded by the elite regiment in the Americas: the Knights of the Green Cross (whose code was to become so famous).

Needless to say, visas could be arranged (price on application to the Chargé D'Affairs) and an intrepid group of would-be landowners (999-year leases available – payment in cash or negotiable securities only, please) booked a passage to the land of dreams. Some concern was expressed about local government, and the resourceful MacGregor agreed to strengthen it (not too difficult in retrospect) by selling Commissions in the police and army. Lieutenant Colonel Hall, frustrated by peace, bought the Headship of the Civil Department; Andrew Picker, frustrated in love, became Clerk to the Government (with an option on a Lieutenancy in the Royal Green Lancers thrown in for free); while a Mr Gauger, frustrated by slow promotion in the City, bought the manager's desk in the Bank of Poyais.

MacGregor was at the dock the day the boat sailed, not just to wave 'bon voyage' but to remind the brave but fortunate 50 that they should exchange their English gold sovereigns for Bank of Poyais paper. The exchange rate seemed magnificent, and MacGregor gave over each of the 70,000 dollar notes picked up from the printers that very morning (handling them carefully so as not to smudge the ink). Like their life savings, they were as worthless as the other papers he had signed for the poor saps heading west.

Sales boomed and sails filled as more ships departed (after paying customs duties, health fees and naturalisation expenses – cheques payable to Poyais Enterprises Inc., please) and by 1822, MacGregor had offices in London, Paris and Edinburgh, with a great future and an even better income. The ability to capture the public's attention (and its cash) took him back home to Edinburgh where he made extravagant claims that he was jointly descended from Rob Roy Macgregor (at a time of great popularity of Walter Scott's novel) and from a survivor of the Scottish Darien scheme. This caught the national spirit (even though they should have been warned: Rob Roy was an outlaw and Darien a human and financial disaster, but these things can't happen again). MacGregor was on top form. People wanted to believe him, so it was easy to take their money.

But the eventual return of the first survivors changed all that. When the first ship anchored off St Joseph's Point off the Isthmus, the Captain thought they were lost – they weren't, but their investments were! The Civil Department met uncivil natives who would not recognise MacGregor's commissions. The only use for the lancers was to cope with the boils. The only bank had crocodiles on it. The shoemaker whose capital had secured the vaunted 'By Appointment to the Princess of Poyais' lay down and shot himself as he had lost his all. Others died more slowly, through malnutrition, malaria and murder. Those who were left escaped by ship home to face the perpetrator of the fraud with an affidavit from the Mosquito king that denied MacGregor's powers.

This put the kybosh on MacGregor's plans to launch a further £800,000 loan through the City of London so he decamped to Paris. As one door closed, another opened, and the French market looked to be receptive to an investment opportunity with such potential. The Parisians' good taste was played to by the pretty certificates in elegant double columns of French and English and they bought land grants that entitled them to vast Poyasian ranches (MacGregor sold more Poyasian acres than the entire land mass of Brazil!). This success tempted him back to sell a goldmine in London where his luck deserted him briefly, spending three days in jail for debt. He got bail (in murky circumstances) and did a bunk back to Paris only to end up in prison awaiting trial for fraud (out of the frying pan and into La Force) but like a good Scots lad he took his porridge where he found it and bided his time until his totally unexpected acquittal.

When he got out, there was still a small market in Poyais land grants which became prettier and prettier as the truth went further and further away. At one point, as the Mosquito king had let him down, he turned Poyais into a Republic with himself, of course, as first and founding president of this new beacon of democracy. Even that failed to create a buzz and by 1839 MacGregor (still handsomely in funds from his ventures) petitioned Venezuela to allow his return to spend his declining years in the country he had helped liberate. Bolivar was dead (and the niece had moved on to better things) so no one was left to oppose the prodigal's return (especially as he had saved enough to 'thank' his former colleagues with golden compliments).

He died quietly in peace, wealth and honour (all ill-gotten) and the old chancer was laid to rest in the Cathedral in Caracas. Today, in the main square in the capital of the State of Venezuela, the monument to the founders of that country proudly carries the name of Sir Gregor MacGregor without the irony we might feel.

While he was a monumental fraud, he captured the public imagination in offering to share the financing of one of the burgeoning new countries leaving feudal control with the consequent repudiation of Spain's monopoly over trade and industry allowing vast tracts of raw materials and huge markets for processed British goods. In his day the enthusiasm for South America was in the public eye. Now in the 21st century, punts on the BRIC countries (Brazil, Russia, India and China) are hailed as the economic engines of future growth, and there have been some spectacular invest-ment successes in those countries, and a few horrendous losses (thinking of the change of fortunes – politically and financially – of several Russian 'oligarchs' or the huge accounting frauds in India) that have made it not too hard to imagine BRIC becoming BROKE. One unusual feature about this current financial crisis is that unlike many heretofore, we have seen no more than average tribulation in the investments in sovereign debt – in fact it's the mighty UK who may be facing a ratings downgrade, so perhaps the international sovereigns are having a good laugh. (Perhaps we could clone MacGregor from his DNA and put him in charge of 11 Downing Street to get us out of this one?)

In MacGregor's boom period, the economic historian Frank Griffith Dawson calculated that seven Latin American nations borrowed about £20 million in bonds in London from 1822 to 1825 (about £1.3bn today). The bankers ate about 60 per cent of the proceeds in fees and expenses (and more fees) and the governments managed to default on 90 per cent of the bonds issued between 1825 and 1829. It's a pity that Nicholas Brady (who master-minded the biggest crash as US Treasury secretary) wasn't alive then, although being in the history books as the saviour of one crisis is enough for any of us.

At the end of the bull run in 1989 statistics show that the big US banks had loan loss provisions on just over half of every Less Developed Country loan. Nicholas Brady realised that there was no way back from this awful posi-tion unless the level of debts could be reduced. Without that the emerging economies would remain stagnant and the banks would be carrying these toxic assets forever. He corralled the IMF and World Bank and presented a menu of ways to reduce the principal amounts outstanding and to ame-liorate the debt service payback too without causing the collapse of the big banks balance sheets. In return the debtor governments would introduce internal economic reforms to promote liberal growth and thus create the potential to meet the reduced interest and repayment plans. Eighteen dif-ferent countries eventually joined in from Bulgaria to Bolivia, with the banks forgiving about US$60bn to this new Brady Bunch, although the overall bill came to over US$200bn.

In between MacGregor and Brady, in the early 1930s, Latin American governments had given up repaying US$3bn in loans from New York banks – that loan crisis took three decades to unravel. So how, pray tell was it a good idea to have US$416bn outstanding in 1989?

It would be unfair to castigate only the nations of South America for reneging on debt obligations to international creditors (particularly as the numbers now look pretty puny compared to the banks' losses – Argentina owes its international creditors a paltry US$6.9bn). Russia and China walked away from their debts as part of their respective revolutions (though did agree some forms of reparations generations later although Russia was back in default in 1998) while even the US State of Mississippi still has two outstanding bond issues in default (though everyone is far too polite to mention them).

And while there are always countries to lend to if that's your poison, there remain the heirs of MacGregor, owners of coral reefs offshore from the Philippines issuing sovereign debt, or National Banks based in PO Boxes above greengrocers' shops. An enterprising group of Sons of MacGregor in 1997 ran a 'boiler room' out of an Essex shed, where investors in the 'Dominion of Melchizidec' (a guano-covered rock off South America which claimed rather more of the trappings of statehood than were truly warranted) could not only turn your deposit of £3,300 into a guaranteed £60,000 in only one year but also get cheap mortgages, car loans and rebates off food from the dominion's bankers. (For the doubters, the dominion undertook to maintain a certain level of wealth in bonds of the Weimar Republic as tangible security of its wealth and bona fides.) No case was ever brought against the promoter, as the investors were too embarrassed at their stupidity, naivety and general poor grasp of history (a Weimar Bond, for heaven's sake...)

Even in the current markets, investing overseas (or cross-border) is less transparent than putting money into your home country, but at the end of the day (or at the peak of a crisis) the economic squeeze affecting a country hits its international bonds quickly (you need dollars to pay those debts) while the political will at home means that it's easier to default on bonds held by non-voters. We have had little in the way of distress in the international bonds on the emerging market economies. Don't worry – it's only a matter of time before these problems reappear. In fact, it's extraordinary that they haven't yet.

For the foreign government, the international investor in a crisis is out of sight, out of mind. Which means, out of pocket. Or to paraphrase Scotland's national poet, Robert Burns,

It's coming now for a' that
That man tae man the warld o'er
Shall creditors be for a' that.

There is no monument on the Mosquito Shore to that wily old crook Gregor, but if there were, it would surely carry this immortal epitaph on my countrymen:

There are few more impressive sights in the world than a Scotsman on the make.

JM Barrie, *What Every Woman Knows*, 1908

ROBBING PETER TO PAY PAUL BY PONZI:
NEW YORK 2009
(Boston 1920 and many places before and since)

> The first theorem of the financial instability hypothesis is that
> the economy has financing regimes under which it is stable,
> and financing regimes in which it is unstable.

> The second theorem of the financial instability hypothesis is
> that over periods of prolonged prosperity, the economy
> transits from financial relations that make for a stable system
> to financial relations that make for an unstable system.

> Hyman Minsky, *The Financial Instability Hypothesis*, 1994

The Ponzi scheme could well become the most overused word in the financial crash. Google Ponzi and Madoff and you'll get over 194,000 hits!

Charles Dickens's novel *Little Dorrit* is a book I enjoy – full of classic characters Dickensing about, more subplots that there are bottles of champagne on a bank's bonus day, each strand of plot glowing with a cynicism about the world and its financiers and the folly of the public in believing in them. At its centre stands the great banker Mr Merdle – impossibly wealthy, an MP, well housed, well married and well connected.

> Mr Merdle was immensely rich; a man of prodigious
> enterprise; a Midas without the ears, who turned all he
> touched to gold.

So, too, was Bernie Madoff. The shock of losing so much (and in such a stupid way) was ameliorated for many of us by the simple pun that Madoff had made off with the loot. From his eyrie in the Lipstick Building, Bernie had kissed off investors to the tune of US$65bn. His track record of success (or at least his own unaudited – i.e. fabricated – figures) had shown month-on-month returns at a rate of 10 per cent per annum. When asked how he did it, he had some spiel about exploiting a gap in the futures market to make this exceptional return, in fact he was sucking in new investors and using their cash to pay out returns to earlier investors. For him, his return on capital invested was 150 years in jail (and not a nice jail either especially for a 70 year old). Of course, such a dramatic fraud isn't new. Far from it.

In the world of Professor Kindleberger, the great writer on financial mania, these are known as Ponzi schemes after the redoubtable Charles Ponzi of Boston who developed this game of monetary musical chairs into an apparently credible investment in the 1920s. This pyramid starts at the apex and builds to the base – every participant is offered outstanding rewards compared with the conventional markets. Ponzi guaranteed his investors '50 per cent profit in 45 days' by investing their savings in Postal Reply Coupons – it was impossible to make any return out of postal reply coupons (even if Ponzi had owned any – which he didn't) and, quite simply, the new rush of credulous investors paid dividends to the punters earlier on in the game until the authorities prevented him from taking new money and the pyramid fell over.

That's the joy of the Ponzi scheme. Its investment philosophy is fronted by an apparently decent guy who makes good returns – very good returns in fact. It depends on a couple of key factors though. Firstly, it has to be a story of compelling return discovered by a 'genius' and attributable to his investment skill. Secrecy – or at least mystery – around the investment technique is imperative. Punters have to be told that, if the workings of this escaped into the wider world, lesser managers would have a free ride as they copied the genius, so it's in everyone's interests to keep the mechanics in the dark and maintain the high profits without competition. This creates the Bouncer at the Door – if you're not 'in' you can't get in – unless you have lots of money and an introduction. In a cruel way, the investors queue up to volunteer to be defrauded.

You also you have to stop the investors from asking to see the books – or even worse – the investments themselves. Ideally you will have a friendly auditor (your brother-in-law's one-man accountancy firm in an office above a kebab shop) and a lazy banker or broker who acts as custodian for your investment portfolio (this should be a specially created subsidiary of the investment company in a jurisdiction which enjoys taking company registration fees more than policing what goes on behind the brass plates). But the simplest thing is just to tell the punters that if they want to play, they play by these rules. If they are unhappy then, alas, they can't share in the big game and the great returns. No exceptions to these rules – that's just the way it works. Come in on these terms and share the largesse or not. Your choice. I'm not forcing you.

The last bit of genius is to work with only professional investors and immensely rich individuals and trusts. The social cachet of being on the inside of a money-spinning enterprise is superb and has a secondary advantage. Local regulators are pretty stretched in staff and resources, so naturally their genes drive them to tick the boxes and to protect the millions of little guys. The top end of the investment market should have enough wit, money and lawyers to work it out themselves (until it's too late). One of the clever developments in the Madoff ploy was to deal extensively with 'funds of funds', which are akin to unit trusts for the wealthy – an investment fund that invests in other funds. By analysing other investment companies and placing, say, five per cent of their fund into each investment, they diversify the risk (I know you've heard this before and I know you know it's not always working). Ideally, they create a Feeder Fund, which bundles individual investors into a larger group to invest en bloc in what they haven't realised is a Ponzi in return for a flat fee of one per cent or two per cent annually on the amount it invests and sometimes a share of the upside yield. All for taking Madoff's prospectus off the shelf, getting an intern to give it a quick read and then stuffing in a précis to your own prospectus. It was such good business, some feeders built up half their investments in Bernie's schemes. It seems a more cost-efficient way of selling investments than having to do all the work yourself!

The temptation was there because you could see and touch the Madoff wealth – he had an apartment in New York City (on a floor as high as the Dow), a house on Nantucket, a villa in the South of France and a place down on Palm Beach. Three yachts (I guess he didn't need one on the Hudson River) and a fair sized private jet were the accoutrements of success. There was a famous fraud in the '60s which carried the strap line 'Do you sincerely want to get rich?' to entice punters into the web, the added frisson was that Madoff didn't seem to want you in on it. It took an effort to force your money on this man.

It takes two greedy people to make a fraud. And given human nature, Ponzi was just another chapter in a long book which should have been written by Dickens, or probably Trollope, but I'm happy to have a bash at it for you and have a stab at analysing the popular English variation which was seen in the Railway Boom in Victorian times.

In a quick summary, you may have noticed that railways are very hard to run and very expensive to maintain (and seem to be getting worse). In the days of George Hudson, 'The Railway King', vast sums were raised to connect the major conurbations of our country. The shares flew from the brokers' hands as everyone wanted to share in the new paradigm (although that specific phrase comes from a more recent bubble). There was certain confusion, however, between the construction activities of the railway promoters and their supposedly independent duties as board members of the railway companies. With their Railway hats on, these gentlemen awarded building contracts to their own construction companies, and bought land from their own real estate ventures. There was no incentive to avoid overruns on the construction (quite the contrary), and so cash budgeted for capital works inevitably ran out quicker than expected. At the same time though, shareholders still expected to be paid dividends so the railway companies would announce plans to build new branch lines (on the theory that more volume equals more profit), so they would make a rights issue to collect new cash from the shareholders and divert some of it from building the new branch into paying the dividend to the old. When the last two places in England that no one wanted to travel to were connected there were no more rights issues. The wheels fell off.

The idea should be to have a huge pool of dupes to suck in, but in 1991 a feminist-themed scheme called Hearts failed in the Isle of Wight because there were not enough women in an island community to feed the exponential growth. This was billed as the way to turn £3,000 into £24,000 in a month. At or near the pyramid top sits the functionary called 'the receiver'. In this case she had to find eight other women to put in £3,000 each. Then she takes out her £24 grand. The eight punters get promoted and are asked to bring in eight new punters each so as to bring in the £24,000 for each of them. And so on. Do the maths and you'll see that no community can support that level of growth.

And this is the recurrent theme as it is inevitable that the same will happen to any Ponzi scheme. Sometimes the schemes can run to an enormous catchment – Caritas in the early 1990s captured about 20 per cent of the population of Romania in its web, spun by a Mr Stoica in Cluj (and four million citizens were less than stoical as they watched their everything flushed away) but that wasn't enough to warn nearby Albania, who stood by while 17 per cent of Albanians lost their savings in a pyramid scheme collapse which stung even the government, who lost over a billion US dollars and plunged the country into bloodshed and riots in 1997. The momentum will fail. People will lose money as they did in Ireland in 2006, Columbia in 2008 or round the corner tomorrow.

This century was encapsulated by Bernie Cornfeld's mantra 'Do you seriously want to get rich?' (You'll guess he did/we didn't – but at least he served a brief spell in a Swiss jail as well prior to being acquitted) and we seem to have seen an inverse correlation between the spread of education and regulation against the rise of financial manias, bubbles and frauds.

Or maybe you should never invest with a guy called Bernie?

One of the most powerful but simple techniques in banking is to 'Draw The Boxes'. Create a flow diagram showing all the interested parties – promoters, creditors, investors and banks. Draw arrows to show where the money comes into the system, and where it goes out. Look at each arrow between the parties and ask how can it be disrupted, how likely it is, and how can the money be replaced?

You won't have a piece of paper big enough to draw a Ponzi scheme, unless you are the one who draws the first box. (Although I do think that several fund managers who feature on the front pages of the *Financial Times* or the *Wall Street Journal* could have made a bit of an effort to understand the underlying Madoff business before taking their hefty fees.)

Think of the ways people have lost savings in the last two years and of people who, with low interest rates, find a terrifying hill to climb in replacing pensions, school fees or horse stabling. It's hardly surprising that we are seeing two effects. The corporate scandals in the early 2000s (Enron/WorldCom etc. etc.) destroyed equity value and confidence in the stockmarkets, so investors started buying bonds which, all things being equal (and it's not that easy…), have less of a risk of loss of your principal amount. The 'bond bubble' is the outcome, as the significant increase in demand is inflating the price and, to a lesser extent, enticing less creditworthy borrowers to come to market. On the other hand, eschewing 'safety', investors move to 'alternative' (i.e. more risky) or 'high yield' (which used to be called 'junk') investments to pick up a higher return (unless, of course, it defaults). Every day, we saw that large financial institutions were buying into secretive hedge funds and opaque derivative transactions. Individual investors were fed up of having to rely on house prices. It's tempting, although ultimately doomed, to see pyramid schemes as offering a geared investment opportunity to a select group.

I am surprised when reputable papers and magazines publish articles supporting these follies – often with a celebrity endorsement (which should be a common sense warning sign – you wouldn't have a brain operation just because a *Hello* celebrity endorsed the hospital – yet you'll trust your money to some decaying sportsman advertising subprime car loans…).

The Ponzi scheme is just another fraud, although rather more sophisticated than the classic scam from Nigeria which has become so popular it even has its own section in the Nigerian Criminal code – section 419. You'll probably have received one of these emails asking you to send your personal bank details to assist someone release a fabulous sum of money that's accidentally blocked in a Nigerian bank. A recent variant of the sting concerns a British citizen killed in 9/11 leaving US$30 million deposited (honestly) in the Central Bank of Nigeria which can be released only on the signature of an English 'next-of-kin'. By great good fortune you share his surname, so as he was a friendless orphan your signature is key to the money's release. If you will help the kind lawyers who have contacted you by sending them your address, your letter heading and (naturally) your signature, accompanied with your bank details, he will wire you a 10 per cent facilitation fee. Make sure you check the debits, not the credits, on your bank statement. (While writing, an impressive new version appeared – purporting to be a disgraced UK bank CEO who had fled Britain and needed to access his bonus and (rather handsome) pension which had been frozen and could only be released into your account!)

Or let's have a essay on Advance Fee Fraud by a sophisticated American who, in return for an initial (and, though you don't know it, non-refundable) US$100,000 will let you invest in the super-secret international market where exceptional returns are made in buying and selling 'risk-free guaranteed standby letters of credit on prime banks'. These instruments are so secret that that neither the Federal Reserve, nor the Bank of England, has ever seen them. Neither will you. Madoff was just one step higher than this – many steps higher if you measure it by either the amount he stole or the sentence he got. Compound interest with a vengeance.

So when an invitation to join an investment grouping with phenomenal returns comes to you, or if share touts call from Bermuda, or timeshare sharks offer a free TV – please, dear readers, remember this important law of banking: 'If it looks too good to be true – IT IS.'

In *Little Dorrit*, Merdle kills himself in his bath as his Ponzi fails. The only pain this time is for Bernie's investors.

> I don't like to see this type of activity. Eventually, if this
> bubble bursts, I think that people will be left holding the bag.
> I don't want to be around when that happens.
>
> Bernie Madoff, 1999

CASE STUDY SIX

MEUM AND TUUM:
FROM ROME 50BC TO NEW YORK 2001AD

Only the little people pay taxes.

Leona Helmsley

'The rich are different from us.' (Fitzgerald) 'Yes, they have more money.' (Hemingway)

Wealth does odd things to people and has done since Jacob defrauded his brother Esau (Genesis xxvii). But it's not just personal wealth that influences behaviour, it's being close to money. It almost seems irrelevant to debate common human greed when dissecting the current financial crisis, but one of the precursors to the present crisis was the inability of a species of corporate executive – often the founder of a great commercial corporation – to distinguish between taking a truckload out of the company validly and on the other hand confusing the personal and fiduciary roles he (for it is almost always a he) plays while getting us shareholders to pay for his (no longer aspirational) jet-setting lifestyle.

In the lists beloved of the Sunday papers, some have tried to rank the richest men of all times. Inflation, accuracy and the passage of time makes it difficult to be scientific (a bit like bank economists' models) but the approach that appeals to me is looking at the percentage of the individual's reported wealth as a percentage of the total GDP (or something equivalent) of the country at the time.

Most commentators rank John D Rockefeller Sr as number one. When he died in 1937, Standard Oil's retained profits in his hands accounted for 1/65 of the whole US GDP (estimated by the appropriately named *Fortune Magazine)* – no wonder he commented at JP Morgan's death leaving a substantial fortune but less than the wealth of Standard Oil – 'who would have thought Pierpont [as JP Morgan was known to the rich and richer] would have died a poor man?'

Go further back, through the Gilded Age into the Gold Standard and back centuries to the Golden Age of Rome and one man still stands out in the top 10 of all time – Marcus Lincius Crassus (nicknamed 'Dives' – the rich guy). When he died, his wealth of 7,100 talents of gold was greater than the reserves of the City of Rome and although inflating that up to today's prices gets us to about £145 million. Another way would be to value a talent at about US$1.1m at today's (albeit high) gold price – which makes Crassus more like Croesus at a total pot of US$7.8bn (unless, like the UK authorities, he had decided to sell gold and buy Euros at a very low point in the gold cycle).

He was born in the difficult times around the end of the Roman republic and the transition to the Roman Empire. He befriended (as much as any man could) the Dictator Sulla who sincerely believed that his harsh policies were trying to clean corruption out of Rome by executing or exiling his enemies (where is he now that we need him at the Fed?). As the enemies of the State were typically influential men, Sulla had many empty prime villas to shift. It was pretty dirty work and many of the nobles felt that profiting from misfortune was unacceptable. Crassus, though, liked the sound of gold chinking in his pouch, and was a regular bidder at the auctions. Buy a disgraced man's home, do it up and sell it on. A nice entrepreneurial real estate venture.

It would be wrong, though, just to see him as a shady developer, as he had an acute business sense. Rather than employ a slew of independent artisans, this pioneer of vertical integration built a team of 500 slaves trained as builders, masons, decorators on the one hand, but with architects and surveyors too. Eventually he even had a school to train up slaves and made a good profit by selling trained men.

He branched out into an even less salubrious speculation. Rome was a cramped city and fires often broke out. Unless you were lucky and had sufficient slaves and access to water, once the fire had caught, the villa was doomed. In those days before insurance, Crassus's spies would hear of a conflagration and the great financier would whizz over to offer a few sesterces – a tiny percentage of the house's worth – to the grieving owner. Most took it on the principle of something's better than nothing, leaving Crassus (whose byline was 'no man can consider himself rich unless he can support an army') to mobilise his slaves to save what he could of the building, refurb it and sell it on at a multiple of what he paid for it.

He was almost unique in the City – he made his millions like a common merchant yet his lineage (although not of the optimal rank) made him a nobleman. The two routes for fame in the Republic were to win a war and to become consul (one of the two annually elected chief executives of the Roman government). The problem for Crassus was that there were several talented rivals who saw themselves as the rightful owners of both highways to the top – notably Pompey the Great and the now immortal

Gaius Julius Cæsar. Crassus wasn't in their league, but he had a unique selling proposition – he was the first to think that the golden rule meant that the man who had the gold could make the rules.

He started building influence at first by lending money to political candidates, or better, standing as guarantor for their debts. Throughout his life, Julius was an extraordinary spender and when he was voted into the significant role of Praetor of the Spains, Crassus stood surety to Caesar's Roman debtors to the tune of 830 talents, otherwise they wouldn't have let him out of their sights. Crassus oiled the political wheels – here a touch, there a dollop – until many men of all political groupings were his clients.

For the upper classes in Rome – the senators and Optimates (or 'posh chaps') – money was vulgar (but a necessary vulgarity) – so Crassus had to bathe his enterprise in a gentleman's perfume. There was a trend away from the austere ancient Roman habits towards a peak of new-fangled, louche oriental luxury, as described in the immortal Satyricon where the gauche, nouveau but definitely wealthy Trimalchio lays on supper for his friends dazzling their eyes and taste buds with the most extraordinary dishes – chosen more on cost than taste – and sounding as appetising as toxic debt:

> Peahen's eggs stuffed with figs
>
> Roast wild boar (with live thrushes inside)
>
> A whole pig filled inside with sausages and black puddings
>
> Cakes and fruit filled with liquid saffron (then, and now, the most expensive spice known to man)
>
> Thrushes made of pastry, stuffed with nuts
>
> Quinces with spines poked in to look like sea urchins

All served by naked slaves, fighting gladiators and dancing girls (or if so minded, dancing boys) and washed down by the Roman premier cru, the Grand Falnerian wines. Don't know about you, but amphora nother.

Crassus couldn't access the traditional Roman powers directly, so he made himself into the nexus of power. He found hungry politicos and fed their ambition with his money and their vices with his dinners. He loved making money and was very good at it. He spent a lot too – not just on the politicians and powerbrokers, but also on the bread and circuses expected by your ordinary bloke in the Forum ('the plebs'); when he was finally elected consul he gave every citizen in Rome three months of free food (and none of your broiled sturgeon stuffed with camel steak tartare either, but real good nosh)! The problem was that he obviously liked coining it in more than shelling it out. Every time he spent, you could see him calculate how much he needed in return to balance his books. This was not appealing – people felt they could actually see the cold behind his eyes while he opened his purse to you. As we say in Latin, nothing is free.

He did get a chance to perform politically and showed a businessman's interest in matters of state while seated on the consul's chair. When Spartacus led the Slaves' Rebellion in a time of economic stress in the city, it was Crassus who bought an army and marched out to quell the rebellion. Like many CEOs he set hard standards for his men – good rewards on victory (to the Boni) but on one occasion, he exacted the penalty of decimation for a unit's failure in battle – all 500 drew lots with one in 10 to be hacked to death by his colleagues (a bell-curve policy still seen in several US corporations, at least metaphorically).

He was best at amassing wealth but he was overjoyed to climb to the traditional heights he had long sought: to be appointed general to attack the Parthian King (who ruled an empire round about where Iran is nowadays and which was a snippy and irritating neighbour to Rome's provinces). Alas, all the gold in the Crassus treasury didn't stop the Romans' defeat in the desert in 53BC, as they were drawn into a terrible ambush and 20,000 legionaries were shot down by arrows in the blistering golden sun. Crassus fell, his head was cut off and his mouth sealed shut with liquid molten gold.

Sic transit.

> Get place and wealth, if possible with grace;
>
> If not, by any means, get wealth and place.

As Alexander Pope translated the Roman poet Horace's spiteful epistle in the 1730s showing the links between human mindsets over 18 centuries...

From Crassus to the Medicis and beyond we enjoy reading histories of extraordinary wealth. Sir Thomas Gresham, for example, who founded the Royal Exchange in London, dissolved his most precious pearl valued at £15,000 in a glass of wine to toast his queen, Elizabeth 1. Wealth often disappears, though not in the seconds of Gresham's gesture. In the North of England they say that families go from 'clogs to clogs in three generations' and in France, the four generations are: Farmer, Rentier, Gambler, Pauper. Savings are built up by the founding generation, invested by the second, and then wasted by the subsequent grandchildren.

The advent of the Industrial Revolution and the firing up of the engine of US growth generated a good slew of pelf (that's a posh word for 'wonga,' or in the USA, 'spondoolicks') for the lucky winners. Of course, Andrew Carnegie (who post plutocracy sincerely held to the philosophy 'that he who dies rich dies disgraced') used few scruples in amassing a huge personal fortune, but gained many by giving it away. These tycoons (to use the Japanese term – 大君 – a great wind which was one of the many titles of the Shogun, which became used for big big money in 19th century business) were founders of businesses and the paterfamiliases of dynasties of wealth.

JP Morgan – the bankers' banker – a man whose metaphorical nose for a deal was almost as big as his famed physical schnozzle, came into his father's banking house in the rough and tumble of merchant banking. His first deal was selling faulty rifles that couldn't fire to the US Cavalry – making a nice profit – and he escaped prosecution as the poor witless general who'd bought the rifles (and had survived the rather more than expectedly one-sided fighting) hadn't the authority to enter into purchase contracts on behalf of the department in the first place, so there was no valid contract over which to sue. From then on JP fought on the side of the big battalions. His peak came in 1911 when his masterful handling of the money market crisis allowed him to call the bottom of the market and make (a) the world a safer place (b) a killing and (c) a reputation in the history books.

It didn't always go smoothly, and his ability to control vast swathes of the US economy through 'Trusts' brought a degree of obloquy in his declining years, involving investigations and corrosive press reports, all of which turned his interests more towards his library and its collection of very early bibles (maybe a cunning plan to earn loyalty points for the afterlife). Big Money is never universally popular (no matter how people crave for a share) – anarchists had even tried to blow up the fabled House of Morgan on 60 Wall Street (you can see the scratches on the building to this day – it's the small one opposite the NY Stock Exchange – when all the skyscrapers were rising and bringing real estate profits to the owners of the footprint, old Pierpont refused to build upwards as he didn't want people to think he needed the extra cash).

New York was the focus of riches in the Gilded Age, and Trimalchio would have called James Buchanan Brady 'brother'. Diamond Jim made his life out of an unprepossessing start in the parcels office of the New York Central Railroad and by dint of hard work and a sharp eye for detail rose to be the assistant assistant to the Vice President of the Corporation (a title that would be Co-SVP and business partner nowadays). He made his money through branching out into supplying the railroad companies with essential supplies in the late 19th century. Just as the American people had an appetite for railroad stock, Diamond Jim had a literal appetite for life. He was a big lad, our Jim, and liked to show off his large physique by adorning himself in diamonds – shirt studs, tie pins, cufflinks, billfolds, and watches – all masterpieces of the jewellers' art. At any given moment he'd be wearing half a million dollars worth of jewels and with jowls to match in size.

The pleasures of the flesh (and remember he had a lot of it) were his forte. Not booze – he lived and died on the wagon, but he made up for it in food. Truly conspicuous consumption.

Captains of industry now usually claim to have no time to start the day with a breakfast – while Gordon Gecko decried lunch as for wimps. Diamond Jim thought otherwise having as much interest in the farmers' market as the futures market.

After a hard day's work (punctuated by a full breakfast, a few oysters by way of elevenses, a four course lunch and a host of teatime snacks) Diamond Jim topped out the business day at dinner, always at the same table in the same restaurant (Rector's on Broadway – the owner did rather well out of this – calling Jim 'his 25 best customers'). His menu usually started with another three to four dozen of Maryland's finest oysters and a half dozen boiled crabs and two bowls of globular turtle soup. Add a main course with varying proportions of lobsters, whole roasted ducks, turtle steaks and beefsteaks rounded off by the dessert trolley (tray by tray) and a snack of a whole box of chocolates on the way home.

He and his redoubtable inamorata, the 200lb (15 stone) Lillian Russell (his other fleshly weakness) maintained their trim figures by cycling around Central Park on solid gold bicycles (adorned, as you might fear, by diamonds). At least they did till the invention of the automobile, when Jim naturally became the first car owner in NY City in a diamond studded vehicle more valuable than the King of Sweden's legendary present to Minnie the Moocher. (Hi De Hi De Hi De Hi!)

It was his money, he'd earned it and By Heaven he was going to enjoy it. And he did, evading the bookmakers' consistent odds on pricing that he'd expire at Rector's in full munch (or perhaps in the wanton arms of Miss Russell), he lasted to a fair old age and left a big fat fortune to Johns Hopkins Medical School and the New York Hospital.

From the South Sea directors to the robber barons of the US, these commercial titans arrogated extra profit to themselves in the form of inflated pay, bonuses, free stocks, and expenses that would sink a battleship. Go to one of America's poshest resorts, Newport, Rhode Island, and see the fossilised remains of their grand living – these 'cottages' by the seaside looking as if the Ritz had sent its children off to play at the beach – the mix of power, money, influence and ostentation is exactly the same as old M Lincius Crassus 2,000 years ago. It's hardly a surprise that F Scott Fitzgerald's working title for *The Great Gatsby* was *Trimalchio*.

The old Romans called this Meum and Tuum – mine and thine. Often shareholders don't mind/care/notice in the boom years – if your dividends and capital returns are jumping by leaps and bounds, why shouldn't the CEO have a Gulfstream 550 rather than having to slum it first class with the ordinary millionaires? And if he takes his wife/mistress/boyfriend off for a weekend using the company plane and the company apartment in Paris, well after a 102-hour week slaving constantly in our interests, isn't a chap allowed a bit of relaxation? And did I mention that under my management the price is up again today? As the old English Duke plaintively asked when debating the high rates of taxation in the 1950s which caused him to sack his pastry chef: 'Can't a fellow have a biscuit nowadays?'

The problems started to arise when shareholders' and investors' money were subscribed in ventures alongside the capital of the entrepreneur – the great man was used to getting his own way and lifestyle that paid for what? While Crassus and Diamond Jim were dining on their own nickel (or denarius) – whose credit card pays for today's CEOs? As always, the pendulum swings – and if you're too slow, it can hit you right in the head. Two powerful men lost their businesses and their freedom for not understanding this.

Dennis Kozlowski was CEO of the US conglomerate, Tyco, and was known as a strong businessman, regularly featured in the media as a thrusting and effective executive. He was a serial acquirer of other companies – over 200 while in charge of Tyco – and the corporation's market cap kept rising – showing investors handsome capital gains and thus enough money to go round.

He was busy, hard working and very, very rich, as could be seen from his lifestyle. His properties – from the Park Avenue apartment (not a small one either) to his beautiful estate on Nantucket – were hung with the finest art from the most expensive New York galleries (hold that point in your head for later), while his planes and yachts were on standby to ferry him between his waterfront compound in Boca Raton or his impressive homes in Connecticut and New Hampshire. Sharp suited, he was well known as a benefactor of mainly educational charities. His alma mater Seton Hall's business school was renamed Kozlowski Hall thanks to a personal (remember that too) donation of US$5m – other institutions including Columbia University and even the Nantucket Historical Society ranked him as a major benefactor.

The board jogged along happily until early 2002 when it came out that one board member had been given a US$20m bonus for introducing the finance and leasing company CIT to Tyco as a huge takeover target (oddly enough, just at the time of writing, CIT had been declared bankrupt yet again). That deal had closed the previous year, and the huge US$9.1bn price was already looking fat. Some lesser paid board members started asking questions. The regulators at the Securities and Exchange Commission had already started looking at the technicalities of the accounting policies behind the financial reporting on some of the Tyco acquisitions but the press had a field day with what was to become known as the Tyco Roman Orgy. M Lincius Crassus where art thou frater?

As is not uncommon in the upper echelons of corporate America, Dennis had traded in the first Mrs Kozlowski (who unbeknown to Tyco was still staying rent-free in a Park Avenue apartment owned by them) for a new trophy wife (Warren Buffett has often queried this term, saying in general they look more like the booby prize). Mrs K2 (there was always another mountain to climb for Dennis) was turning 40 and so the annual Tyco offsite was moved to Sardinia (that's Sardinia, Italy, not Sardinia, NJ – very close to the holiday home of that other fascinating businessman and politician Silvio Berlusconi) where the kind treasury of Tyco offered to pay half of the US$2m party bill. As if the toga-d look of Mr & Mrs K were not enough to grab the front pages of the papers, the life-sized ice sculpture of Michelangelo's David was the centrepiece containing a huge supply of premium vodka being dispensed (in homage to the famous Manneken Pis of Brussels) in a constant jet of alcohol from David's icy member. As befits any great financial party, the evening was graced by Buffett himself (Jimmy that is, not Warren). A bad enough idea to spend the money, but a stinker of a plan to have it videoed for posterity (or as it turned out, for the Grand Jury). Gatsby would be turning in his swimming pool.

The New York district attorney got in the first shot. It transpired that when Dennis was acquiring his art works at a pretty considerable expense, he balked at paying the NY sales tax on top, so he had the galleries pretend to export it to one of his other homes out of state. It was these same percentages that tripped him up. Reminiscent of Al Capone falling foul of income taxes or the late Leona Helmsley's cry that only 'little people' need to pay taxes, these eight per cents came home with interest.

Once investigations started, it became clear that the financial relationship between Tyco and some of its top executives was far from clear. Kozlowski seemed to have used funds from a loan scheme to allow him to buy Tyco stock and a generous relocation allowance scheme to fund his lifestyle without the schlep of buying stock or moving house. The planes, the boats, the picture, the jewels, even the charitable donations all came from these Tyco-based sources. What was even more surprising is that, having lent this money to its executives on rather generous terms and for various unusual purposes, the executives then arranged that the loans be 'forgiven' – effectively cancelled without repayments (something that my credit card company has yet to consider for me, I must admit). Add in a bit of sloppy accounting, and poor regulatory reporting, and soon Dennis and his cohorts were on up before the Judge.

These are complicated areas of law – were they legitimate perks and privileges that were expected by senior executives and maybe liberally but unintentionally over used? Was this just a case like getting a taxi home on the company's expense, of squeezing the team Christmas party through exes or the traditional 'back to school' raid of the office stationery cupboard. Or was this, as the DA called it, a case of 'looting'? The first trial mistrialled as the jury couldn't agree, the second sent him down. The video of the toga party and disclosure of the line–by-line expenses in refurbishing the mansions (including an infamous US$6,000 shower curtain) or a multi-thousand dollar 'dog umbrella stand' (whether an item of furniture shaped like a dog for holding umbrellas or a special receptacle for specially designed canine weather protection, I still don't know!) – was sufficient to convince the second group of jurors that this was not a case of innocent over-enthusiasm.

This was not the first case where a CEO to fail to persuade 12 good men and true that their lifestyle, spending in a day what the juror took home in a year, was justified. My favourite fallen executive is Horatio Bottomley in England who was sentenced not just to jail but to hard labour – manufacturing mail sacks – for his frauds. The prison chaplain found him at work: 'Ah Bottomley sewing I see': 'No Padre, reaping', came the reply.

The story repeats and repeats. At a time when imbalances in wealth are horribly apparent globally and even domestically (the Walton family of Wal-Mart fame is as wealthy as all the bottom third of the US population added together) this is an acute question.

Plutarch said of Crassus: 'The Romans say, it is true, that the many virtues of Crassus were obscured by his sole vice of avarice.' At least it was his own money (albeit rather sharply come by even by the standards of the day). There was a public backlash in the wake of 9/11 and the end of the dot com boom against corporate greed and excess (one investment house went as far as to ban travel on private jets 'even if self piloted' so they were taking it seriously). We will see this again – bankers' bonuses and executive compensation will move again from the remuneration committee to the back page of the *Financial Times* and thence to the newspapers of the world.

Perhaps old Andrew Carnegie (approximately the seventh richest man in history) got it right – he made his pile with some hard tactics, sold out to a bigger player and gave it all away to good causes (well, nearly all, he went to his grave with a little left, us$25–30 million). Or maybe it's just a good idea to live within your salary. But that's always so difficult when the CEO next door has a bigger plane...

> A man who has a million dollars is as well off as if he were rich.
>
> John J Astor III, 1890

CASE STUDY SEVEN

DOT COM OR DOT CON?
TECHNOBUBBLES – A NEW WAY TO LOSE MONEY FAST
ENGLAND 1830S/40S, USA 1850–73, USA 2000

> An industrial revolution, a revolution which at the same time changed the whole of civil society.
>
> Friedrich Engels, *The Condition of the Working Class in England in 1844*

There comes a time in history when one innovation captures society with its capacity to change production exponentially. I am sure that the caveman who invented the wheel bartered it for a bigger share of the mammoth, while Archimedes did all right by selling his inventions to the tyrant of Syracuse. Paper, gunpowder and printing presses all added to the sum of human endeavour, allowing more to be achieved, made and consumed.

What's this got to do with finance? A lot actually, for an idea is just that – an idea – it becomes an invention once some seed capital is spent, and then becomes a product or solution once a large enough investment is made.

Just imagine if there is an invention that would multiply the country's output, and you were given a chance to invest in a share of that. The upside is limitless and you have a direct share. This has happened on two dramatic occasions – the financing of the railways in England in the 1840s (with a similar enthusiasm in the US later that century) and recently in the technology boost in the late 1990s – or as these apparently limitless pots of wealth are known in history: The Railway Mania and The dot com Crash.

In the early 1800s, the United Kingdom had gathered the fruits of the agricultural revolution and was increasingly focusing on revolutionising industry as the next step to building the trade and produce of its growing empire. International trade was growing apace, but internal communication was a significant drag on moving raw materials (including the expanding labouring class) and of distributing finished product. Initial projects to break this logjam centred on cutting a network of canals (or 'navigations' – the working men became known as 'navvies' which is still used as a term for a civil engineering labourer) but it was a hard, laborious and expensive process (though some of the network remains in use today, albeit mainly for pleasure craft).

The steam engine had been used successfully by Trevithick to transport materials within the environs of coal mines, and it was the legendary George Stephenson who saw the potential to revolutionise logistics. There were a few horse-drawn 'railways' where carriages were dragged along wooden rails. It was Stephenson's dream to adapt the technology of James Watt and Matthew Boulton (now the heroes of the UK's £10 note) into an engine which would turn wheels by dint of steam power and generate *loco-motion* with a pulling power greater than the strongest team of dray horses in the kingdom.

This he did, and triumphantly fired up Locomotive No 1 to transport 600 signatories (on benches in converted coal wagons) for 26 miles from Stockton to Darlington on 27 September 1825. At first the expense of the steam locomotives was off-putting and so early lines mixed horses and engines, but the accountants noticed quickly that the locos could pull more weight than the horses each day, and so the initial higher expense was recouped out of higher productivity. But to get tomorrow's benefits, you have to pay today. The large amount of cash needed for the machinery ('capex,' or capital expenditure) needs to be paid out to the seller of the kit before the benefit flows back to you in cash over time.

There were some who expressed concern about the change and the safety of the new technology – rather sadly this got up a head of steam after a leading politician and cabinet minister, the Right Honourable William Huskinsson MP, inadvertently and fatally stepped in front of Stephenson's Rocket in September 1830 at the opening of the Liverpool and Manchester railway (which goes to prove that if you don't understand technology you should get someone else to do it for you). Or maybe standing in the way of a bull market is bad for your health?

There were clergymen who were concerned about the sexual feelings that travelling at that speed would arouse in young women (who flocked to try the experience – takes my breath away!) and the rival canal interest tried to prove that the technology was dirty (an early if unconsidered green argument) and innately hazardous. One of the leading canal advocates, Thomas Port, is buried in my local church, St Mary's on Harrow-on-the-Hill. He was convinced the new-fangled engines were dangerous and ironically proved himself right, as his tombstone attests:

TO THE MEMORY OF

THOMAS PORT

SON OF JOHN PORT OF BURTON UPON TRENT

IN THE COUNTY OF STAFFORD,

HAT MANUFACTURER, WHO NEAR THIS TOWN HAD

BOTH LEGS SEVERED FROM HIS BODY

BY THE RAILWAY TRAIN. WITH GREAT FORTITUDE

HE BORE A SECOND AMPUTATION BY THE SURGEONS

AND DIED FROM LOSS OF BLOOD

AUGUST 7TH 1838
AGED 33 YEARS

Bright rose the morn and vigorous rose poor Port

Gay on the train he used his wonted sport

Ere noon arrived his mangled form they bore

With pain distorted and overwhelmed with gore

When evening came to close the fatal day

A mutilated corpse the sufferer lay

The railways were now literally unstoppable if only we could get our hands on capital. We had the brand-new modern technology, but now we needed the same old-fashioned cash to buy it.

Let's jump back a few years to rural Yorkshire, the wealthy northern county in England (which almost considers itself to be a kingdom with its capital in the beautiful medieval city of York). In 1800 a son was born to Farmer Hudson and his wife. They named him George and a pretty average lad he was, living a pretty average life until his dad went to plough the celestial fields, leaving George apprenticed to a drapery business in the city with a tidy little legacy when he reached his 21st birthday. Now, out of the rural shadow, we see the lad blossom in the mercantile environment of the city.

He had a great uncle living nearby and if blood ties were not enough to encourage George, financial prospects ensured he would call and say hello. What better to do than befriend Uncle Matthew for, despite being a boring old bachelor, he had a pot of investments that positively called out for a good family member to visit every day to ensure those riches stayed within the happy family circle. Many questions were asked in 1827 when the old gentleman died and the family round the solicitor's table were told that the bulk of the estate (£30,000 – maybe a couple of million Sterling today) had gone to George who promptly threw over his poor relations (and the draper, too) set up house and started thinking about how to make a real fortune.

Not for nothing is the old guild in York called the Company of Merchant Adventurers (its motto is 'May God Prosper Our Affairs') – so our George was emboldened to play the railway game as no one had played before. At the relatively young age of 33, he bowled up to the offices of The North Midland Railway and handed over Uncle Matthew's legacy in cash in return for a substantial shareholding. This early investment yielded strong returns and George actively protected his investment and grew to understand the business, being elected to the board (partly on his merits but substantially because of his wealth).

The railway lines had not yet come north to York or arrived to serve the industrial North East round the Tyne. York was a proud community of hard businessmen and county wealth; it was Hudson's idea to raise more capital to build a new line to connect York to the infant network.

Forming a company in those days was difficult. After the South Sea Bubble the traditional overreaction resulted in the Bubble Act meaning that companies could be formed only by Royal Charter or by a private Act of Parliament – the former was impossible without high political influence; the latter, however, could work if you found a way to appeal to the vested interests in the House of Commons.

In 1833 Hudson fronted a bill in the House of Commons, confident that he could raise the £4.5m odd capital at home, he didn't mind spending a paltry £3,000 in bribing members to support the bill (or at least to find a good reason to be absent rather than speak against it). This was a theme in which he grew to be a virtuoso: calculating to the penny how much to buy this man, or sell this other. Sometimes the bribes were substantial cash amounts, later on the foolish legislators accepted shares in the railway companies. Oftentimes, the board of directors would welcome one or more MPs into their midst with privileges such as per diem board fees, free lunches (they did exist in those days), gold railway tickets allowing unlimited travel in

First Class Carriages and, best of all, they were given options to buy shares cheaply before offering them to the punters.

Stephenson was the technical director on the project and, after Royal Assent had been granted and the line was completed in 1839, he became wary of his partner's philosophy (and to be honest, probably much else about Hudson's style) and so stepped quietly out of the limelight.

The next project, The Great North Railway, followed hard on its heels with the staggering capital requirement of £5 million. Hudson led from the front and was the largest initial investor – for by this time he had multiplied Uncle Matthew's nest egg into one of ostrich proportions. Not only did his wealth allow him to participate in the increasing business of building railways, but he had become active in the Tory party, joining the City Council and receiving the highest accolade when he was made Lord Mayor (he wangled an unusual second term in the following year to preside over the city's festivities for the coronation of young Queen Victoria) – a new era in monarchy, in capital and technology.

And while there was a new Queen in London (after whom Victoria railway station was named), York enthroned a new king itself – but a single station was too small for his monument. The whole system was his empire, so he was acclaimed as THE RAILWAY KING. Hudson was not alone in seeing this new speculation as a fixed route to new levels of wealth unseen in the Three Kingdoms, as the effect of new technology multiplied output in a generational change. Many men and many plans were calling for more lines between more towns. Railways were needed for collieries, railways were needed for goods and, above everything, railways were needed for people. Civic pride was inflamed as rival towns demanded direct rail links. Some legislators, notably Gladstone, expressed public concern about the growth of rail and the unplanned nature of the growth. The Railway King stepped up his 'educational payments' (please never say 'bribes') to Westminster and bought more time and yet more acts of parliament. But there were many others around him with similar machinations and the demand for capital was rising as fast as the share prices.

It was time to move to a higher game – consolidation. Rather than build an empire line by line, why not pull together a whole swathe of tracks and so establish an effective monopoly to guarantee a growth in profits. There would be opposition to any monopoly in such a vital and growing industry, but that could be diffused by telling people that the overall control could create a coherent national timetable which was an undoubted boon and a benefit to all with improved connections and better customer service.

Out of this plan came the Midland Railway – an ambitious scheme even by Hudson's imagination.

He used his position in society, politics and the railway industry to approach three other railroads in the Midlands to suggest that they all amalgamate, with him as chief executive officer and largest shareholder. He had to offer generous terms to secure control and raised a fortune from investors in preference shares (so as not to dilute his voting control) at the dizzy coupon of six per cent per annum – and with real chutzpah, Hudson personally guaranteed the coupon payments out of his own pocket.

He started picking up other lines and adding them to his network like a hungry man at an all-you-can-eat buffet until, in 1845 at his peak, he controlled nearly a third of the railways in Scotland and England – over 1,000 miles in total. The people of Sunderland were so appreciative of their industrial town being plugged into the techno-network they elected him as their Member of Parliament, while the richest men in England held a dinner in his honour and gave him the present of £60,000 in gold as a testimonial (coals to Newcastle, but that's another story).

He was popular in the House, too (hardly surprising since a quarter of members sat on one Railway board or another – they were known as the guinea pigs as they received a fee of one guinea, £1/1-, per board meeting) and grew chummy with the old Duke of Wellington himself (it was expensive being a duke, so George's helpful hints on when to buy and when to sell helped pay the bills and stop him from worrying about the mundane world at the Cabinet Table). They say that he took virtually no recompense from the great old hero and PM except once and then in kind, his daughter being at school in London and her friends teasing the newcomer's accent and origins in trade, Hudson asked the duke to call on her and impress the peer group. (Although almost the same story is told about NM Rothschild, but still, it is a good story.)

Now the building of railways had become a national frenzy. To start the process of winning a private Act of Parliament even today you have to submit a prospectus and a host of papers to the authorities before 30 November each year to start the stages of the legislative process on the draft Bill; miss that date and it's a 12-month wait. In the summer of 1845 the demand for architects and surveyors to prepare railway plans was so high that foreign papers carried adverts and the government's own ordnance surveying department lost 60 employees as poaching technical staff became a necessity! As the deadline approached, printing firms across England were vainly trying to set the text and carve lithographs of the complex maps.

Lawyers and bookkeepers sat up all night writing out forms, estimates, affidavits and lies. As the 30 November fell on a Sunday, the Board of Trade was persuaded (by about 150 'interested' MPs) to open especially for the deposit of papers. Now the fun began. One enterprising promoter bribed the printer to hand over his rival's printed maps, boxes of papers were stolen and burned in the hope that there would not be enough time to print them again. Clerks were bribed to work slowly, printers were paid to run out of ink, skulduggery was the order of the day.

One new Northern company needed to get to London to submit its own bid and so approached the incumbent railway company to run a special train to London. The existing company (looking to maintain its fine monopoly) refused to carry them point blank. Little did they know that the funeral train which ran on Saturday 29th had the enemy's prospectus in the coffin, while all the engineers and lawyers were disguised as weeping relatives and pall-bearers in full mourning dress.

Outside the Board of Trade's offices, the police were called to maintain order as tensions mounted in the face of the deadline. Some late arrivals tied rocks to their papers and tried to throw them in through the windows to save time; so it goes without saying that a few fist fights enlivened the proceedings and at the end of that long day, 320 new applications for railway bills were piled on the desk of the President of the Board of Trade with an aggregate capital requirement of £650m (c. £46bn nowadays). With the backlog already before Parliament, some 500 applications were ready – and of the amazing 272 which passed in 1846, 32 alone were sponsored by the Honourable Member for Sunderland. He was at the pinnacle of his career, his railway shares were worth over £300,000 and he owned country estates in Yorkshire and all the perquisites of a self-made man.

On the surface at least Hudson was in clover. The middle classes piled into the share issues, and the stockmarket frenzy increased apace (a bit like the 'Tell Sid' privatisation campaign in 1986).

But 1847 was to be the year of crisis. Firstly, out of these myriad schemes a chap called Denison had the temerity to lodge a Bill for a rival London to York line – trying to check the King in his own home. Hudson wasn't ready to let a whippersnapper bite his ankles, so he oiled the wheels of the House – 80,000 wheels in fact (at £1 each) – but he'd grown overconfident. Sentiment was turning, and a poor English harvest reduced the cash available to spend on the mania. Hudson's normally prescient antennae failed to notice this and he launched a bid to buy the Eastern counties line to block Denison's project. This was a step too far or at least a step too late.

With less cash slopping around the country and literally hundreds of railways schemes, the bubble burst, wiping out thousands and thousands of investors and obliging the Bank of England to intervene to protect the country's banks that had lent vast amounts against railway shares as collateral. That security looked pretty toxic next day.

The MPs were outraged (especially those who had lost their cash and revenues as directors) and an investigation was set up to find the culprits of the bubble (or scapegoats).

The examiners found an incredible tale. To be fair, it wasn't just Hudson. Everyone had cut corners. It was only that George's empire was so vast, he had many more corners to cut.

- Land was sold at inflated prices from a Hudson property company to a Hudson railway, without a valuation (in the case of the Great Northern transaction, he cut out the middleman – selling land out of one company to another but just pocketing the cash personally)

- Hudson would buy small branch lines with his own capital and borrowed money and then sell those shares to his holding company at a far greater price (repaying the loan to himself and retaining the profit as well)

- If the railway line wasn't generating enough profit to pay an increased dividend every six months, he would announce a new capital raising for a branch line, or some improvements, and use that new capital to pay the old dividend (and of course with his shareholdings that produced cash for him to invest in the next scheme)

- Acquiring other lines caused expenses and fees, some of which flowed to Hudson (and many fees to his associates as douceurs)

- If your rivals wouldn't sell out then you'd promote a bill for a railway line parallel to theirs – no intention of building it – but they'd have to buy out your rights to prevent that competition – early Greenmail but good money if it worked

- Getting permission for more and more tangential branches and branches to branches – providing a continued pool of shares for gullible bubble investors

- Announcing spectacular future dividend growth or high-preference share coupons to draw more money in

- One of his accountants admitted that the company accounts were kept in pencil to make it easier to effect changes if later required by Mr H.

- Fees payable as directors and expenses and perks rolled in to George's pocket day-in-day-out.

Our George was a fighter – and, importantly, an MP still. His reputation and millions were crumbling, but the folk of Sunderland stood behind the man who linked their factories and collieries to the outside world. Many ordinary people had seen the economic benefit and (at this point at least) didn't begrudge their king his crown. The evidence at Committee was killing, though, and Hudson had to undertake to repay his defalcations, though these were, he said, the oversights of juniors as he was so busy and couldn't attend to detail. York was less forgiving than Sunderland and expelled him from the City Council, renaming George Hudson Street as Railway Street in 1849. Even Madam Tussaud melted his waxwork down in disgust.

His personal bank – the great railway firm of Messrs Glyn, Mills & Co – had provided serious amounts of unsecured debt to the Railway King's privy purse, and in a gentlemanly way, tried to claw it back. One partner's letter is a joy to read:

July 31 1851

Dear Sir,

We feel it right to call your attention to the state of your account which is overdrawn to the extent of £2,700 and to mention that we have no means of preventing its being known to our clerks whose attention is called to the fact when cheques are presented for payment.

Your obedient servants

GLYN MILLS & Co.

With his investments ruined, his remaining wealth melted away and he stood down as Sunderland's representative 12 years later. He hadn't repaid the debts he promised and fled to France to avoid imprisonment as a defaulting debtor. When he came home he thought that it had all blown over, and stood in the elections of 1865 at Whitby, hoping that his Yorkshire friends would propel him once more into the world of power (and on a more mercenary level, MPs couldn't be imprisoned for debt) but his creditors had kept an eye open and he was finally arrested and ignominiously thrown into debtors' prison until a band of well-wishers helped him out of his predicament. He lived quietly thereafter in London on a small annuity and died, reportedly worth less than £200, in 1871 to be shipped home – by train of course – to his last purchase of land, a six-foot long by three-foot wide plot in a Yorkshire churchyard.

As the grass was growing over that Yorkshire tomb, 5,000 miles away the same farce was being played out in the US by the robber barons. And just over a century after that a new bunch of outsiders with a brand-new revolution in technology looked to the internet to be the railways of the future. The dot com Boom (or Dot Bomb as it became known) followed very similar follies.

The technology WAS a revolution but it would take time to build a stable network (when boo.com opened to sell fashion in 18 countries few of them had sufficient dial-up capacity to download the pictures).

The public felt this was a sea change in society and the global economy and were persuaded to jump in and invest like fury – every business was going to be revolutionised by the internet and no old technologies would survive. This truly was the increase in production that would change us and the world forever. If only it was better managed: if you have a business where the sales margin is negative, you can't trade your way into profit by increasing customer sales.

Investors need to analyse rather deeper than investing because the title has 'railway' or 'dot com' in it. Hudson would have been proud of the dot com guys. Technology changes our lives, our society and the productive capacity of our economies, but not all new entrants – or participants in the broadest sense – are going to be winners. Just because Coco Chanel's New Look changed women's fashion not every dressmaker who could run up 'a little black dress' (LBD) was guaranteed to be rich – just as not every girl who wore one would be sexy.

Tech crashes tend to cost their investors a lot. When the Great UK Railway Mania broke over the head of George Hudson, share prices fell dramatically with investors losing up to 65 per cent of their investments and seeing the exceptional dividend income they had lived off simply vanish. In the two waves of investment starting in the 1830s a total of £200m was invested in the UK (which represented about 40 per cent of the country's GDP) of which the real mania investment of £130 million in the 1840s lost half its value in the crash. In the US the almost forgotten 'Long Depression' started in 1873 with the collapse of Jay Cooke's railway empire when it failed to meet a margin call. In the ensuing panic a quarter of all the railroad companies across America went bust, triggering a recession in the general economy which lasted a decade. Of the trillions invested in tech stock less than 10 years ago, if invested is not too strong a word for companies that rarely paid a dividend or made a profit, shareholders lost over US$5 trillion while the banks had loan losses a plenty. Railways all over again.

Although, to be fair, in context by some measures, bank and financial share prices are down 84 per cent from their peak in February 2007 while the dot com stocks we have just been pillorying only collapsed by 78 per cent from the high of their bubble in early 2000, to the bottom of the market in October 2002.

And by the way, in 1971, a hundred years after his death, York Council restored the street signs on George Hudson Street while Sunderland never flinched from its hero. Last year The Monkwearmouth Station Museum in Hudson's home in the North East ran an exhibition on its railway 'hero', ironically sponsored by the Northern Rock Foundation. That's an exhibition that will run and run.

> We were a fast-growing company, and I was a demanding boss.
>
> Bernie Ebbers (Former CEO of dot com darling WorldCom, now otherwise employed), 2002

REAL ESTATE – FOUNDATIONS OF SAND: LONDON 1774, NEW YORK 1930, LONDON 1990
(and more in between)

> Of all the Sufferers I am the most concerned for the Adams,
> particularly John. But their Undertakings were so vast that
> nothing could support them: They must dismiss 3,000 Work-
> men, who, comprehending the Materials, must have expended
> above 100,000 a Year. They have great Funds; but if these
> must be disposed of, in a hurry and to disadvantage, I am
> afraid the Remainder will amount to little or nothing... To me,
> the Scheme of the Adelphi always appeared so imprudent, that
> my wonder is, how they could have gone on so long.
>
> David Hume writing to Adam Smith, 1774

Three brothers from another country with a reputation as successful property developers came to London and, with the help of powerful friends,
obtained parliamentary support to reclaim a half-derelict waterfront site
in London in an attempt to create an address to rival the old-fashioned
accommodation in the prime heart of town.

Just over 200 years later, the Reichmans tried to do the same in creating
Canary Wharf. There comes a point in every banking cycle where the
number of visible cranes seen out the office window is the ultimate hazard
warning sign – get out now! Typically, it involves too many banks lending
on too generous terms to too many developers (many new to this particular market) with certainly too few potential tenants. As so often happens,
bank capital encourages bad deals.

In the 1760s the name of the Scottish architect Robert Adam was synony-
mous with style: he had done for the 18th century what John Major did
for grey in the 20th. His undoubted genius was assisted in business by his
two brothers who, on the death of their father, a noted builder (funny that
I describe myself as a landowner; you as a developer; he/she/it as just a
builder), formed a partnership to take the Adam style south. They were the
Marx Brothers of Architecture: Robert, the ebullient genius, William the
pragmatist with the accent and the Silent One, James. Robert designed,
William promoted, and because James had no real strengths, he was put
in charge of the books.

Patronage was crucial, as the King was not convinced by the Adam approach and the brothers feared some sign of the royal displeasure (luckily George II could not spell 'monstrous' or 'carbuncle' so felt no urge to interfere in matters architectural unlike his GGG-GGG-grandson, Prince Charles). Equally fortunately, they had a natural pool of supporters – the Scots.

Since the Union of 1707, London had seen an influx of Caledonian spirit. Despite Dr Johnson's savage and witty remarks (the 'Rivers Of Blood' speech of its day) teasing the new class of adventurers with put downs like: 'The noblest prospect which a Scotchman ever sees is the high road that leads him to England!' or the famous dictionary definition he wrote, describing 'Oats: A grain, which in England is generally given to horses, but in Scotland supports the people.' They kept on coming south.

But even Grumpy Sam had to acknowledge a spark in these financial and economic immigrants from the North, as he wryly admitted (through gritted teeth) that 'Much may be made of a Scotchman, if he be caught young'.

Scots nobles, bankers, politicians, navvies and beggars established a strong expatriate community, and had even started the sad process of moving from being Scots to merely Scot-tish. The Adams were close to two of the leaders in this society: Lord Bute, the First Lord of the Treasury (the first deeply unpopular Scottish Prime Minister) and Lord Mansfield, the Lord Chief Justice who was a remarkably small man, but an equally great judge (one of those little things sent to try us).

Through their influence, the Brothers tasted success, but how could they combine unlimited talent with all-too-limited cash and still walk away with a full sporran?

Property Development!

They had made good fortunes out of all the ancillary business supporting property speculation: designing, refurbishing, interior décor and furniture – so why not go into the first stage – building the building as well? But not just one house, rather a brand new quarter – two dozen palaces by the Thames, to be called 'The Adelphi' (which is Greek for 'The Brothers').

There had already been a number of prominent developments, notably the Grosvenor Estate, where six worthless fields given by a rank old miser as dowry when he married off his only niece to a man of rank were transformed into Mayfair. Developers had very little cash (thankfully some things have changed!) and while things were going well, little was needed as a system of barter operated. Most developers were tradesmen – each would swap materials and craftsmanship on each other's projects leaving cash, typically, to pay ground rents. The risks remained great with one in every eight bankrupted by having insufficient capital to hold completed houses until sold to their new occupiers.

The Duke of St Albans was facing a heavy jail sentence unless he could pay off his immense gambling debts. He owned part of the foreshore along the Thames (when the Strand was a strand) and his lawyers offered the Brothers a 99-year lease on a plot 400-foot by 400-foot at the phenomenal ground rent of £1,200 per annum. This was a sum more closely correlated to the Duke's needs and debts than to the market value of this undeveloped land. If they were to take up this noble offer, the Brothers would need to create a revolutionary new product that could command a super-premium price; in fact, the highest ever paid for a London house.

There were only two problems: how to build it and how to pay for it. The Brothers paid the first quarter's rent on Lady Day 1768 and Robert (now MP for Kinross) lobbied Bute to introduce a Bill to permit them to embank the Thames, thus providing both a foundation for the palatial houses with a series of high-vaulted cellars beneath for commercial use. The plan was to pre-let the vaults to the Board of Ordnance for storing gunpowder (potentially the first property boom). The Brothers only needed to cover the ground rent until the vaults were ready for occupation, when the rental from Her Majesty's Government would pay for it. As for the houses, they would be built in batches of twos and threes, and sold quickly, releasing cash for the next phase. That cautious approach would mean that the capital need not be injected all at once. The family resources provided a contingency (which would, of course, never be needed). Easy peasy!

The first, small cloud on this sunny horizon came from the City of London, who objected to the embankment. The ensuing tangle in court, cut short by Mansfield's influential shears, cost the Brothers several quarters' rental. So, without those incoming rentals to pay the Duke, cash was already running low and the contingency fund in the old tartan shortbread tin was near exhausted. Just as well that work had started, and nothing else could go wrong...

Of course, the embanking works cost that bit more than planned. But if a job's worth doing... it's worth doing at someone else's expense, so James borrowed some money from his own bankers and everything went swimmingly. Literally so at high tide, when the vaults flooded, being two feet too low. Not even Bute could cajole his officials to sign the lease for the gunpowder store. It was a damp squib.

Bad luck was becoming to be called bad judgement. At least, some houses were built (or nearly so) but in a change of plan these had to be mortgaged to raise the shortfall. By the halfway stage there were only three tenants – Robert Adam, William Adam and James Adam (and they couldn't afford to pay the rent themselves). Everything had fallen behind plan (except cost), and more and more workmen were brought on site. They, too, were under cash flow pressure, but happily one innovative bank (Messrs. Fordyce) had sufficient market knowledge in this highly specialised industry to discount contractors' bills of exchange to lend them working capital. Needless to say, they went bust, and took down many of the Adams' subcontractors (the little artisans who actually did the hard work in the vain hope of riches from the great new residential quarter).

Robert's famous collection of Italian statuary went to Christies (and the proceeds into the Adelphic black hole) but even then £218,000 was needed to complete the project and pay out the mortgages (or vice versa, depending on your priorities). The brothers all chipped in their remaining assets at a bargain price – anything to stay afloat.

Beg? Borrow? Pray for a miracle? All choices were considered and each was – ruefully – rejected. The Brothers simply needed hard cash (and found that it's called hard because it's hard to get when you really need it).

Only one final burst of political influence could rescue the ailing entrepreneurs. They proposed to promote a lottery. A total of 55,360 tickets at £350 a pop were authorised by Robert's parliamentary colleagues to raise the sum needed to finish the Adelphi. The only sad part was that the prizes had to be worth at least the £218,000. Any profit over that was available to rescue the Adelphi.

There were 108 prizes: you could win houses in the Adelphi, or a host of other properties and antiques. James ran an advertising campaign extolling the wonders of a competition where, for a meagre outlay, you might recoup £50,000! The populace went wild, and the Adams' office was besieged for three days while punters clamoured for tickets. Every single ticket was sold and, in a hubbub around Jonathan's Coffee House (where the embryo stockmarket met in those days), tickets were drawn and prizes awarded.

The creditors were paid in full and, eventually, the houses were let. What about the Bros. Adam? They salvaged just enough from the debacle to allow them to do what developers invariably do when they have narrowly escaped from financial ruin: find a new bank, and start again!

In 1986 we hit the peak of the New York real estate market. Following Mitsubishi's capture of the iconic Rockefeller Centre, the Exxon Building was put on the market at US$375m but was sold quite quickly for a staggering US$610m. Why? Mitsui's president had been given a copy of the Guinness Book of World Records which had the most expensive building in the world in at $600m. He wanted to beat that. Can you beat that?

It took three subsequent owners and many dollars of carrying cost before the Rock wasn't a millstone round the owner's neck. With luck and inflation, the best cure for a real estate crisis is time and a forgiving bank manager.

Whether it was the Adam Brothers creating the Stand centuries ago or the Reichmann Brothers realising Canary Wharf, speculative real estate development is a hard and chancy way to make your living. Over time, you could be lucky, in London the visionary schemes of new office space were Canary Wharf in the docklands and Broadgate over Liverpool Street have seen changing fortunes.

Canary Wharf was a gleam in the Reichmann Brothers' eyes in 1988 when construction started, but the London market tanked just after the UK's tallest building was opened in the centre of the wharf and the estate went bankrupt in 1992. Over the next years, the buildings were built out and filled by mainly financial tenants until the occupancy rate hit 75 per cent when a consortium including Paul Reichmann bought the company in late 1995. They continued to work at the project and when it was virtually fully let, they floated on the London Stock Exchange generating a handsome return. By now the Wharf was humming and growing apace in the long period of financial euphoria. This led to a hostile takeover by a group including Morgan Stanley who won majority control and took Canary Wharf private again in March 2004 financed by a large leveraged loan. Reports in 2009 that loan covenants were under strain make it look as if the cycles of financial history are still turning in the Docklands.

This is not an isolated story – the founders of London's Broadgate lost control in the last property crisis, and the company which bought it then has recently sold a stake in it as part of its financing strategy in this downturn. Even the Empire State Building was known for years as the 'Empty State Building' as depression hit New Yorkers wouldn't take on new leases.

They say property is all about 'location, location, location'. It's more about 'liquidity, liquidity, liquidity'. After all, this is the most cyclical business after banking. Particularly when you are building new offices for investment banks! The old saying goes that as they're making no more land, it's a good long term investment. For the real estate barons (literally in the case of the Duke of Westminster or Lady Howard de Walden and of course, The Crown) who inherited all those lovely acres hundreds of years ago that's probably true. But if you are a parvenu who has to buy the land and then also incur the construction costs, you are at the hazard of the market. Buy badly and it will take years (if your bankers let you survive that long) to recoup your investment.

Many's the developer who has had to thank his funders in the words of a prominent borrower in 1991: 'We owe you a debt we cannot repay'! But of course, it's the next generation – it's the investors, not the developers, who come in after the construction and take over the project – they are the organisations that reap the rewards of these massive new quarters. It was thus in the 1770s and remains so today. The trials and tribulations of the commercial real estate market globally are still very real indeed.

The banking cliché is that you should look out your office window every day, and when the number of cranes has doubled, stop your bankers lending to real estate developers. We have seen the first pain in commercial real estate (and house builders) as the final stages of output came on the market just as demand was falling. Real estate often has an unreal quality.

That being said, go down to the Adelphi, or even better Canary Wharf, or the Empire State, the Rockefeller Centre or the World Financial Centre in New York – or somewhere near you. Empty they were and many lost money. But, location, location, location (plus a helpful bout of Collective Amnesia) brings everything round in the cycle if you can stay holding on.

> As a development it was admirable but as a speculation it was unprecedented.
>
> David Hume writing to Adam Smith, 1774

CASE STUDY NINE

SPIRALS:
LONDON 1980S, LONDON 2009

Over the head of the crier hangs a huge ship's bell, a bell of
fame, a bell of ill-omen. It is the Lutine Bell, and it rings when
news has to be announced of overdue ships, one stoke meaning bad news, a loss or wreck, two strokes meaning good or
hopeful news... At the first stroke of the Lutine Bell, there falls
a sudden silence. The room waits for the second stroke, which
comes or does not come...

Collin Brooks, 1931

From ancient times traders have risked life, limb and capital to import and
export goods for profit. Whether by quinquiremes of Nineveh from distant Ophir, stately Spanish galleons or dirty British coasters, the flow of
trade goods and commodities has always been a key part of economic
development. The histories of great merchant cities – Tyre, Carthage or
Rome; Genoa, Lucca or the powerhouse of Venice; London, Bristol or
Glasgow – share many common themes over the centuries, and one important shared characteristic is the innovations in finance to promote the
growth of trade. From the oft-asked 'what news on the Rialto?' in old
Venice up to browsing your Bloomberg today, the finance of trade remains
a key part of financial enterprise. But no lender can take the risk of the loss
of a ship and its contents, so insurance is an essential feature of global
trade, and has been for centuries.

Primitive forms of marine insurance started in the Mediterranean as the
Italian city states began their long domination of the trade routes, but it
was in London during the reign of Good Queen Bess that what we would
recognise as a formal market began to form. With the defeat of the Spanish
Armada the seas were open for our merchants to grow trade with England's
fledgling colonies in Virginia. Within a few years there were a couple of
dozen full-time brokers who would arrange to find groups of merchants
who would commit to pay out an agreed amount if a ship was lost or its
cargo ruined (in return for a premium paid in advance).

The British Empire and its trade grew over the next century and a half, and
at the time of the South Sea Bubble there were over a hundred London-
based investors willing to underwrite British and foreign vessels. As we

discussed, the Bubble Act prevented all but Royal Exchange and London Assurance from forming insurance companies as we know them today, so they held a corporate monopoly for a century. There was nothing in the Bubble Act, though, to stop individuals from taking on insurance risks and so those merchants who used to hang about the coffee house of one Edward Lloyd (where you could get a nice cup of latte and a bun while picking up the gossip and news about which ships were docking or missing) became an increasingly formal marketplace for underwriting insurance: a market which became known as Lloyd's of London.

The Lloyd's market is still there today, now housed in the ugly Richard Rogers building where the inner workings of the building's plant and equipment festoon the outer walls. It is often said that Lloyd's started life in a coffee shop and now lives inside a coffee machine. The City of London has a long history of financial innovation wrapped up in the coat of tradition. Things change imperceptibly here but people outwardly carry on as usual; so no one in the insurance world blinks an eye at the liveried staff (still called 'waiters' from the coffee house days) checking security passes on the steps of the Lloyd's Building, nor stare at the old ship's bell that hangs still in the centre of the underwriting room, which was salvaged from a wreck of a ship once insured here and which is traditionally rung once for bad news and twice for good news. Every working day men and women in formal pinstriped suits rush in and out with their unusual leather portfolios bulging with papers. This activity reaches its peak in the early afternoon and then, as there has always been a social element to the conduct of business in this market, the traditional long lunch takes over, filling the restaurants, pubs and myriad wine bars which cluster around the district.

Lloyd's is unique – a marketplace for insuring ordinary and extraordinary risks. But it, in and of itself, is not the insurer; it is simply (if anything is simple about Lloyd's) the market – the venue, the infrastructure, the culture and, nowadays, the regulation and control of its members who are the providers of the actual insurance policies. It remains in essence, Edward Lloyd's coffee house, housing a community of underwriters, and it competes with the large insurance companies across the world, not just in marine insurance but in every kind of risk.

It is proud of two things: however many times the Lutine bell has rung, Lloyd's is proud to proclaim that it has met every single claim in full in its history and, secondly, that there is nothing on the planet that can't be insured there.

Many a shapely actress's legs (and a few more prominent body parts, too) have been insured there, a comedian insured against the risk of any member of his audience dying of laughter and the risk of the silent actor Ben Turpin's eyes uncrossing and Ugly Betty's smile vanishing have joined wine tasters' noses, vocalists' vocal cords and explorers' lives on policies underwritten in the Lloyd's hall, but the bread and butter for many years was the insurance of shipping and cargoes.

You can't just phone Lloyd's to get a quote – firstly you must find a specialist broker, whose firm is regulated by the market. He will prepare a proposal form and take it into the market by visiting the great Underwriting Room. Here, the underwriters sit making decisions on what to insure and at what cost. It isn't the underwriter, though, who bears the risk. He acts as the risk manager for the group which puts up the capital and takes the risk: the syndicate.

The syndicate, even by Lloyd's quirkiness, is a unique concept. A group of investors called 'Names' (once all private investors – some market professionals and some external investors, but now mainly companies) put in the initial capital to form the syndicate and, rather startlingly, can end up with unlimited liability for the policies the syndicate agrees to write. A syndicate is an 'annual venture' where the individual's involvement terminates at the end of the year. In practice, the syndicate often reforms for a new year under the same number and largely or completely the same participants, but legally it is a new partnership, and as such is not responsible for the losses in any year but its own. When the syndicate closes at the end of its year of operation, it takes two more years to ensure that all the profits and losses are calculated and then typically distributes profits (or losses) in proportionate shares to the syndicate members.

Historically, the unlimited liability of the capital providers was a great strength of Lloyds. The policy holder would have his claim paid out of the syndicate's capital, and if that weren't enough then the wealth and houses of the individual Names would be liquidated to provide more cash to pay the claims. As a final security Lloyd's itself set up a central fund (financed by a levy on all participants) which could be tapped if all else failed. The principle of unlimited personal liability has been watered down of late but it defined Lloyd's for many years. One old Chairman used to check a new Name's understanding of what 'unlimited' meant by asking the prospective Name to sign three cheques payable to the Chairman personally but blank as to the amount! So you can see that the business model was very high risk for the Name if something big went wrong. Over time the sum of profits on the good years should exceed the losses in the bad years, but the Name needs a lot of liquid capital to ride out any insurance catastrophes that occur. That is, after all, what insurance is for.

Nobody wanted to take losses, but a curious tax distortion became important. As UK taxes rose after the Second World War, income tax reached the impossible top rate of 98 per cent, while capital gains tax rates did not exceed 40 per cent. Some bright sparks at Lloyd's started running the business to make a gross loss on the underwriting income but a much bigger capital gain on the syndicate's investments. The underwriting loss was offsettable against income tax (reducing each Name's income tax bill) and the investment profits were accounted for in the lower tax band. As always, when a business model is changed to achieve a certain tax consequence, there's usually an unintended consequence in the real world too. One such consequence was that an increasing number of 'non-working' Names – pure investors rather than participants in the industry – rolled up to play.

Originally a potential Name had to be a UK male with a significant fortune in liquid assets to hand, about £70k in old money – and that was a lot of old money in the 1970s – before being allowed to join, but in a move to be more inclusive (or at least to get more capital in the market) overseas residents were allowed and 'even' women in 1970 (to the chagrin of the old school). But the real change was in the 1980s when they announced that one's wealth could be in the form of property or a guarantee from a UK bank (which in practice would be secured against the Name's home or homes). Now Names were joining who had limited liquid funds. This is an important point – for until then, hard as it may have been, if a Name made losses he has cash or other assets to hand over to meet the obligations but still have a roof over his head and enough capital to stay in the game the following year in the hope of a profitable year to claw back his losses. The new rules meant that new Names were often relying on the value of their family home which would need to be sold if the losses were significant – a different equation altogether.

You'll remember that a syndicate writes business for one year only. There's a bit of an oddity in this, though. Imagine you have car insurance (please tell me you do…) and let's assume that some careless trucker reverses over your Audi on the very last day of your policy. You have a claim to make but it will take a couple of weeks for the garage to look at it, call in the loss adjuster, have the police assign a reference number, complete the forms in squillions of copies and so forth. The syndicate has to make an allowance for these claims (in the jargon 'incurred but not reported' or IBNR), which will be paid out in time. Fortunately, explosions, hurricanes, etc. shouldn't take too long to sort out – and these are called short-tail risks – the catastrophe strikes and the fall-out is clear to see when the dust settles.

On the other hand, there are long-tailed risks (nothing to do with lemurs). Health policies are the classic long-tailed risk and asbestos the nastiest of them all. As it can take decades for the disease to show, it will be many, many years ahead before the underwriters are certain of the quantum of payout needed. Changes in the law, particularly in the USA, aggravated this, as judgements against the insurance industry meant that an asbestos victim who had been insured years ago but didn't claim still had a valid claim against the syndicate decades later when the disease was finally diagnosed. All of a sudden it was very difficult to achieve a close if your syndicate was tied up in these long tails.

Enter the concept of reinsurance. This is a specialist discipline within Lloyds and is effectively insuring other insurers. A classic reinsurance contract says to the primary insurer that losses on a contract greater than an amount (like the deductible or excess) will be borne by the reinsurer in return for a premium. This is a longstanding and albeit risky, standard working in the insurance markets (not just Lloyd's as there are corporate reinsurers too). A standard product was offering to 'reinsure to close' ('RITC') effectively to give a syndicate an insurance policy to cover the event that an unexpected claim surfaced later. After paying a premium to the reinsurer, the books could be closed. The RITC premium would be deducted from the P&L and the resultant figure could be divided up amongst the Names who now had no outstanding insurance obligations if any claims surfaced at a later date.

In the boom of joining Names in the 1980s thousands of new chaps (and chapesses) entered the market for the first time looking for a way to deploy their capital to make money. They didn't know how; as greenhorns they were only interested in a share of the return, not the mechanics of the Lloyd's market. So they asked their agents to sort out a good plan and so their money started to flow not only into the reinsurance policies that closed off syndicates, but a variant that was called London Market Excess of Loss (or LMX) which reinsured syndicates either for huge one-off hits or the aggregate effect of a major catastrophe or catastrophes.

At one level, the idea was sound, LMX gave certainty to the old syndicate and by spreading its potential final risks around a number of other syndicates, the danger of a catastrophic long-tail problem is shared and diluted. In return the LMX syndicate would take a nice cut of the premiums and could afford to pay the introducing broker a good fee (allowing a few happy lunches along the way). All apparently prudent and profitable. Virtually free money was the popular belief (which only encouraged more activity).

In the nature of the beast, growth had to be maintained, so a particularly ingenious broker suggested a way to multiply the returns. Why didn't the LMX underwriters sell LMX cover to other LMX syndicates? So they did. And then they reinsured those contracts with another syndicate and then that syndicate's and so on and so on. The structures, documents, management and regulations were not up to the explosive growth so no one really noticed that the end effect was that everyone had a bit of everyone else's danger in the portfolio maybe two, three or many times over as the risks had been bundled and rebundled again and again (or sliced and diced in the more current phrase). Many syndicates wrote policies which were unwittingly reinsuring their own reinsurance! It was a bit like the poor village where everyone made a precarious living taking in each other's washing. No great shakes if it's the normal distribution of small or containable losses. But a catastrophe would turn out to be a catastrophe.

It happened on 6 July 1988 when the North Sea oil platform Piper Alpha erupted into a fireball that engulfed its crew and set fire to Lloyd's itself. It's not cheap to insure an oil rig, and if there's no accident it must be a nice earner for the underwriters, but when there is an accident it results in a total loss that's over £300 million. It wasn't just in the North Sea; other catastrophic losses at that time included the oil pollution scandal of the Exxon Valdez, Hurricane Andrew and Hurricane Hugo ripped through the US coasts and California experienced an earthquake. By 1990 these major losses were looking to cost Lloyd's nearly US$10bn on top of the long-tail asbestos and pollution suits which were at least double that. Now these losses had to be paid, and to do that they had to chase all the way backwards round the spiral. Up and down, across here and there, unbundling rapidly as thousands of unsuspecting Names found out their huge liabilities as many had insured or reinsured the same risk several times. For the first time counterparty risk started to be of concern – what would happen if these losses brought down a syndicate who was supposed to provide reinsurance to another? These multiple risks were all within the Lloyd's market: the coffee machine had turned into a pressure cooker.

In the ensuing saga, Lloyd's Names lost over £8bn in aggregate and many were personally ruined, losing their savings, homes and livelihoods (which is the downside of unlimited liability) and the venerable institution itself wobbled under the financial and reputational implications. As the combination of the loss of confidence in the market itself and growing allegations of incompetence and fraud from the burned Names (some of whom they alleged a master plan of 'recruit to dilute' that Lloyd's knowingly brought in new Names and capital as patsies to absorb the long-tail losses thus letting the old Names evade the pain that they had first underwritten) investigations and working parties grew like mushrooms to cover the problems (and pin down the blame).

The near-death experience was just that: Lloyd's didn't die. Radical surgery cut out the dangerous risks preceding 1993 into a run-off company (the equivalent of a bad bank) called Equitas, which is still running off and will be for another couple of decades, leaving the core market to return to its knitting with a new management. The market is the same in many ways today, but features a stronger regulatory framework overseen by the UK authorities and the introduction of corporate Names and more limited liability, but many people lost everything.

From pessimists to optimists to idiots. 'Never let the perfume of premium disguise the smell of the risk' was a saying attributable to Hank Greenberg of the giant (and now effectively bust US insurer) AIG. So, looking back at the LMX spiral, while the Lloyd's building's workings are vulnerable to the naked eye, the business practices remained fairly arcane. So arcane for many years that the tsunami of losses simply were not understood. It bears staggering resemblance to the modern market in Credit Default Swaps (CDS), the derivative bets (sorry, insurance) on a company going bust and the Collateralised Debt Obligation (CDO), which sliced and diced all sorts of bonds into diverse bundles. We saw:

- Weak regulation of experienced market traders

- Bespoke and complex documentation that few read and fewer understand

- Trying to mitigate risk by selling it in the market, which then sells it again, and again until everyone has a bit of it

- Excess capital looking for better yields

- Huge bonuses and rewards for the originators who created these risk spreading instruments

- Counterparty risk with your contractual partner

- Exponential growth in the market

The combination of good market conditions, new player capital and opaque risk is never a good mix, whatever you call the underlying product, be it LMX insurance, collateralised debt obligations or credit default swaps. Playing slicing-and-dicing can cost you a few fingertips – a very dangerous way of playing 'Pass the parcel'.

> Unless we take radical action now to produce a solution which is acceptable to our policyholders, our regulators, and to you, the membership, I do not believe that [Lloyd's] will be able to survive in anything like its present form.
>
> David Rowland, Chairman of Lloyd's of London,
> May 1995

CASE STUDY TEN

RUNNING ROUND IN CYCLES:
SCOTLAND 1772; SCOTLAND 2008

> Considering that the business of banking, when carried on
> proper principles, is of great public utility, particularly to
> the commerce, manufactures, and agriculture of a country,
> at the same time that it may yield a reasonable profit to the
> bankers concerned in it; and likewise considering the necessity
> there is in the present situation of the country, that a Banking
> Company should be created on proper principles at this
> juncture ... resolved to establish a Banking Company upon
> a solid, creditable, and respectable footing.

> Deed of Co-partnery, Messrs Douglas, Heron & Partners
> (The Ayr Bank), 1769

I've written on many occasions about my home town of Ayr in Scotland, an ancient burgh where the oldest school in Scotland trains its lads and lassies still under the school's Latin motto – appropriately for this book *'respice prospice'* (look backwards, look forwards). In the time of Scotland's national poet, Robert Burns, who was born beside Ayr, there was a Scottish banking collapse almost as shocking as recent events: the fall of the Ayr Bank.

Scotland was at the brink of her greatest period in history, the Enlightenment, and the start of the great industrial revolution that would see Scottish manufacturing and shipbuilding cover the Empire. Scotland had three joint stock banks, founded by law: The Governor & Company of the Bank of Scotland (founded by an Act of the Old Scots Parliament in 1694); The Royal Bank of Scotland (created by Royal Charter in 1727 in a complicated act of restitution for England destroying Scotland's only overseas colony, Darien) and The British Linen Bank (which started trading in 1746 to support the trade of linen manufacture). In most towns and cities there would also be traditional banking partnerships that would have closer relationships ('correspondences') with one of the big boys, or with the larger private banking partnerships such as Forbes of Edinburgh.

In the 1770s there was a great capital strain on the Scottish economy. Growth in the West Indian sugar trade and vast profits out of Virginian tobacco helped create a boom in house building in the beautiful 'New Town' of Edinburgh which meant that there was a strong demand to borrow from the banks to finance this new cycle of growth and conspicuous consumption.

The Honourable Archibald Douglas and Mr Patrick Heron of Heron lived in Ayr, which was then a prosperous town in a very prosperous county with many prosperous landed estates. These two gentlemen had the idea of starting a bank in between the publicly quoted banks and the partnerships – the Ayr Bank would be structured as a partnership to avoid the long-drawn-out costs in getting legislative approval but it would be a partnership of hundreds of wealthy men, more like shareholders than working bankers.

Each of the partners (or 'proprietors' as they called themselves) undertook to invest £500 (about £4.5m in today's money) which would be paid in instalments as the business grew. But unlike investing in shares in a banking company, every investor was an equal partner which in legal terms made them unlimitedly liable for the obligations of the enterprise. Greed, not fear was in the ascendant, and everyone focussed instead in the equal shares of profit which would accrue to them, amounts which should be far in excess of the conservative bank dividends.

No more stuffy Edinburgh banking methods – this is a way to be modern and fulfil the modern needs for leveraged capital! The first round of fundraising went well, with 136 new partners contributing £96,000 in August 1769. Headed by the Duke of Queensberry, they ranged from the heights of government members to ordinary tradesman on Ayr High Street, from owners of the beautiful estates round Ayr to a bundle of Edinburgh lawyers and their trust monies. They were all shapes and manners of men – the only linking feature was that none of them had any banking experience.

On the positive side, the many merchants and businessmen who sat as 'directors' on the board of the branches in Ayr, Edinburgh and Dumfries (each of which were managed independently and without reference to each other) all had flourishing businesses which could certainly flourish further and faster if the new bank would be pleased to furnish credit. So at a very rapid pace, the bank lent the entire new capital and all the deposits to the businesses of its own partners. It's quite easy to be a banker, they must have thought.

The demand for credit still grew. On the positive side, new New Town houses were now built and needed kitting out in Adam furniture and liveried servants, causing a supply chain boom through the country. On the negative side, the older banks were ca'ing canny – and increasing their obligations slowly and cautiously. So our lads of Ayr filled the gap. The only technical issue was that the capital had been lent out already. It was possible to draw down the next instalment from the partners, but that would take time, so to bridge the gap the directors authorised the printing presses to run off as many banknotes as were needed, with no worry about maintaining any more than a tiny cash reserve. So the loans continued to flow.

The plan wasn't quite so smooth, though. While the lucky borrower got his loan and collected in brand-new (ink still damp) notes of the Ayr Bank they often had need of hard gold to pay tradesmen and mechanics, or to ship payments overseas. The cashiers of the Bank were constantly vexed to see the loan department bundling out notes in the morning, only to see them come back for encashment that afternoon.

Now you mustn't think that this was unique. Bank notes were a constant worry in those days. Even the mighty Bank of England had some tight moments. Once there was queue of banknote holders all the way from the counter out of the door onto Threadneedle Street itself and the world's most venerable bank was only saved by paying out slowly in sixpences until 5 o'clock when they could close intact and run round town overnight to get political supporters to be there first thing in the morning to pay in ostentatiously. There was also a great rivalry between issuing banks. One cute trick was called 'note picking' (or 'beggar your banker' perhaps) and worked like this: as your depositors pay in other bank's notes (or maybe seek change) you gather in your rival's notes and pay out yours, then once you have collected together a tidy sum, you nip round to his counters and demand to exchange his notes for gold as he was obliged to do. Your gold reserves have just jumped, allowing you to increase business, while his have fallen, pressurising his balance sheet.

That being said, the lads behind the Ayr Bank were pretty reckless. It juggled from hand to mouth for a few weeks until hitting on the idea that we would now call 'wholesale funding' – going to the London interbank market to raise cash to be a substitute for new deposits. The creditworthiness of the bank was dependent on its rich partners and their underlying estates – there must be a go-ahead banker in the Capital who would place his capital at their feet on the basis of all that lovely collateral.

And it worked. The directors made a 'rights issue' call of an extra 20 per cent on the partners (who were happy to get more skin in the game) and the London end was sorted through a loan facility with Messrs Dinsdale & Co. who advanced cash against the deposit of bills of exchange in return for a healthy commission. During the next 12 months, that London funding grew alarmingly, until it amounted to over four times the capital of the bank!

The huge amount of credit the bank could raise in London encouraged the directors to lend it out to each other and their close friends in ill thought and compromised credit decisions. Simultaneously, to try and keep the reserves growing in line with the increased London funding, note picking became effectively a third department of the business, causing real antagonism throughout the Scottish banking community. To increase the rate of growth they even started to acquire weaker banks in the West of Scotland at silly prices to build market share and remove rival note issuance. There was still enough cash to announce a healthy profit share for the growing base of partners, who took their payout and looked for ways to reinvest it in their cash cow and thanked the boards heartily for being such enterprising businessmen.

Businessmen certainly, but hardly bankers! With hindsight at the end of 1772, the *Scots Magazine* hit on the magement problem (echoing critiques of some recent bank boards in terms of seasoned banking practice):

> The direction was composed almost totally of young gentlemen of the law, many of them of genius and spirit, but not conversant in matters of trade.

Another 12 months of this splurging brought the bank to its balance sheet calculation in May 1772. The churn of money had maintained the growth momentum of the business but the slower growth in deposits meant the inevitable reliance on borrowing in the London wholesale markets who realising the nearly insatiable demand from Ayr, had jacked up the princing to eight per cent per annum. Even the least trained banker could see that as they were charging their borrowers around five per cent there were significant problems in the business. The directors looked at the balance sheet numbers with unalloyed horror.

What a mess. Firstly there was virtually no gold in the tills to pay out any withdrawals by depositors or encashments by noteholders. The reserves had been depleted to maintain loan growth. The cupboard was bare. Even if they gained a bit of time by calling on the partners to pay in the final uncalled capital (which amounted to a further £30k) to give about a five per cent reserve on deposits and notes, that would be dwarfed by the bank's mountain of London paper which needed refinancing at the quarter end. Most of the bank's loans were long term and so their repayments were years ahead (on the rather generous assumption that they would be repaid: the bank has not set aside any reserves to cover loan losses or defaults either!). Any pressure from London over the financing and the business was ruined.

Assets	£ 000s	Liabilities	£ 000s
Loans and advances		Client deposits	300
To clients	467		
To related counterparties	361		
Bills of Exchange	409	Notes in circulation	220
Cash and Specie 'limited quantities'	0	London interbank loans	600
Fixed Assets 'value unascertained'	13	Capital	
		Called Up and Paid	130
Total	1,250	Total	1,250

The managing partners, or directors, had to maintain confidence to avoid a run on the one hand, or a liquidity crunch on the other. So they swaggered in the public view, strolled amongst the county set and the merchants and projected a bonhomie that comforted the markets. How long could they keep it up?

The Scottish banks, particularly in Edinburgh, did everything in their power to distance themselves from the upstart and refused to take Ayr Bank notes in settlement at all, putting extra strains on Ayr's tiny cash position which meant that even more money was needed to be raised in London. The Minsky Moment, the moment the boom turns to bust, as always came unexpectedly.

In May 1772, the good folk of Edinburgh watched as, up the Canongate, following the road from London, a booted and spurred messenger charged along on a horse as flogged as the Douglas Heron balance sheet. The rider had covered the 400 miles in a record 43 hours, for the news was of the blackest. In one of the periodic crashes a small English house called Messrs Neale, James, Fordyce & Downe had closed its doors and failed to pay its notes! The story was that Fordyce (whom you'll remember from our Adam story) himself had personally shorted the East India Company in a foolhardy speculation and broke his own bank, absconding to the continent to escape the collapse. No dice Fordyce.

The Ayr Bank directors breathed a sigh of relief for they had no dealings with that bank and maybe the hand of fate had fallen elsewhere: as Ayr was still standing, that would increase the confidence in it. While they were sitting tight with an increasingly fixed grin, Fordyce's cousins who had an Edinburgh bank collapsed on the 15th in the consequential wreck of the English firm, and the whole Fordyce network started to unravel the next day. The failure of these smaller firms was not helpful to Ayr, but wasn't the fatal blow. But cold words started to pass around – if these minnows should be in trouble – what about the great pike in the banks of the Ayr? Ill informed (but substantially correct rumours) were rife that Douglas Heron were next to fail.

Now was the time for chutzpah. The good folk of Edinburgh saw this poster on each corner:

> Whereas the Branch of Douglas, Heron & Co., here, have for these two days past had an immense demand for specie, from the lower class of people, in exchange for notes, owing, as it is suspected, to some ill-grounded reports raised by foolish or malicious persons respecting said branch, a reward is therefore offered of one hundred pounds Sterling, to any one who will discover the person or persons who have been concerned in raising such an infamous report; the reward to be paid by Mr Hogg, cashier, upon conviction of the offenders.

I don't know where they could have found even a hundred pounds by then to pay the spurious reward, but the pronouncement was enough to hold the flood for a day or so until three of the largest Edinburgh firms ran up the white flag on the 24th. That was the death knell. The directors maintained a positive outlook issuing a conciliatory message on the 26th as the last of the cash had been paid away and as far as could be calculated, most of the partners were destined to be ruined financially.

> Ayr, June 25, 1772. — The company of Douglas, Heron & Co., Bankers in Ayr, taking into their consideration the present state of the credit of this country, and the uncommon demands that have been made upon them for specie, owing to causes sufficiently well known, have come to a resolution to give over, for some time, paying specie for their notes. But as the country, who have received the most liberal aids from this company, cannot entertain the smallest doubt of the solidity of its foundation, it is hoped that, on occasion of a national

emergency of this kind, the holders of their notes will not be under any alarm.

The knock-on effect was terrible. The following Monday, the Ayr collapse caused the failure or at least temporary closure of most of the banking partnerships in Edinburgh and Glasgow – only the big three banks and the three oldest Edinburgh banking partnerships (who distrusted any innovation and thus had avoided dealings with the nouveaux pauvres) walked away unscathed.

Now there was the vexed problem of a bank to bury. (We still don't have an easy way to close down a bank today.) Once the old directors were replaced, it was obvious that there was no way the bank would ever recover. As a partnership, each and every single partner was personally liable to repay the failed bank's obligations. It had to be wound down and hopefully that could be done in an orderly fashion. But how to generate the liquidity? Even with the Duke of Queensberry on board, who knew a few good strings to pull, the Bank of England refused its assistance (partly because of the rivalry between Scotland and England, but practically since its own customers had deposited some £150,000 of Ayr notes and bills as security already – so it already had a lot of Ayr Bank paper already to shift at the risk of a big loss). To raise the initial cash needed to meet their personal liabilities, the partners had to sell annuities – they'd pay £100 each year they were alive to the Bank of England in return for a loan of £700 (£800 for a married couple) – that scraped together enough to keep afloat, nearly half a million Sterling.

Naturally the partners (who had enjoyed spending their profit share in the good years) were shocked at the mismanagement of their bank and firmly bolted the stable door by arranging a committee to investigate and report in a beautifully bound volume that the Ayr Bank was (read all about it) a ruinous folly – even the 'sensible' lending for agricultural improvement was carried out on a scale that could never have been repaid out of the reformed production of the county, while the nepotistic support of the mercantile adventures of its directors and partners exposed the firm directly to the equity risk of those troubled businesses. If you add to this the speculation in funds and New Town properties the collapse of the Ayr Bank was modern in its scope. Adam Smith gave a trenchant summary:

> The essential errors of the Ayr Bank were — trading beyond
> their means; divided control by permitting branches to act
> independently; forcing the circulation of their notes; giving

credit too easily; ignorance of the principles of business; and carelessness or iniquity of officers.

The loans were called in, and of course there were losses. The speculative enterprises that had been built up wiped out a fortune, while many of the bills of exchange that had been discounted turned out not to be linked to underlying trading business, but were just bits of paper often guaranteed by the very shareholders who were facing ruin. With the burgeoning liabilities and the dwindling assets, every single partner faced a capital call of £2,600 to try and balance the books of the bank. That's over five times the initial capital investment – an extraordinary loss!

A dismal final meeting of the partnership in August 1773 saw the dispirited partners thrown up the sponge and start to account for their personal losses. It caused a disaster in Ayrshire, where many of the oldest and wealthiest families had no choice but to sell up – contemporary estimates guess that £750,000 value in country estates went under the hammer to meet the losses which totalled £663,396 to be shared between the 241 forlorn partners. By 1775 just over half of them had been bankrupted and it took another forty years to wind up the whole fiasco finally (with a few pennies returned to the surviving partners). That being said, I am sure that you will find it comforting that most of the banking partners resurfaced in other forms, one even running for parliament. It was a great financial and emotional shock not just to Ayrshire, but to Scotland as a whole. James Boswell summed up the country's feeling in a paper he called 'Reflections on the late alarming bankruptcies in Scotland':

> War, famine, and pestilence, used formerly to fill up the
> general number of the calamities of mankind; but, in the
> present age, one has been added, viz.bankrputcy. The year
> 1772 will ever be remembered as a year of confusion, dismay
> and distress. All Scotland has been shaken by a kind of
> commercial earthquake, while, like a company connected by
> an electrical wire, the people in every corner of the country
> have almost instantaneously received the same shock.

With heedless lending on the asset side ballooning the balance sheet and a huge debt to the vagaries of the interbank market, the Ayr Bank literally became a Bank of Air – does that sound familiar?

As we will discuss later, the goldsmith became a banker when he lent not just his own money, but also the cash that others had deposited with him, such that he actually multiplied the amount of capital in the system. The stress is how to fund that gap between the banker's capital and the loan he makes – this latest boom saw many many banks follow the strategy of the Ayr Bank, to pile into a good thing on the asset side of the balance sheet while financing it through shorter term wholesale liabilities. The market was creaking, but when the US authorities decided to make an example out of Lehman Brothers the interbank market became a cold and suspicious place to be. As the worries about what assets we all had on our balance sheets became common talk so as the asset values crumbled, the ability to renew funding eroded.

This is the real insight into banking. It's playing with other people's money. To lend to anyone you take a bit of your own capital and borrow money (either from depositors who tend to leave their money with you, from bondholders who expect to be repaid in some years or from the wholesale markets effectively for a few weeks or months). Just as the people the bank lends to have to pay interest regularly and repay the whole amount one day, so do the banks on their wholesale funding.

Forget that and you run a huge risk.

A risk that's only going to end one way.

Disaster.

The only difference is that it unravelled a lot quicker in 2008 than in 1772.

> There is already quite a crowd around the jug [bank] again, as it is always very difficult to make people who live on the lower East Side understand about such matters as busted jugs. They are apt to hang around a busted jug for days at a time with their bank-books in their hands, and sometimes it takes as much as a week to convince such people that their potatoes are gone for good, and make them disperse to their homes and start saving more.
>
> Damon Runyon, *Broadway Financier*, 1932

WEAPONS OF MASS HYSTERIA: CALIFORNIA 1994, THE WORLD 2009

> I view derivatives as time bombs, both for the parties that deal in them and the economic system... The derivatives genie is now well out of the bottle, and these instruments will almost certainly multiply in variety and number until some event makes their toxicity clear. Central banks and governments have so far found no effective way to control, or even monitor, the risks posed by these contracts. In my view, derivatives are financial weapons of mass destruction, carrying dangers that, while now latent, are potentially lethal.
>
> Warren Buffett, 2002

Strong, wise words from the Sage of Omaha himself, but of course, derivatives can be the source of huge profits, too (which is why, despite his reservations, Berkshire Hathaway has a proportion of its investments tied up in long dated equity derivatives which are doing rather nicely thank you).

Are derivatives inherently toxic? Or is there a more balanced view of risk and reward? Throughout history *caveat emptor* – Let the buyer beware – has been an older and more visceral warning than *cave canem* or Mind the Gap. The dog can nip your ankles, or you might lose your footing on the Tube, but handing over your money for nothing hurts most of all. Mad bargains are the stuff of legend. There are some once-in-a-lifetime bargains: Jack trades his mother's only cow for the magic beans; the settlers on Manhattan get the world's richest real estate for a bundle of beads (not such a good trade for the Native Americans, mind); Faust makes a devil of a bad bargain. Then there are the mundane bargains from BOGOFs and Twofers in the Malls, the punters flocking to buy Chanel No 5 for five cents in Canal Street. All Bargains which we can see daily.

Let's look at what happened to Orange County, California. Orange County is a pleasant and prosperous community famed as the home of Disneyland in Anaheim. As we write this, the state of California is facing a great financial crisis with Governor Arnold Schwarzenegger issuing IOUs to keep the Golden State from getting tarnished. But there's a great history of financial trouble rooted in the heart of dear little Orange County which should teach us that buying anything you don't understand is dangerous.

In the early 1990s the county ran a fair budget surplus and had modestly left the cash in deposit accounts with local banks, earning a bit of interest in a sleepy Californian fashion. The Orange County treasurer was a man called Citron (honestly) and deep inside this municipal functionary was the gold prospecting spirit of the old '49-ers who built the state in the great Gold Rush era. So when a party of derivatives salesmen called one afternoon and showed Robert Citron how he could magnify the return on the County's pot by using these new derivatives, he felt that he, after 20 years had struck gold at last with the help of the new generation of Wall Street financiers.

It was fool's gold, of course. The whizzo derivatives initially produced phenomenal results which prompted Citron to grow and grow the strategy until the good folk of Orange County were left with a real big lemon. When the market turned, the county filed for bankruptcy just before Christmas 1994 after announcing to stunned markets that its US$7bn investment fund (a pool of monies earmarked for spending by school districts, local municipalities and public bodies) had racked up losses of a billion and a half dollars (or so) by following an investment strategy devised by Merrill Lynch and enthusiastically supported by treasurer Citron and his team.

OC had gone OD.

Does this prove that derivatives will kill you in the end? Or is it a simpler tale: the more risk you take, the more cash you make. Until it goes wrong! The Orange County strategy, at its peak, had Wall Street firms lending huge amounts to OC through an instrument called a 'reverse repo'. Here OC effectively borrowed from the investment banks by selling the investments in its portfolio to the firms with a simultaneous contract to buy them back at a higher price some weeks ahead (thus giving cash to OC and a security and a financial return to the broker/dealer). Additional borrowings could be made by using other securities as margin for traditional secured loans. Interest rates were low so the cost of borrowing seemed to be marginal when compared to the fabulous returns on offer.

The County took that borrowed cash and then invested it in high-paying (i.e. high-risk) derivatives with a plan of making many times more income on those deals than they would have to pay as interest back to their lenders. The investment they were sold was called an 'inverse floater' which means (roughly speaking) that the return your get by investing in it is inversely proportionate to the prevailing short term market rate. If rates are low (as they were then), the inverse floater pays you a high return. If rates are rising, then that yield falls rapidly. Typically you will have to lock your money up in the derivative for five years, and you only know what the payout will be as the interest rate is calculated each quarter. At the end of the five years, you get your capital investment back.

So in the low interest rates of that time, Citron could borrow cheap in the short-term markets using his conventional bonds as security and use the borrowed cash to buy medium-term notes which had a very much higher return. The net interest income was jam and certainly was a key joy in OC's budget. That's probably why the borrowings spiralled until the county owed over US$14bn to the investment banks.

It looked like a one-way bet – and would have been if interest rates went only one way.

Guess what? Yes, interest rates started to rise in 1994. The effect of the derivative strategy turned too – and the leverage that was locked into the derivatives magnified the downturn in the same way it had boosted the upturn.

As interest rates rose:

- borrowing costs increased, eating into the profit;

- bond prices in the market fell, so the lenders made margin calls, asking for additional bonds as security, thus eating into the profits even more; and

- the yield on the inverse floaters backtracked, wiping out the profits and generating huge losses.

The mathematics that guaranteed riches in a low interest rate environment was guaranteed to destroy the County in a rising interest rate environment. Citron was well and truly squeezed. Hence, December 1994 saw the County go bust and court cases and suits started flying around.

(The upshot wasn't as catastrophic as you might think – OC was in bankruptcy for just 18 months, and with agreed 'no fault' settlements from some Wall Street firms, investors did get paid out in early 2000. Citron, who made no personal gain, was treated relatively lightly by the courts with a year's house arrest and a US$100 grand slap on the wrist.)

Of course, Treasurer Citron's problems were not an isolated occurrence and soon other plaintiffs brought their sorry tales to the bench and (more importantly) to the public. 'Mis-selling' and 'misrepresentation' were the new bywords. In a highly prominent set of law suits in London, a handful of English local borough councils escaped the Citron-like debacle they nearly got themselves in as it was ruled that they did not have the legal power to enter into the swap contracts in the first place so they couldn't be forced to pay the losses. Soon, the only people making money out of derivatives seemed to be the trial lawyers. Although in my researches, I can't find a single case of an investor enriched by derivatives that complained he didn't understand what he was pressured into buying...

The Wall Street rocket scientists had followed a couple of strategies to create mind-boggling potential returns – all based on optionality.

Options are a kind of bet and every option, like every betting slip, has a value to someone. Complex derivative investments take an option and use its value to enhance the income paid to the investor (until the option is triggered). It's usually all bundled together so you can't see the financial mechanics. All you'll have is a note which gives you the right to receive a specific return under certain conditions. Very broadly, if you pick a bench-mark (say an interest rate) and are happy to bet that rate will never reach a given level (say 10 per cent compared with one per cent today) within a specific timeframe (say at any point over five years) the investment bank can calculate how much that option is worth (it's the product of the potential extra income times the probability of the interest rate rising so high in the period). They can use some of that value (after taking their profit up front) to increase your investment income (or subsidise your borrowing costs). Of course, if the unimaginable happens, you will be under the immense burden of the scenario you felt could never happen. Then, as you started off being sure it would never happen, that was a risk you were very happy to take. Because it could never happen. (Or could it?)

This example is the wrong way round, however, for it was not the com-panies who were suggesting the parameters for the options, but it was the sales desks of the investment banks setting the triggers. Some large deriv-atives trades were disputed by large companies like Procter & Gamble (who exhibited too much gamble and too few proctors) on the basis that the investment banks at least held undisclosed information about the risks involved, and probably exploited that asymmetry of information and experience. While this was the daily grind for the bankers with their teams of mathematicians, the corporate looked at something like this once in a blue moon – could they really comprehend it and make considered assess-ment of the risks and rewards? (One case revolved round a trade where the interest rate was linked to the wholesale banking rate of interest, LIBOR, but on the calculation if the option were triggered, the rate would jump up to LIBOR cubed – LIBOR^3. In evidence in the court case against the bank for 'mis-selling', the assistant treasurer of the company saddled with the derivative timebomb said that he had read the contract but couldn't find 'footnote 3' to the definition of LIBOR).

You'll recall in the musical 'Guys and Dolls' that Sky Masterson, the highest playing gambler of all time, was warned by his old Dad that one day, a guy would show him a brand new deck of cards and would bet him that the jack of spades would jump out of the deck and squirt cider in Sky's ear. Dad's advice was simple; don't bet because if you do, you'll end up with an earful of cider. That's the danger of asymmetrical information. The guy with the cards has worked out the risk in advance and has set a price at a level that will seem attractive to someone who has less knowledge of the component parts of the proposition. Remember John Law and his challenge of throwing six sixes in a row? They have worked out the odds before setting the bet.

The danger in derivatives is not, as many will tell you, in the concept itself. We'll see in a moment that there are centuries of safe trading in derivatives to hedge (or insure in a way) many risks businesses face. It's merely that these contracts allow companies to leverage up risk – often because they believe that the downside will never occur. Now that does sound familiar?

Welcome to the great powers of strength and destruction inherent in the set of financial tools called Derivatives. Warren Buffett's quote above famously denounced them as 'weapons of mass destruction', a phrase not without its own hyperbolic element) and countless politicians have denounced these instruments as tools not of financial wizardry but of monetary devilment. Part of commentators' fears arises from the sheer size and dramatic growth of the derivatives industry: The total value of the unregulated derivatives market (the 'over the counter' or OTC market) in terms of the face value of contracts in currencies, interest rates, hog bellies and grain, bonds and shares, gold, death and default has been calculated as rising from a mere US$72 trillion in June 1998 to a whopping US$592 trillion in December 2008. That's about US$85 grand for every man, woman and child on the planet. It represents over five times the size of all the equity and bond markets put together! No wonder people get anxious!

The numbers are not quite that simple however. While the face values are astronomical, the real risk at any time is really the difference in the current market price of the underlying commodity (or interest rate or index – whatever the derivative is base off is called the 'underlying') and the price in the derivative contract. That gross market value in the last reported figures stood at about six per cent of the total notional value (the face value of the contracts) – OK – the opportunity to lose US$33.9 trillion is still a big pill to swallow when you could be using the money productively by rescuing banks instead. In fact, the number is further reduced by about 70 per cent through the effect of 'netting' – where big trading counterparties have many derivatives trades between them, some of which effectively cancel each other out (if you have the correct legal documents in place that is). Finally, many derivatives traders take security from their counterparties, which roughly halves the remaining exposure. After all this boiling down of risk, the final net unsecured position is only about one per cent of the gross numbers, albeit that US$4 trillion is still roughly equivalent to the whole GDP of Germany or China!

Like so many things, the derivative in concept and theory is a valuable tool to aid the prudent in the management of their risks in business. Like almost all the examples in the book, it's only once every fool is creating new variants to sell to bigger fools that this goes awry. How can we tell who's on our side as nobody's wearing a white cowboy hat and if we don't know who is wearing the black hat – how can I tell if what I have just bought are magic beans or jumping beans?

Let's get the boring bit over, and then we can get back to the stories of greed and stupidity. What is a derivative?

It's a contract between buyer and a seller to exchange a cash sum upon a given specific future date (or series of dates) based on the rise or fall in price of a commodity (in the broadest sense). Please keep that in mind. It's a cash transaction based on (or derived from – hence the name 'derivative') an underlying commodity or index (such as an interest rate). Sometimes it does involve having to deliver the physical underlying, but mainly they are what is called 'contracts for differences' – a bargain between two parties to pay the cash difference between the actual market price on a specified day and the target price agreed between them earlier.

Take a simple example, if I am a farmer and you are a miller, I might enter into a contract to deliver 50 bags of grain to you at the end of the harvest. You will then plan to mill that cereal and to sell it onto the bakers to bake loaves to be sold then to the great public.

As the farmer, my real concern is how much I get paid. I have the costs of buying the seed and running the farm, of harvesting and threshing the crop along with my own living expenses to recoup. That means there's a minimum price I can sell my grain for. My worry is that if turn up in September the miller may offer me much less because there's just too much grain on the market (and as there are more sellers than buyers, the price will be lower).

I need to 'insure' this risk – and I can through derivatives.

So I enter into a binding contract to sell my 50 bags (or bushels, pecks, tonnes or whatever) of wheat to the miller at the market price per bag for at the end of the harvest time, say on 1 September. As long as old Dusty Miller is still in business and has the cash, I'll turn up in the tractor, drop off the 50 bags and he'll give me the prevailing price per bag. At the same time I go to my friendly derivatives bank and agree a forward price of £5 a bag for that same day in September.

Come delivery day, I have two sets of interactions: what happens in the real trade with the Miller – and what happens with the bank under the derivative.

Market Price	Cash Market	Derivative Market
£4	I sell 50 bags at £4 each = so the miller pays me £200 cash.	I pay the £200 (50 times £4) earned in cash to the derivative counterparty but receive £250 (50 times £5) so making my budgetted profit (avoiding a loss).
£6	I sell 50 bags at £6 each = which is a £300 payment from the miller.	This time, I still have to pay the market price to the counterparty (£300) but receive the agreed fixed price per bag totalling £250. I've lost my excess profits but have secured my budgeted profits.

So adding together what happens in the cash market plus the derivative contract gets you to your budget.

Basic derivatives come in three forms:

- **Swaps:** where the parties agree to exchange cashflows over time (the largest segment in the market is swapping between fixed interest rates and floating interest rates)

- **Forwards:** where they agree to receive/deliver a set amount of the underlying at a future date at a price agreed at the beginning (the subset of these which are traded on specialist exchanges are called Futures)

- **Options:** where one party has the right, but not the obligation, to buy (or 'call' as it's often termed) or to sell ('put') a specific amount from the other at the agreed price (either on one specific date, or sometimes up to that date). For this right, you will pay an upfront premium – if you chose not to exercise your option, that will be the total cost to you.

These structures, or variants of them, have been used for centuries to hedge against the risk of price changes in the future. From Babylonian sheep farmers through to major airlines today, prudence dictates that if you have big costs in the business (like jet fuel or the cost of borrowing) you should aim to fix those costs to ensure there will be no untoward surprises – if those costs rise, your profit will be insulated against it and you won't have to increase your prices to your consumers (say through an unpopular fuel charge supplement on the tickets). Nothing is free so you now have the opportunity cost – if oil prices fall, you are contracted to pay a higher price (which could be an issue if a competitor has not fixed and can then pass on that price fall to the market, undercutting your prices), which is where options can play their part.

There are other ways to look at derivatives: not as a means to an end, but as a means to generating trading profit. The joy for a speculator (or to use a value-neutral term, a trader) is that investing in a derivative costs less cash and less capital than investing in the underlying. You need not buy the physical oil, or grain, or yen – use a derivative and the cash cost to you will be the option premium or the margin called for by your counterparty. If the margin is say 10 per cent then that allows you to trade in derivatives with a face value 10 times higher than the amount of the underlying – you've invested in 10 oil tankers cargoes, not just one. Ten times the profits. Ten times the bonus. Ten times the grief if it all goes wrong. It's this leverage element that can come back and hurt (as is always the case when you gear up, as we have seen).

While 90 per cent of the derivatives business is on the OTC market, the remaining 10 per cent carries on under the aegis of the formal futures exchanges across the world. Whenever there's a financial crisis, the papers will usually have some poor trader in the market in his (or her) brightly coloured jacket with his head in his hands as he considers his losses. For most of their history (until quite recently) the trades were done face to face in Open Outcry – the registered traders (wearing the snazzy coloured jackets to mark them out) would stand in a 'pit' and shout out what they wanted to buy and sell, emphasising their bids and offers by hand signals – until another trader signals that he wants to do the opposite and a deal would be done between the two. The exchange's strength came from the closed structures that the allowed themselves to operate under more defined and transparent parameters than the OTC side of the business:

- Contracts were standardised: the underlying commodity was defined in terms of quality (West Texas or Brent) in fixed multiples or amounts, with all contracts payable on specified quarter days,

- The exchange traders had to be members – abiding (broadly in many cases) with the legally-binding rules and ethics of the market,

- Your derivative contract will be completed at settlement by the Exchange not the individual trader (at the same time the Exchange completes a mirror trade with him so it takes the risk that he goes bankrupt and it stands personally liable to you),

- Contract parties had to put up 'margin' or cash collateral if their 'mark to market' (i.e. the difference between the cash and strike prices) moved beyond a certain limit. Failure to provide this saw your contract closed out (this is now a common feature in OTC trades too).

These elements made a futures contract readily determinable by value – you know exactly what you are getting and there's an overseer to ensure that fair play occurs.

The reason that the OTC model is so dominant is simply because there are many commercial needs, that are less homogeneous – buying and selling foreign currency to pay for exports or imports is a great example. Here you want to buy a precise amount of dollars (not rounded to the nearest 100k) and have it on the day you need to settle your invoice (which probably won't be the quarter settlement day on the exchange). The standard contract just doesn't fit.

Of course when we talk of 'Over The Counter', there is no physical counter and there is no marketplace especially in the glorified world of electronic trading (which has its own risks – there was a trader eating a quick lunch at his desk – eggplant parmigiana from memory, in one of those polystyrene clamshells. He was keeping an eye on his trading screen and noticed as he was eating that some mug was putting up a price way out of market and was making a mad loss every time his bid was hit. He only noticed that the bid went up every time he stabbed his fork into his lunch, pushing the trading button on his own Bloomberg terminal (and losing US$100,000 a forkful).

It is the flexibility of the OTC market that is its strength (and weakness) and players can set a bespoke set of terms and quote a price. The vast majority of OTC derivatives are simple interest rate swaps (swapping a stream of floating interest rate payments for and equivalent fixed rate or vice versa) and by and large they follow market-standard documentation. But critics see a vast unregulated market where poor clients still get fleeced. The gross nominal numbers are eye watering, but they boil down to a much smaller risk number and most contracts are relatively 'plain vanilla'. The real risk in derivatives is when a number of different elements get bundled up together and you can't see what you are buying in total. Is that the fault of the structure? Partly, but you have to ask yourself why you'd buy anything you didn't understand. That's one cider-wet ear you've got again.

So quite simply, remembering Robert Citron and the Orange County imbroglio, you shouldn't sign anything you don't understand and you certainly should work out how much you will lose if your bet (sorry, strategy) goes the way you didn't predict.

> There are two sorts of wealth-getting, as I have said; one is a part of household management, the other is trade: the former necessary and honourable, while that which consists in exchange is justly censured; for it is unnatural, and a mode by which men gain from one another. The most hated sort, and with the greatest reason, is usury, which makes a gain out of money itself, and not from the natural object of it. For money was intended to be used in exchange, but not to increase at interest. And this term interest, which means the birth of money from money, is applied to the breeding of money because the offspring resembles the parent. Wherefore of all modes of getting wealth this is the most unnatural.
>
> Aristotle *Politics* I.X, c.320BC

Part II
Banking Basics Gone Wrong – But How Does Banking Really Work?

The plumbing that underpins not just the financial world but the whole world too

> The distinctive function of the banker begins as soon as he
> uses the money of others; as long as he uses his own money he
> is only a capitalist.
>
> Walter Bagehot, quoting David Ricardo, 1873

Before we look at the current fiasco, let's start with the simplest question of all.

What is a bank?

This is as awkward a question as when people ask me 'what do you do?' (At this stage in the economic cycle it's more prudent to claim to be the proverbial whorehouse pianist than to admit to working in a bank.)

In the good old days, the bank was a safe home for the community's deposits, a provider of short-term working capital to the local business, the source of a fair and stable dividend for the shareholders (who were typically the most cautious of equity investors: widows and orphans as they used to be known – recently dismissed as 'grannies' by a senior UK government figure) and the provider of a gold-plated pension for the lifetime's service given by the solid and fundamentally dull bank managers. Banks in those happy days were based in huge marble temples on the best corner of every High Street, they were the fourth organ of the Establishment: the Armed Service, the Civil Service, the Church (morning service, I suppose) and the City (the financial service).

The theory is that a bank is a mechanism that collects many people's savings (in the form of deposits held safely and paying interest) and then simultaneously lends amounts to people and businesses (in the form of loans and mortgages, again adequately secured and paying a higher rate of return to the bank than it pays its depositors).

These concepts sound rather complex and dry, but an easy way to understand how a bank works is by looking at the very early beginnings of the financial sector. This business of 'intermediating' the needs of both borrowers and savers, making a profit on the 'spread', started as a sideline in the goldsmith's trade. Goldsmiths, being master tradesmen and members of a guild of craftsmen had three important attributes:

- They had reputation and social standing in the community as skilled members of a craft guild,
- They owned large vaults in which to store gold securely,

- They had a monopoly of trade in a metal which was both a craftsman's raw material and at the same time a medium of payment and exchange (and a store of value).

The first banking trades were simple. Imagine the case of a merchant who owned a fine set of six golden goblets which were held safely by the goldsmith in his vaults. The merchant needed a few golden coins to settle an account ahead of the landing of his next cargo at the Rialto. Unfortunately, our merchant is a bit short of ducats, shekels or mazooma. Once his boat comes in he'll be giving out little fishes on silver dishes like no tomorrow, but right now his purse is as empty as a cuckold's codpiece. Our merchant (let's call him 'Antonio') could generate hard cash in a couple of ways: he might take one of his goblets and sell it, or he could get the goldsmith to melt it down into coins, but he only needs a modest few coins for two weeks – a tiny percentage of the goblet's worth – so he doesn't really want to part with it if he can (as it would break up the set!).

Let's think laterally: the goldsmith (called 'Cosimo') has many golden objects in his vaults, including other clients' coins. He lends three of those golden ducats to Antonio against a promise to be repaid out of the profits on landing the ship's cargo when Antonio will give Cosimo back four ducats – three to replace the loan and one as Cosimo's reward for making the credit available in the transaction.

Here we see the two fundamental risks of banking.

The first is obvious. Will the merchant repay? Antonio could abscond without repaying (though this seems unlikely as his precious golden goblets lie within the goldsmith's power – and this security or collateral is worth much more than the loan); he might experience a delay or worse in getting his cash – his merchantman could be delayed by poor weather, a broken rudder or Somali pirates (a disaster if he's shipping perishable fresh fruit, but no real problem if it's a shipment of silks and pearls from India); or he might be prevented from repaying by dying (Antonio looks pretty fit to me, but these days everyone's worried about Black Death and swine flu...) or by bankruptcy if his entire business fails. This is *credit risk* – the possibility that your debtor fails to repay you in full and on time. In this case and in wise transactions generally, the banker mitigates this risk (a) by having a good assessment of the underlying business and (b) by having security (or 'collateral' which is worth more than the loan made (after taking account of the costs and expenses of turning that collateral into cash).

Cosimo, our goldsmith/banker has to assess the likelihood of the merchant going bust ('the potential for default') and then he has to predict the severity of the loss that he will incur should that happen ('the loss given default'). This crystallised loss is then an amount that must be met out of the goldsmith's own wealth – the capital invested in his own business. In our example, for Antonio,

- The **worst case** would be that the vessel sinks, losing the entire shipment of goods. If this occurred, Cosimo still has the right to sell the one of golden goblets (worth 50 gold coins each) taking his four coins and returning the remainder to Antonio (or to Shylock and the other creditors who financed the ship and its contents). Of course, the security is not without its own risks too: on the day Cosimo goes to sell it, there may be many other goblets in the market to sell, or perhaps people only buy goblets in sets of six. There are many problems that might arise – that's why the security is always worth more than the advance – even if Cosimo has to drop the goblet's price to get a quick sale, he will receive enough to get repaid

- The most **likely case** is that Antonio's expertise in selecting Indian goods will result in the whole cargo flying off the shelves, garnering a huge profit, out of which the four coins are repaid to Cosimo (and in fact, many more coins are deposited in the account, an ancillary reward for Cosimo's support). So both men's businesses prosper and they will do business together again in a comfortable long term relationship between banker and customer

- And somewhere in between, perhaps Antonio's not bought as wisely as usual, or perhaps there's a Venetian credit crunch and prices fall – Cosimo has to be happy that the size of the advance (the three coins) is appropriate in the light of the worth of the shipment when it lands in the Venice market – three versus 300 sounds OK, maybe 300 lent against 500 worth of goods would take more thought (fine if it's for bread in a famine, but probably too much for fashionable consumer goods), not, of course, forgetting that he still had the golden goblet in case of emergencies (in fact he's probably at home now having a large G&T out of it while he's waiting). Of course, it's much more preferable just to get the coins back rather than having to schlep about with the goblet!

The other risk for the goldsmith/banker concerns the deposits his customers make with him. In general, people can withdraw their deposits instantly (or on a defined notice period, for which they are compensated by a greater rate of interest) so there is a risk that the depositors will want their own coins back from Cosimo not knowing that they've been lent to and spent by the merchant. This is *liquidity risk*. By-and-large, ordinary folk tend to leave their money in the same place – inertia and neophobia (and the similarity of product and return) lead to a 'stickiness' that the banker can rely on from day to day while he can attract longer term deposits by offering an enhanced interest rate to those who forego the right to have their cash delivered back to them the moment they ask for it without having to give notice.

What happens if all the clients who deposited coins need them on the same day? Perhaps the Doge enacted a new tax and everyone needed to pay it unexpectedly all at once? Ironically, what happens if all of Venice wants to buy Antonio's wonderful new goods and so they all want their golden coins back from Cosimo to go shopping? Or rumours about the business acumen and solvency of the goldsmith might make depositors worried and run to withdraw their savings first. This is the classic 'run on the bank'.

Of course, the goldsmith arranges his affairs to have a suitable percentage of gold coins on hand at any time (his 'reserves') to cover what his experience tells him is the likely demand for withdrawals, and has maybe some large candlesticks or golden ornaments of his own that he could use as a pledge to another banker to raise credit in his own name. In time, the business expanded as people worried about the weight and inconvenience of lugging coins about, or the practicalities of sending them long distances, or even the risk of having one's pocket picked on the way home. To resolve these very practical issues, the goldsmith would agree to issue a receipt for the deposited coins which could be used as a proxy for the coins themselves – whoever turned up at Cosimo's counter with the valid receipt could draw off the coins described within it. In time other goldsmiths (even in far away towns and abroad) who knew and respected Cosimo would also agree to take these receipts and exchange them for gold, knowing that they could pop round to visit Cosimo one day and redeem them for gold: the first bank notes.

There are a number of good social effects out of this simple transaction. The merchant's trade is increased by using capital sourced from depositors (which otherwise would sit unproductively in a sock or under the mattress) through the intermediation of the 'banker', resulting in higher profits, bigger investments, increased employment, and the building up of Venetian consumer demand.

In fact, the productive capital is even greater than the sum of the deposits made with Cosimo, for now his paper receipts are 'as good as' cash. Cosimo can actually create 'money' – not gold, for alchemy is as big a lie as a free lunch – but as his paper notes are accepted by traders and others as if they were real gold, he can multiply the monetary effect of his gold deposits and reserves by issuing as much paper as he wants, on the assumption that only a proportion of the receipts will ever be presented for payment on any given day. It's like the way he manages his deposits, but on a grander scale.

Little Zebedee is a happy lad. His Granny has given him two bright scarlet Bank of England £50 notes for his birthday. Being a good lad, he pays this into his young savers deposit account with Amalgamated Bank. Let's follow Zeb's savings through the banking system. A bit like the primary school composition you were probably set as at Zeb's age: 'A Day In The Life Of A Penny'.

Amalgamated Bank	Takes Zeb's cash deposit of £100.	Am Bank puts £10 prudently to its reserves.	Then it lends Yolande the remaining £90 to buy a car from Xavier.
Beneficent Banking Corp	Takes Xavier's £90 cash on deposit.	BB Corp puts 10% (£9) prudently to reserves.	Then lends £81 to Willy who spends it in VeryCheap the local supermarket.
Clever Chaps & Co	VeryCheap banks the £81 as part of the day's takings with its bankers CC&Co.	Who prudently put 10% (£8.10) to reserves.	And you're getting the pattern, lends £72.90 to Una who makes a deposit for a holiday.
DaftBank AG	The travel agent puts £72.90 on deposit here.	And its bankers prudently put 10% (£7.29) to reserves.	Lending £65.61 to Tam who spends it on a bottle of malt whisky.

Extreme Finance Limited	Scott who sold the whisky deposits his £65.61 at his own bank.	EF Ltd prudently sets 10% (£6.65) of that to reserves.	And lends the remaining £59.05 to Roberta.

And this can carry on and on, but let's take stock here. Zeb's birthday present of £100 has managed to create deposits across these five banks of over £400 (£409.51 to be exact) and at the same time has created loans of £368.56. This is the money multiplier effect that banks have. By a bit of simple maths, if the process of depositing and lending continued, Zeb's £100 will burgeon under the banking system to build up £1,000 in aggregate deposits, with aggregate loans of £900 (and, of course 10 per cent of the deposit base as banking reserves).

In our simple example all the banks adopted the same 10 per cent rate for reserves. If that percentage is lower, then the volume of money created increases and if it is kept higher, then the bank's book grows more slowly.

On the downside, the banker has to steer between two pitfalls.

The first is that he lends his depositors' money foolishly. If he does, then losses on these loans eat up all the capital he has personally invested in the firm and so when the entire loan book is called in and repaid, there is insufficient cash to repay the depositors. This is *insolvency*. The banker goes bust. The old Italians used to break the bench that a failed merchant had used as his trading post – the medieval Latin phrase for broken bench was *banca rupta* whence comes that stigma of our age – bankruptcy.

The second crisis is more one of timing – *illiquidity* – the banker may have made all the right credit judgements and his debtors are paying him back with interest according to the loan contracts but the depositors need or want to have their money back now. The depositors are well within their legal rights and the borrowers cannot be forced to repay faster than the loan agreement has determined. So the banker goes bust again. But not necessarily (to paraphrase: had he but liquidity and time/ this credit crunch were no crime). And this will become important later on. Just don't forget that the banker needs to take in money from depositors and the wholesale money markets to augment his capital to have enough cash to hand out in loans. The banker is often the biggest borrower in the street.

The illiquid banker, if given time, may well be able to persuade his depositor to wait (and again reward him with a better interest rate) or perhaps find another banker who is liquid enough to lend him money or even buy loans from him for cash. This is because the illiquid asset has a verifiable value in excess of the deposit, unlike the insolvent position where the value of the asset is 'under water'.

This curious but crucial distinction between a lender under pressure and a lender under water will be an important point of discussion later, for it was only in Victorian times under Walter Bagehot that the mechanics of this were focused upon with theoretical clarity. He argued that it was in society's interests to support 'illiquid' banks over their period of stress and back to health (charging well for the rescue), but to allow 'insolvent' banks to go broke Now some regulators find that a difficult concept as so many of their banks are either too big, or too interconnected to fail – for if they went down, then they would take many others with them in their ruin.

But back to sunny Venice and to Cosimo, our medieval proto-banker. The business model he has followed thus far has brought in two welcome streams of revenue: the profit made by charging interest on loans ('the offer' price) after deducting the interest payable to depositors ('the bid'). This life-blood of a bank is the positive difference between these two: the net interest margin.

Our goldsmith has a new problem. A good problem to have, for he is riding high on success: the demand for loans has been so strong that he has lent every single gold coin in his vaults, so he is without the wherewithal to continue lending unless he develops a new source of physical specie to pay out to borrowers. Of course, the net interest margin flows in and can be recycled in the business, but it would be quite nice to take a cut of that on the way through to live in the style to which even a proto-banker should aspire (after a particularly good deal, he might award himself even more for being a good man – a 'bonus', in Latin, but we'll have more on bad men and good money later). He could also issue receipts for coins that he didn't actually hold (quite a high-risk strategy as he has to remember that a certain proportion of these will be brought back to be transformed from paper promises into hard cash) but the development that followed and allowed his business to burgeon was for Cosimo to become a borrower himself.

When you think of it, he already was, albeit borrowing relatively small amounts from the breadth of his customers in the form of deposits. Imagine he knows of a fellow goldsmith, let's call him Lorenzo, who lived not in a port but in a hill town surrounded by the beautiful arable lands of Tuscany. His clients are farmers and they have most gold at the end of the harvest, in fact so much that old Lorenzo needs to find a second vault to help him store the largesse. So he could become a large depositor with our man or (the other side of the coin) our goldsmith could ask to borrow a chest of those coins until the farmers needed to spend them on seeds next year. Rather than letting the farmers' gold lie fallow over the winter, it can be put to good use temporarily by the merchants down in the port, earning a return for both Cosimo and Lorenzo (and even Lorenzo's clients).

This is the beginning of 'wholesale funding', where professional counter-parties in the market lend to each other in larger amounts. As both parties are respectable financial institutions and dealing in big sums, the rate paid to another bank for wholesale deposits will tend to be higher than for the widows and orphans, the ordinary depositors; and likewise, the interbank borrowing cost will be lower than for a loan to a tradesman or merchant.

It's not without its risks though. One or two small depositors withdrawing their gold unexpectedly will be manageable but it takes extra planning and reserves to have that plan B if one very large wholesale funder (accounting for a percentage of the whole deposit book) calls off his money. When Lorenzo comes to collect his chest of coins, that will be more than the reserves normally kept in Cosimo's vaults, so he needs to match the loan repayments so that coins flow in to him before Lorenzo calls. And those considerations apply to the lender/depositor too, who is chancing a significant sum on the creditworthiness of the deposit taker/lender.

So wise Cosimo will always keep enough gold or readily sellable objects as a reserve sufficient to cover any losses, any unexpected withdrawals or any financing that fails to be renewed by his fellow goldsmiths. These reserves will represent only a fraction of the total sums – Cosimo's reputation is the balancing figure.

Credibility is king.

Changing plays for a moment, Cosimo might well quote from Othello:

> Good name in man and woman, dear my lord,
> Is the immediate jewel of their souls.
> Who steals my purse steals trash; 'tis something, nothing;
> 'Twas mine, 'tis his, and has been slave to thousands:
> But he that filches from me my good name
> Robs me of that which not enriches him
> And makes me poor indeed.

Notwithstanding all these potential pitfalls, over time, it seemed a lot easier to make money than to make candlesticks, and so the goldsmiths, whether our fictitious Cosimo or the devious Medicis of Florence or the clever Fuggers of Antwerp down to the old banking houses of London (including Coutts), left the artisan quarter and set up in banking parlours instead.

But wherever they hung their signs, the fundamentals of the banking business that had developed remained the same, and broadly speaking remain in place today. One antidote to Collective Amnesia is to strive and remember that you make, and importantly, you lose money in just the same ways as your ancestors. Forget that at your peril!

> Up, and after doing some business at my office, abroad to Lombard Street about the getting of a good sum of money; thence home, in preparation of my having some good sum in my hands, for fear of a trouble in the State, that I may not have all I have in the world out of my hands and so be left a beggar...
>
> [I] received £2,000 and carried it home – whereof, £1,000 in gold, the greatest quantity, not only that I ever had of gold, but that I ever saw together...
>
> Samuel Pepys, *Diary*, 6 July 1666

Men that hazard all
Do it in hope of fair advantages:
A golden mind stoops not to shows of dross.

William Shakespeare, *The Merchant of Venice*, 1596/98

Another fable I hear you say – what's that to do with today? Everything – for the basic risks in banking remain exactly the same. The US regulators used an analytical model called CAMEL for years focusing on the business just the same way as the goldsmiths did:

- **Capital** – does the bank have sufficient capital resource in readily realisable form to cover losses and withdrawals?

- **Assets** – are the loans and investments made within an acceptable understanding of the level of risk?

- **Management** – is the bank owned and controlled by people of integrity, credibility and financial expertise?

- **Earnings** – can the net interest margin (plus any trading profits) cover the bank's running costs and out-goings (including bonuses)?

- **Liquidity** – how does the bank raise funds to finance loans for borrowers and how quickly can it turn its assets into cash to meet the withdrawals of depositors and the maturity of any wholesale funding?

As we walk further through this book, I think you'll see that this camel has one hump that matters, not five. It's asset quality that drives behaviours, results and disasters. In the old way of printing a balance sheet, assets were on the left and liabilities on the right (a convention often described as 'debits to the window; credits to the wall'), hence the formula for a broken bank:

If on the left, nothing's right then on the right, nothing's left.

And don't we all know that now.

THREE KINDS OF BANK

Banking was conceived in iniquity and born in sin.

It is easy to dodge our responsibilities, but we cannot dodge the consequences of dodging our responsibilities.

Sir Josiah Stamp, a Former Director, Bank of England, 1928

The goldsmith's model is still the basis of banking, but it is a mistake to see all 'banks' as identical, for the model has evolved and expanded to create banks which carry out more roles in finance than the 'narrow' bank which recycles deposits into loans. As we saw above, the goldsmith's operation morphed into a banking partnership but followed essentially the same business model: encourage wealthy depositors and lend short-term money either as working capital for business or for families and issuing banknotes as a medium of exchange. Confidence was all important.

As the banking partnerships consolidated and grew into the High Street banks as we know them today, these retail banks became the engines of working capital for the economy. A banking crisis (like we have seen now) not only potentially lost depositors' money in that particular failed institution, but made other depositors wary of banks in general, so the broader market experienced a withdrawal of cash as people put it under the mattress at home (or left to find the traditional refuge in either government bonds or the ultimate queller of fear solid gold in your own vault or in the safety of a discrete office on Zurich's Banhofstrasse). This reduced the amount that banks could lend, stifling economic activity.

In a developing pact with the state, retail banks agreed to oversight from a central regulator which gave the man in the street the (sometimes mistaken) belief that the institution was well managed and double checked by the brightest and the best of government service. In return for that the banks obtained two benefits from the government: the provision of a Lender of Last Resort and state guarantee to protect ordinary people's deposits.

We'll talk of the regulations and last resort later – it's a subject that even now the lenders of last resort don't quite understand – but at its basic level it's ensuring that the banking system continues to function when things go wrong (such as now) by specifically supporting illiquid banks.

The deposit guarantee is more straightforward. The government makes little depositors comfortable with any given regulated institution by promising to repay the savings of any individual up to a certain financial limit. Companies, corporations and the wealthy who can deposit large amounts are expected to use their own wit to assess the risk and are not guaranteed. What the authorities are saying is that no matter how stupid the management of the bank, the small depositor (or voter at a cynical level) does not get let down.

The devil is, naturally, in the detail as seen in October 2007 in the UK when there were photographs across the newspaper front pages of queues of people outside Northern Rock waiting to get all their cash out of the troubled bank. The deposit scheme at that point covered most people's deposits (the calculation was a bit convoluted: 100 per cent of the first £2,000 in any bank including 'Northern Wreck' as the City was calling it – and 90 per cent of the next £33,000 – giving a maximum payout of £31,700 if a bank did go bust) but with the high-level television coverage there was uncertainty in the public mind (and probably the official mind, too) on how the process would actually work and more importantly how long it would take. No one seemed able to explain to the public what was happening. Rather than calculate the complicated deposit protection maths, the punters decided to 'take away the number they first thought of' – i.e. the lot. In the end in a political judgement, after a good dither, all deposits were covered to stop the rot.

So the first family of banks in the system are the retail banks (also known as commercial banks). Traditionally these tend to be large national institutions, generally quoted on the stock exchange, offering a wide range of money transmission services, savings products and lending to the personal and business markets. They controlled the clearing system for payments – in the UK, in fact, they are still known as the 'clearing banks' – and they balanced that monopoly with the implicit understanding that depositors' money was not to be used in high-risk, long-dated or speculative transactions (at least not intentionally).

You might look on these institutions as supplying the financial plumbing of a country – which is why sometimes they are called 'utility banks' although the phrase being used increasingly is 'narrow banks' capturing a very defined and socially important role in the community, therefore warranting government oversight and deposit protection.

A banker is a fellow who lends you his umbrella when the sun
is shining and wants it back the minute it begins to rain.

Mark Twain, 1890s

By the nature of any utility, there are some things that work well and are
simple commodity transactions which are usually repeated in large
amounts with many different customers. There are parts of financial life,
however, that aren't so straightforward, so other kinds of bank developed
one family of institutions to look after long-term transactions (typically
housing finance) and another to supply risk and trading capital.

If you read the papers today, you'd be expecting the millions of small
savers and borrowers to be about to re-enact the last scene of *Frankenstein*
– to take their last pennies and invest in burning torches to march and
overwhelm the creator of the monster and burn down him and his evil
machinery, destroying that inhuman creation of his. Now of course, it's not
body parts, it's financial products; not electricity but investor demand; and
not the Monster, merely a monstrous collapse. Those of you who have
read the book will remember that Victor Frankenstein started off with
good and kind motives, but who remembers that now?

But Frankenstein is a myth. So is much of banking.

Remember old Cosimo? His banking model is fairly simple but can't be
expanded without limit. Look at one of the biggest investments a family
makes: buying a house in which to live and raise your family. How can the
goldsmith model cope with lending a large amount over a very long time?
There is an old saying 'An Englishman's home is his castle' – it is certainly
his primary topic of conversation (and fills more column inches in the UK
press than even discussions of soap stars' sex lives) and indubitably will be
the largest investment in his lifetime.

Let's look at a version of our goldsmith banker, but in a sector that might
seem more familiar to readers today.

Just as industrialisation was taking off in Britain, a movement started in the
small parish of Ruthwell in Scotland where the Reverend Henry Duncan
started the first 'savings bank' for working folk in 1880 when he proposed
'the erection of an economical bank for the savings of the industrious'. It

was a great success, although the terms were strict – every family joining had to promise to save a fixed sum each week or face penalties, and attendance at the annual meeting was compulsory. It gave a real vehicle for the ordinary people to save money and 'improve themselves'.

Property ownership, the vision of a prosperous blue-collared class safe in the sanctity of their own home and hearth (and probably through that more conservative in their politics!) was a great ambition, so after the savings banks were well established, the next development were the Building Societies.

The earliest form saw a group of workers band together in a savings bank but with the express purpose of building each member a house. Every member contributed a fixed amount on each payday and promised to do so until all the members had built a standard house. The society then terminated. The popularity of the principle gave rise to a new generation of 'permanent' Building Societies, which acted like tightly controlled banks allowed only to take deposits and lend 25-year mortgage loans (with the interest rate being reset to prevailing market rates once every year) for the purchase of family homes in their own town or locality.

Extreme prudence was the watchword, for the mismatch between deposits and mortgages is the widest possible – loans that will repay over 25 years compared with deposits typically withdrawable tomorrow or at a few weeks' notice at best. So these specialist mortgage banks arose with an exclusive mandate to provide this product while regulators excluded the mainstream banks from getting involved. The quid pro quo was that this mandate had to be operated within a very tight framework and the mortgage banks (Building Societies or Savings & Loan Associations) could neither undertake any other real utility banking business like overdrafts and current accounts nor any other kind of lending or investment.

Each aspect of the model was tightly defined: for example, before borrowers could be considered for a mortgage, they would have had to be depositors with the society for a number of years. As the Building Societies were not companies but mutual societies, they were owned not by external shareholders but by all the depositors. This gave a strong incentive to remain cautious (particularly as the depositors and home owners all lived in the same town as the managers!).

Similarly, any loans would only be made against the security of family homes within the footprint of the local community. The Society would see a very significant proportion of the housing stock in its area and could compare and monitor pricing developments. (Of course, with 'rationed' levels of finance, house prices were less volatile.) The maximum loan would be set at a conservative two-thirds or perhaps 70 per cent of the value of the house, and it was illegal to refinance to draw out equity (except for strictly controlled renovations or additions that would increase the value and utility of the home – so no flights to Florida on the back of the housing boom in those days).

The ability of the family to make its repayments promptly ('serviceability') was the key factor. The maximum loan would equate to a multiple of the base pay of the primary earner in the family – traditionally two and a half to three times earnings (after *discounting* overtime, perks and most certainly bonuses). It was not a question of credit scoring by a computer model, as every borrower would be obliged to provide formal written evidence of their income (say payslips and a reference from the employer) and would submit a calculation of the family budget to prove that the surplus of income over expenditure was enough to pay the loan. The social structure then prevailing made it unlikely that there would be two wage earners in the family, but if there were, the loan serviceability would be calculated on the breadwinner's (typically the man's) wage alone. So the society knew that the family could afford to live in their new house and pay the loan off as part of their household budget. (This concept will return!)

That assumes of course that the wage earner stays in employment for the period of the loan. To protect the lender above and beyond the mortgage on the house itself, the borrower would have to have life assurance to pay off the whole mortgage on his death and often unemployment insurance would be required to cover any temporary loss of income.

In risk terms, this second family of banks took one big risk – the liquidity risk of having all the lending long term and all the deposits short term. This risk was substantially mitigated by the conservative lending policy and the local nature of the loans so that depositors in that same community had visibility on how well the society was run, breeding the confidence necessary to leave their life savings in as deposits that they would never draw out. Of course, this was emphasised as the only way to buy your own home was to be a depositor yourself, so it was in many ways a virtuous circle.

But virtue is rarely enough to succeed in business. The Societies (first by their own rules and latterly by regulation) created strict limits on what they could do. Typically only two activities were permitted: the taking of deposits from individuals and lending in the long term against the security of a single family dwelling. Archilochus, the ancient Greek poet and philospher, talked of foxes and hedgehogs – the fox does a little of many things pretty well (eating chickens, sleeping in holes, rummaging through bins and poo-ing in suburban gardens) while the hedgehog has only one trick (curling up in a spiky ball) which it does to perfection. So it was with the mortgage banks who undertook effectively one socially useful risk while happily bound in a straightjacket of regulation and surrounded by protectionism that forbade retail banks from lending for house purchases.

As part of deregulation in the 1980s, the big retail banks were finally permitted to offer long-term mortgages, and equity loan restrictions were waived away as part of the Thatcher years. The big banks piled into the market using their nationwide chain of branches, cross-subsidising their new capabilities, prompting the hedgehog building societies to seek new freedoms – a process which ended unhappily. Many societies faced such competition in their core markets, they used new found freedoms to expand into the commercial banks' riskier hinterland, incurring huge losses. But more of that later.

She can not think that one who owes his great wealth to contracts with foreign governments for loans or to successful speculation on the stock exchange can fairly claim a British peerage.

However high Sir L Rothschild may stand personally in public estimation, this [investment banking] seems to be not the less a species of gambling because it is on a gigantic scale and far removed from that legitimate trading which she delights to honour, in which men have raised themselves by patient industry and unswerving probity to positions of wealth and influence.

Queen Victoria writing to WE Gladstone, 1869

Now for the can of worms (although today many of the public think that worms are a higher form of life than investment bankers).

The modern view of The Masters of the Universe is a rather new concept. Thirty years ago the integrated Investment Bank did not exist. In between the clearing bank's conservative short-term lending and the mortgage bank's long-term loans to householders, there were a number of specialist finance partnerships who filled the gaps in the financial market, dealing amongst each other in professional markets, and which were actually prevented from having any direct contact with 'ordinary' folk like you and me. (The Good Old Days indeed.)

The most visible specialists were the arrangers and underwriters of longer term finance for business, whether through the equity markets or the bond markets (or in the bond markets there would be a subdivision specialising in raising finance for local and international governments). These firms displayed a range of appetites for taking risks. There would be those involved in trade finance and merchant banking (broadly speaking taking a share of the risk and reward in a commercial venture) – these activities grew into a more general trading on the firm's own account, not for underlying clients, so became more like direct 'capitalism' rather than pure 'banking'. At the other end of the risk spectrum firms started advising companies on takeovers, dispositions and capital raising which required no capital other than a brass plate with the firm's name at the front door (latterly an HP 12C calculator too). In a famous phrase, one of the senior Lazards heroes maintained that the only capital needed in investment banking was 'a yellow pad and a pencil'. Mind you, it was the same guy who believed that one of the principles of banking was 'why be unpleasant when with a bit of effort you can be unbearable?'

Alongside these 'white shoe' (us) or 'blue blood' (uk) firms, shares and bonds were bought and sold in a curious form of tandem bike. A member of the public (usually wealthy) could buy shares only from a broker (a member of the regulated stock exchange) and that broker could only act as the agent for his own clients. He never bought or sold shares for his own account with his own money, so he had no position to cover and so had no personal pecuniary interest in whether you bought or sold or at what price (as his commission was fixed by regulation). His role was to approach another firm called the 'market maker' or 'jobber', which represented the flip side. All the jobber could do was buy and sell wholesale with other jobbers, or to brokers in the retail market for their clients, thus making the market in the company's instruments. His obligation was to quote – without definitively knowing if the broker wanted to buy or sell – a price that he would sell shares at and also the price at which he would buy shares (a two-way price – offered blind to the broker). From the client/investor's viewpoint there was no conflict of interest – the person selling him the shares couldn't influence the retail price by having a personal shareholding he wanted to dump. This 'single capacity' provided a fire break for the client. Of course, the clients able to invest in these markets were the wealthy classes, not the wide range of people we see investing today.

Then there were a host of little fishes, each important in their own little niche – bill brokers specialising in short-term debt, accepting houses who bought and sold trading bills of exchange, commercial paper dealers and many others who would have a specialist role in one financial centre, in one type of investment and often specialising in a sector or group of clients.

The key differences were that these institutions were partnerships, not limited companies, where the whole personal wealth of the partners was at risk, and no retail customers were directly involved in these markets because of the strict demarcation between the dealers/jobbers who took the market risk and the brokers who served clients. (With some exceptions, but in those days, for example, the ordinary man or woman would not buy stocks and shares, so it was a high net worth market at the very least, where the investor knew – or should have known – that the investments were at risk so there was much less consumer protection for the personal client investor).

A good example is the collapse of Baring Brothers. Not the Nick Leeson time in 1995, but a century before when an injudicious punt in underwriting the Buenos Aires Draining & Waterworks Company brought this proud bank to its knees (proving that you can't make your increment out of excrement). The Barings rescue was in the form of a lifeboat fund from the major London banks, which was partially repaid out of the partners liquidating their personal homes and assets which made up the shortfall on realising the old 'bad bank' assets. We'll have fun looking at this in depth later. The model for these single capacity investment banks was, like our goldsmith, a partnership – the principals were personally liable for any losses which arose. With no structural conflict of interest and strict personal liability, there was a strong incentive to be straight.

In the 1980s these multiple, fragmented specialist submarkets, all self-regulated (oftentimes a euphemism for hardly regulated at all) fused together after competition regulation demanded an end to monopoly practices and cartel pricing in these markets. On one day ('Big Bang' in the UK and ironically 'May Day' in the US) the Darwinism of finance took all these hedgehogs and built brand-new foxes out of them. The positive side was that we had larger, more 'efficient' businesses where costs, processes and risks were netted off inside the larger firms – the old structures involved several independent steps each needing to be paid – but no one every really got to grips with the concomitant conflicts of interest in the new market structure.

The first professional division to go was the split inside the bond and equity markets whereby some firms (market makers, jobbers) had to quote a price to buy and to sell a given quantity of an investment to other professional firms (brokers) who in turn could only perform matched trades with the public. Once that was bedded down, the distinction between firms trading in shares and firms trading in bonds vanished as both disciplines combined inside the new larger banks alongside the advisory business (guiding companies on mergers and acquisitions and similar strategic input). In a move to build a one-stop-shop or financial supermarket, last of all, they adopted an appetite for trading risk and keeping the profits for the firm (and, alas, often the losses). Add all of those functions together and you have a modern investment bank. For good or ill.

The interesting philosophical change came next as retail banks in the UK and Europe were permitted to acquire the integrated investment banks (or build them piecemeal by poaching staff from the existing firms), effectively funding the increased risk of running investment banking risks on the back of guaranteed retail deposits. The USA, with the depression still a real memory, held out against this only repealing the Glass Stegall Act (which strictly separated commercial and investment banks) in the go-go years with President Clinton in the White House in 1998.

At the same time, the mortgage banks were chafing at the new competition from retail banks and successfully campaigned to change status from mutual ownership into bank corporations quoted on the stock exchange. It became possible for these last hedgehogs to pluck off their own spikes and compete against the foxes (sad to say, a lot of people thought this was a good idea), and the management by and large persuaded the depositors by distributing the 'windfall' (the hundred years of profits that had been built up inside the mutual) to the existing members if they agreed to vote to float on the stock market. Almost all of the largest building societies converted into full retail banks and they distributed healthy sums to their new shareholders. The naked hedgehogs did their best – which wasn't good enough – and one by one they were either eaten alive by large retail banking conglomerates or froze to death when the sun stopped shining.

Politically it was easy to look at the credit market in the same way as other social needs. Certainly, the need to have a credit card in the USA to make basic payments without cash is important (as anyone who has ever worked temporarily in the USA probably knows) and the internationally rising levels of home ownership has a voting siren song that is widely heard and heavily supported by lawmakers. Just as there are kids in poor schools who have the intellectual capability of going to college, but perhaps neither the parental history nor formal exam record, so the subprime market evolved.

The initial concept of subprime is both good and valuable. It is simply that there are families with a weak or no credit record, but who could still be trusted to repay a loan for the car they need to get to work or for the house they'll raise their family in. By definition, the risk of lending here is higher, but with more detailed analysis on the part of the bank, strong in life management of the loan (a partnership between bank and borrower) and appropriate security should it all go to blazes, the subprime borrower can be a good customer for the bank. It will be hard work and not every borrower will make it, so the subprime banker has to put aside more capital for losses and must charge a higher interest rate to reflect the higher risk.

Add to this a growing political and social imperative of home ownership in the Anglo-Saxon economies and you have a good idea, with a good social aim, that it is going to end up distorted and costing everyone a truck load.

Clearly, sustained low inflation implies less uncertainty about the future, and lower risk premiums imply higher prices of stocks and other earning assets. We can see that in the inverse relationship exhibited by price/earnings ratios and the rate of inflation in the past. But how do we know when irrational exuberance has unduly escalated asset values, which then become subject to unexpected and prolonged contractions as they have in Japan over the past decade?

You know who said this – Chairman Alan Greenspan, December 1996

In the long dark evenings of the forthcoming financial nuclear winter, a happy parlour game will be sitting in the dark (hiding from the repo man) playing 'guess when the crunch really started'.

You'll have guessed from the opening chapter that the real start of the crisis was the expulsion from the Garden of Eden – or if you rule that out of order then certainly the coup against the Knights Templar in 1307 has a lot to answer for. (If only Dan Brown would write a bestseller about the Da Vinci Bank... remember you heard it here first, Dan!). It seems an essential and problematical human trait to want to believe that 'this time is different' and that we can make money over and over again without risk of losing everything. There is a bench in the City of London outside the Dutch Church in Austin Friars, one of those Dickensian twisty streets once filled with clerks and top hatted financiers – this bench has been given an elegiac plaque:

> # IN LOVING MEMORY
> # OF EASY CREDIT

Most sensible commentators look to the effect, not of a butterfly's wing in the Amazonian jungle, but of the rapid and effectively uncontrolled growth of the riskiest kind of mortgage loans in the USA which were (so we thought) transformed by the alchemy of structured finance into investments which were promised to be (rather ironically in hindsight) 'safe as houses' – created by reputable bankers in the biggest banks in the world, under the prudent regulation of the canniest central banks and effectively audited by the powerful and independent rating agencies. Such a wealth of talent, expertise and misplaced confidence.

So does that take us back to the pleasant summer days of 2007?

There was a growing nervousness in the financial community. Not enough to encourage anyone to change the habits of a bull market, but just look at the headlines on one page of the *Financial Times* on 12 June 2007:

- 'The bond market panic hasn't spread further – yet'

- 'Private equity checks for banks'

- 'Not so super woman – raised just £33M in two years'

- 'Ford hires advisors to sell off Jaguar and Land Rover'

- 'Avis starts probe'

- 'N Zealand central bank tries to stem Kiwi rally'

- 'Carnegie quizzed... over trading scandal'

- 'Doughty Hanson dispute'

- 'CDO sales reached a record US$251Bn'

- 'Contagion from the Asia-Pacific region has been a concern for a while'

- 'Seacliffe fuels ABN fear'

All from page 17, the front page of the 'Companies and Markets' section. Add these to the growing caution evinced by the Federal Reserve (The Fed) and the Securities and Exchange Commission (SEC) in the USA, The Bank of England (BofE) and the Financial Services Agency (FSA) in the UK and other major central banks, notably the European Central Bank in Frankfurt (ECB) and the Bank of Japan (BOJ) and you can see the storm clouds gathering. While there were some oblique or opaque rumbles from some central bank commentators, in a demonstrable bout of Collective Amnesia, no one in the regulatory or the commercial world actually took steps to slow down the level of activity.

So while the crisis in the pot really started cooking in late 2007, between a Northern Rock and a hard place, there were worries which should have been seen earlier and acted upon too. Over the summer of 2007 some swallows fell out the sky – in the public domain you'd see two of the large German banks (IKB – which should have been a candidate for the most boring bank in the world and Sachsen Landesbank) take surprising hits in their investment banking departments on highly structured investments and loans into the US subprime market. As large German banks are sometimes accused of intermediating the fat deposits of the German economic miracle abroad into large international loans and over-reaching themselves in some quarters the response was a cry of 'same old, same old' but this was just part of an emerging wider problem. And a phrase that had not been seen previously by the non-financial reader – *subprime* – made its dash for the front page, public consciousness and the history books. It became apparent that parts of the machine were creaking. Investment funds (arranged by major banks but not wholly owned by them) experienced strain – typically these entities would have a small amount of capital and would borrow many times that in the funding market to make hundreds of investments. Some banks and insurers felt that the reputational risk of having investors with money tied up in a loss-making fund with the bank's name on the packaging would potentially poison the parent brand (and crucially, would jeopardise future business between the parent bank and the investor), and so they announced help for their funds in the form of taking over responsibility, or by adding capital and liquidity to balance the books of their 'vehicle' and thus shelter their investors from a catastrophic loss. However, not every bank/sponsor was ready, willing or most importantly able to do so as it involved the substantial injection of liquidity and a significant capital burden that the bank had wanted/needed to avoid subscribing in the first place.

The summer saw asset valuations continue to fall, wiping out one by one the Structured Investment Vehicles and opening the second act of the drama in September on the High Street of the UK as Mr & Mrs Punter queued round the block to get their money out of the Northern Rock while the UK regulators tried to agree who should do what – and to whom. (The Trinity is a difficult theological concept and the muddle over these few crucial days showed that a tripartite bank regulator is almost as opaque). We watched the scary sight of people taking a day off work to stand in line to remove every penny from a regulated bank in England. I am not sure if this event is called a run on the bank because customers run as fast as possible to be first at the counter and so take the limited cash reserves of the ailing bank, or if it is because the bank literally runs out of cash to pay the depositors. Either way, there is not enough money in the vaults to give everyone back their money. Don't forget it's lent out to the bank's borrowers. And those subprime borrowers weren't all paying it back.

Britain's first banking run in over a century – the 'Run on the Rock' – in many ways was what started the public face of *the crunch*, but it wasn't the first step. Six months before, in the last lazy sun of the old boom, on

5 March 2007, the famously conservative bank HSBC announced to the stock exchange that a particular portfolio of subprime mortgages was showing 'stress' – that more mortgages were in arrears or default than had been built into the model forecasting the performance and the return on investment. This presaged losses. The Bank of England, amongst other informed commentators, uses this as the shot that echoed around the world, but I think there is a good case for digging even deeper to find the building blocks that made this crisis.

HSBC Financial USA, where that problem surfaced, was built on the core of a business acquired by HSBC in 2003 called Household Financial Corporation. Household was headquartered just outside Chicago and had a long history of making finance available to 'blue collar' families that would not meet standard banking parameters for lending. The American Dream for 25 per cent down. (If not less!)

Home loans, auto loans and the like were its staple business and its customers were, mainly, families who hadn't built up that all important US credit rating (or who had got into trouble and had a blemished report). As mentioned briefly above, it's one of the hardest lines to draw in finance – the line between a person of integrity who borrows at the top end of his capability to repay but by bad luck (say job loss or injury) finds circumstances have changed and needs more time to pay off the debt – as compared with the improvident person who is reckless in his use of credit, heedless of the smash which he is bound to take sooner or later.

The practicality of household finance is a delicate balance for all of us – remember Mr Micawber's definition of financial planning in David Copperfield?

> Annual income twenty pounds, annual expenditure nineteen nineteen six, result happiness. Annual income twenty pounds, annual expenditure twenty pounds ought and six, result misery.

Household would define its success on bridging those sixpenny gaps across the USA.

However, the USA has never really felt comfortable with banks at all. The most famous diatribe against the industry was by President Andrew Jackson (who regarded bankers as an even greater threat to the USA than the Native American tribes against which he also conspired). He used his presidential veto to close the experiment of a joint stock bank, the Second Bank of The United States, on 10 July 1832:

The Bank of the United States... enjoys an exclusive privilege of banking ...and, as a necessary consequence, almost a monopoly of the foreign and domestic exchange. The powers, privileges, and favours bestowed upon it in the original charter, by increasing the value of the stock far above its par value, operated as a gratuity of many millions to the stockholders...

Every monopoly and all exclusive privileges are granted at the expense of the public, which ought to receive a fair equivalent. The many millions which this act proposes to bestow on the stockholders of the existing bank must come directly or indirectly out of the earnings of the American people...

... if this monopoly were regularly renewed every 15 or 20 years on terms proposed by themselves, they might seldom in peace put forth their strength to influence elections or control the affairs of the nation. But if any private citizen or public functionary should interpose to curtail its powers or prevent a renewal of its privileges, it cannot be doubted that he would be made to feel its influence.

It is to be regretted that the rich and powerful too often bend the acts of government to their selfish purposes. Distinctions in society will always exist under every just government. Equality of talents, of education, or of wealth cannot be produced by human institutions. In the full enjoyment of the gifts of Heaven and the fruits of superior industry, economy, and virtue, every man is equally entitled to protection by law; but when the laws undertake to add to these natural and just advantages artificial distinctions, to grant titles, gratuities, and exclusive privileges, to make the rich richer and the potent more powerful, the humble members of society the farmers, mechanics, and labourers who have neither the time nor the means of securing like favours to themselves, have a right to complain of the injustice of their Government. There are no necessary evils in government. Its evils exist only in its abuses. If it would confine itself to equal protection, and, as Heaven does its rains, shower its favours alike on the high and the low, the rich and the poor, it would be an unqualified blessing. In the act before me there seems to be a wide and unnecessary departure from these just principles.

> Experience should teach us wisdom... If we can not at once, in justice to interests vested under improvident legislation, make our Government what it ought to be, we can at least take a stand against all new grants of monopolies and exclusive privileges, against any prostitution of our Government to the advancement of the few at the expense of the many, and in favour of compromise and gradual reform in our code of laws and system of political economy...

This was the political fiat that defined a tradition of geographic and functional fragmentation in banking in the US. Hard words from the President, in pretty much the tone that the banking committees in legislatures across the globe would use to excoriate today's banking management.

A consequence of this was that US banks remained relatively small and more like the private banks in Britain in Victorian times, whose services were beyond the reach of ordinary folk. So institutions grew up, such as Household Finance, to allow 'working class' families access to credit. Household's traditional business model was to spend more time in the underwriting process, looking at families who would fail the standard credit check, and identify those which represented good risks to offer them well-structured secured loans within the borrower's capacity to repay out of his wage packet and underpinned by sound valuations of the car or house given as security. Generations of experience formed a virtuous circle as Household's own experience of the losses that occurred recalibrated the model which was managed by experienced career loan officers and underwriters who were close to the real customers – for remember that making a loss in and of itself is not a problem in the bank – in many ways if you lose no money ever then you are probably too conservative – what matters is that you lose less than the percentage budgeted against the overall value of your portfolio – the 97 loans which pay out in full should make more than enough profit to pay the cash loss after realising the underlying collateral on the remaining three loans which go sour.

A key skill that Household had was to keep in touch with borrowers and to notice when things were going awry. Early corrective action such as delaying a payment, or adjusting the terms following an unexpected event in the family, was a key discipline. That being said, the business wasn't without its critics, and accusations of predatory lending and sharp practice were commonplace over the years with the largest case costing Household over US$500m in settlements with 41 of the 50 US States.

In the powering US economy in the late 1990s and 'noughties' (or maybe 'naughties' is a better description of that decayed decade), this was an attractive proposition indeed for that section of society which couldn't lever up as quickly as the middle classes. Household's business grew and with it, its own funding needs expanded. To continue the pace of growth, the debt markets were consistently tapped from overnight commercial paper through to securitisations, syndicated bank loans and long-term bonds, for, by definition, the subprime universe of clients has few savings to deposit with its bankers.

The aftershocks of 9/11 and particularly the dot com boom (which ended more like a bomb) hit many ordinary folk in the USA hard, so you would expect that Household's customers would take a greater share of the pain. Growth in the loan book and hence revenues and profits were looked for by the market, so even in a weaker economy, Household was tied to the wheel of stockmarket growth almost regardless of the credit cycle.

Investors tend to be brighter than you'd think, often just a little slow to realise how good times have morphed into bad times. As the economy looked weaker, by simple logic, Household's share price looked a bit weaker too – but the loan book fundamentals seemed relatively resilient so fixed income investors held on and kept buying paper. The business model, so they felt, gave the reassurance they needed that there was sufficient equity in the company to cover even the higher expected (or feared) write-offs.

Everyone 'knew' that the management knew their business.

In late 2002, a couple of signs started to worry investors. The delinquencies were not as severe as had been expected, but that was partially because when a troubled loan was refinanced (say it was agreed to have a longer payback period with a higher interest rate to fit the borrower's reduced income), that new loan was 'rebased' – it became classified as a new loan and automatically fell out of the troubled loan statistics. This caused a feeling amongst investors that maybe it was harder to read the portfolio than had been thought, and gradually major funders started to draw in their horns. Bond issues which formerly flew out the door took longer to sell at higher prices, even the asset-backed commercial paper buyers eventually said they'd rather not roll (or renew for another period, except at a huge cost). The cost of funding ballooned and the volume of finance decreased until, at last, to meet maturing debts in the month ahead, Household had to sell common shares in the market – the most expensive way of financing a business. So now both sides of the net interest margin equation are being pounded, making the business model look increasingly uneconomic.

The underlying business, though, was felt to be solid, so a sale was negotiated to HSBC (founded as the Hong Kong & Shanghai Banking Corporation and now one of the largest and most globally spread banking businesses in history) who owned a huge deposit base (partly through its old Midland Bank franchises in the UK and USA). It offered to buy Household in a US$15.5bn deal in late 2002. As Household was pressured by its need to generate funding, HSBC was the ideal big brother owner bringing the other side of the balance sheet (deposits) to make an integrated and profitable business proposition. Rating agencies, investors and regulators hailed the deal as monumental. The Household CEO signed up as an HSBC director on a three-year package estimated to be worth a super-prime US$37.5m.

Fast forward to March 2007 and life isn't quite as rosy. As the second largest subprime player, HSBC reported higher delinquencies in some portfolios which had been bought from third parties, starting an inexorable process which led HSBC to write off every penny of its investment in the two years to March 2009 as the renamed and expanded Household slipped further and further into losses.

All that looks pretty like a microcosm of today's crunch. It's not that this particular company was the cause of the troubles merely that its travails were a clear warning of what was happening in the financial markets with increasing force. (In some ways, HSBC was lucky to take its pain first ahead of the crunch). It's just that this was seen as an isolated incident within one specific line of business. The implications hadn't been thought through.

Collective Amnesia was at play again. The building blocks of disaster are plain to see, though:

- Lending appetite at the lower end of the range of credit-worthiness
- Weakening credit terms and structures
- Rising levels of bad and doubtful debts
- Lack of transparency on the assets that make up the bank's security
- Loan book growth aggressively financed in the wholesale debt markets – with a wide spread of investors in various (increasingly complex) structures
- The average maturity of the funding is shorter than the average maturity of the loans.

The ripples started when capital and liquidity were weakest – or at least strained by the demand for growth. There was a growing realisation (albeit a dangerously slow one) that not only were there problems in individual subprime mortgages, but the way that these had been packaged into bonds to sell to third party investors – bits of this and bits of that combined together – had involved a great analytical change for the purchasers of these structured investments (known as Collateralised Debt Obligations or CDOs in the alphabet soup of finance). Investors were now analysing a mish-mash of multiple loans, rather than a traditional bond with one single company's cashflows underpinning it. To undertake 'due diligence' in this complex world, the investing community was relying on three fundamental principles in choosing their assets:

(a) *Diversification* – intuitively, mathematically and according to all fundamental economic laws, it must be better to invest your £100 not by buying one £100 mortgage but instead to have 100 £1 shares in a hundred different mortgages in different towns. The spread of income sources from the borrowers, and mix of house price markets in the different towns and villages, sounds appealing as you don't have all your eggs in one basket. Intuitively, they can't all go wrong at once. (Or can they? Of course they can, it's unlikely but not impossible.)

(b) *Structural protection* – in any mortgage, the first person at risk is the home owner/borrower. Before the bank loses a penny, the owner (or mortgagee in the legal terminology) has to lose the whole of his own investment/ deposit in the property. The bank takes losses once that equity is eroded. But it's very rare for the bank to lose all of its money. At the simplest level, you imagine that every house in the country has a value to someone, even if only 'vultures' are looking to take it off the bank's hands for a song. So even after costs and expenses you'll never make a total loss. This is where the rocket scientists started to develop what would become a nuclear time bomb.

Let's use some arbitrary numbers. Suppose we've been running a bank for generations, through good times and bad, and have a pretty good track record through a range of economic conditions in our town/area. Our data shows that no repossessed house has ever been sold for less than 15 per cent of the mortgage loan outstanding. Effectively then, if you make a home mortgage loan, you are pretty certain (a phrase that comes close to 'guaranteed') to get that 15 per cent back come what may. If I could isolate that slice of the mortgage then I could sell that to you and you would know that was a pretty safe investment. After repossession and sale, you get your 15 per cent first before I get any share of the proceeds to pay off my bigger slice of the loan (and after that, the borrower would get any remaining cash). This was known as the waterfall, an agreed priority of payments between creditors in the event of a default. If I add (a) above – the port-folio effect – and I say to you in our history we've always recovered at least 15 per cent on each house, and only two per cent of houses are ever repossessed – so I'm offering you 100 houses (which on average look like a typical cross section of my business) – but only the 'top slice' – that seems like a pretty safe bet as you will buy the risk that many borrowers default, making losses so large that (i) the householders lose all their deposit; (ii) the market is the worst in history – with houses selling at a fraction of their purchase price; and (iii) these losses eat up all the profits from the good mortgages. That seems an extreme and unlikely scenario, so may appeal to a conservative investor. (As we now know, though, the extreme and unlikely happen rarely, but they do happen.)

Within our structured loan we can create differing levels of risk and reward – each called a tranche – each level with a bit more risk. As the originator I'll pay each slice of investors differently – less yield for less risk, taking more risk gets you more yield. Now rather than sharing in the whole risk of the whole portfolio, the investor chooses where his risk appetite is. Instead of buying the rainbow, he can specify red only, or all the blue end of the spectrum and participate in that alone. There is dangerous territory here, for argument's sake say that in our historical data there is usually a run rate of a few per cent of loans that will go bad – typically investors would want to see the originator hold this first loss or equity risk on his own balance sheet so he takes the loss as it occurs and only gets paid back – if at all – at the end of the deal once all the other tranches are paid (the crock of gold at the end of the rainbow). Losses greater than the first loss go to the incoming investors as part of their risk/reward.

(c) *Ratings* – The last set of risks is that investors need to be certain that the originating bank can assess the creditworthiness of the borrower and that it can make an accurate valuation of the house. It's not just the credit underwriting that they need to be sure of; they need to have confidence that all the legal documentation and insurance is effective and in place so that if we need to reclaim the house we can do it quickly and legally. They also need to be sure that the originator is efficient and effective procedures are in place to identify problems early, and above all to trust that the data used is correct and that all the calculations are right. That's a lot of trust.

In the olden days, the word of a Morgan or a Rothschild would have been sufficient to mark any deal with the stamp of success. I mentioned earlier a tale told of NM Rothschild who knew a young entrepreneur who needed to raise capital – Nathan Meyer Rothschild wouldn't advance the funds himself, but promised do something as effective for his friend. He walked across the floor of the Royal Exchange arm in arm and in deep conversation with the chap. In those days, being seen in close private conversation with Rothschild was as good as cash in the bank – and as predicted, many other lenders rushed to invest with the Rothschild's new protégé. Nowadays, investors need more 'due diligence' yet the volume of work in determining all these risk factors could only be completed in the biggest companies globally. So 'Trust Me' was outsourced to the rating agencies.

For years the core of the ratings business was analyses of the bond issues of large companies and of local and national governments. Now they became the janitors of structured finance. Originating banks diverted resource from selling the structures to the end investors and created teams who prepared submissions to the agencies so that a set of public ratings would be given to the various tranches. Should be good news for the buyers to have an independent assessment of all the risks not just of one deal – but of virtually every deal in the market.

That outsourcing of risk analysis permitted banks to get even lazier. Once you've understood one deal that's been rated by an agency – the temptation is to set your appetite solely by reference to the external rating and not to review the specific deal at all (so traders would work on a set of policies defined by rating:, e.g. we'll take US$10M of any deal rated Triple A by at least two agencies (by two of the three majors – Moody's, S&P and Fitch) if it yields more than a given percentage return to us.

In a perfect world, this is a risk-free trade.

I forgot.

This isn't a perfect world.

The thing that we forgot in our assumptions is that diversification doesn't help if the whole world is in crisis. It seemed such an unlikely event, we felt it was safe to ignore it, especially as we had independent professional advice on this from the purportedly scientific approach of the rating agencies. What we chose to forget was that even the one-in-a-million chance has (an albeit unlikely) chance of happening. When it does, and you've caught the long tail of a black swan in the blink of an outlier's eye, it comes as a surprise – and not a pleasant one at that.

Alas, the rating agencies are (contrary to popular belief) staffed by humans too. So when the banks start structuring with the rating in mind, when they are asking you early how far they can 'tweak' without changing the rating, those are intellectually interesting questions. However, there was a niggling question – was a structured 'Triple A' rating as safe as the 'Triple A' rating of a country (like Ireland when it commanded that lofty height before becoming a real estate hedge fund) or of a corporation (like GE)? In some cases it seemed not – it's a shock for a corporate rating even to be put on watch (i.e. under the microscope for possible downgrade), let alone suffer a one-notch downgrade. In some securitisations in extreme cases the downgrade threw the bond from the top of the stairs all the way to the coal cellar: from the top Triple A rating (supposedly as safe as the US Government) a full thirteen rungs down to default in one fell swoop. For unlike a corporate bond, where a corporation's decline in credit typically happens over time, here the structure either worked or it didn't and there was no middle ground for it to slide down on a glide path to doom. Experience showed that structured debt defaults and downgrades were more common than corporate ones so how could a 'structured' Triple A be as low risk as a 'corporate' Triple A rating? Didn't this show a dysfunction again between relying on the model and not the world?

To be fair, the rating agency analysts had a lot on their plates as originating banks explored (or perhaps in both senses, exploited) these new ideas. Innovation and competition inevitably weaken structures – at first by tiny amounts, but then exceptions become the norm. By definition those exceptions are untested historically but we assume that the historical patterns will continue and so therefore the risk profile is thought to be the same as before, even though it has new risks unnoticed inside the structure. Add to that the short run of data on new structures, compared to decades of results of established companies, and you have a much less robust model.

The second stage is to take these tried and trusted concepts from being tools designed to be sold to the biggest and most sophisticated companies in the world to adapting them for smaller corporations. And then the next tier down and so on and so on. Similarly, the investor base was widened from the largest and most technically capable investors to all comers. It's an essential component of the growth needed in a highly competitive marketplace. How else can the bank team make its budget and pay bonuses and dividends too? Innovation and globalisation are two key drivers of growth in the competitive phase of any boom, often without thinking if the expansion of a tested product into a new asset class or into a new jurisdiction is as valid as before.

And the whole point of this was to have third parties buy the credit risk from the originating bank and by doing that, shrink originator's balance sheet and reduce the amount of regulatory capital needed to sustain the banking business. *Credere* as we said earlier – as an investor I need to believe in the originator, in the asset class and in the rating agencies. If doubts appear – possibly in my mind, but certainly if my boss reads something negative the *Financial Times* or the *Wall Street Journal* then I probably won't buy from you today Mr Originator, I'll sit back and think, maybe do some more research, or just keep an eye on what my rivals in the investment world do (safety in numbers...).

When that happens, the originator has to finance the whole portfolio on his own balance sheet, and more importantly, hold the whole risk on the portfolio. That takes extra capital and crucially, it needs access to funding in the markets.

Nae man can tether time nor tide.

Robert Burns, 'Tam o' Shanter', 1790

Now these events started to happen faster and faster. The decline in the value of these now called 'toxic' assets hit directly at the heart of the funding market. The Duke of Wellington famously described interpreting the events and management of Waterloo:

> The history of a battle, is not unlike the history of a ball.
> Some individuals may recollect all the little events of which
> the great result is the battle won or lost, but no individual can
> recollect the order in which, or the exact moment at which,
> they occurred, which makes all the difference as to their value
> or importance...

So too, here, I have simplified my battle (or crunch) from my viewpoint, but the important thing is the underlying principles and how they tripped up each player (or set of players).

It was like being on the beach and watching the tide go out – liquidity receded tidally and one by one institutions without natural liquidity were left exposed to burn in the heat of the noonday sun.

The first invitations to the global financial wake of the 21st century landed on the doormats of the special investment companies, or SIVs as they were known. These golem banks existed on an initial injection of equity and a running refinancing in the debt markets to finance a predetermined investment strategy to acquire (and trade) a portfolio of investments within a defined level of risk (which would be set in stone in the vehicle's constitutional documents and mirrored in its lending facility covenants). They raised the money to invest by borrowing in the commercial paper market for periods from overnight out to a maximum of six months. (Commercial paper – or CP – is a form of short-term IOU bought and sold by strongly credit-rated companies as an alternative to borrowing from, or depositing in, a bank). Big companies issue unsecured CP, but structured vehicles supported their obligations by securing them against the investment portfolio (asset backed commercial paper, or ABCP) so that the CP investors (lenders) will have security over the investments. So if there's a hint that something is going adrift in a SIV, there is no big brother behind it obliged to inject more capital and there is a risk that the CP investors will fail to roll over their short-term loans. This is mitigated by a funding 'insurance policy' where the SIV pays a bank (or syndicate of banks) a modest annual fee for a backstop lending facility which can only be drawn to repay short term investors if they decide to pull out of the ABCP market. The investor gets his money back straight away (and is happy) and the bank is in a good place as the SIV will sell sufficient assets to repay the backstop first of all. So unless the market tanks wiping out the value of the assets, the backstop banks should get out OK. Unless the market does tank.

The early casualties in this group were called the SIV Lites. Maybe this was unconscious rhyming slang. (Same old story – Alpha Finance came up with a good idea, then many imitators joined it all the way through the Greek alphabet to Omega – too many people doing the same thing and in consequence, each 'innovation' was inevitably a weakening of the protections given to investors and lenders in previous deals.) Naturally, they were popular as investments but as investment yields were falling, some bright sparks decided that it was time to juice up the structure to increase return (i.e. remove some of the planks in the floorboard and throw them on the bonfire to make an even bigger blaze). SIV Lites took the worst elements of SIVs and CDOs, focused on high-yielding sectors (i.e. deliberately choosing riskier sectors such as Home Equity Loans – not called HELs for nothing) and took the traditional SIV leverage of 15 or so times (i.e. borrowing US$15 for every single dollar of capital) up to 40 or 50 times (which was necessary to maintain competition with the commercial banks who had themselves upped their leverage from 8–12 times to 30 odds). Even as they were being launched, commentators opined that a raise in CP rates from LIBOR flat to LIBOR plus 30 basis points (or 0.3 per cent)would make these new structures unprofitable (even without losses on the underlying investments) – the arrangers told us to sleep doubtless and secure because the CP investor market was much cleverer than that. At first SIVs borrowed cash at the same rate that a large international bank would borrow large sums in the wholesale funding market, but in these changed market conditions, pricing started to ratchet up to Libor + 100 basis points (that's ouch territory – remember that the SIV makes its profits out of the differential between low interbank funding rates and higher long-term investment rates). Some were brought into the arms (and on the balance sheets) of parents, some failed, all wound down before the whole US$400bn sector died, with Sigma the final firm to close coincidentally being run by the team that started the very first one at Citibank 20 years previously.

It is expensive for banks to raise capital to support the balance sheet in the way the regulators want. Many developed a form of SIV to help reduce (arguably even massage) their total assets. This subsector was known as the conduits. Like SIVs they had an independent existence from their parents or sponsors. A bit like an undergraduate child's independence – at the first financial trouble, (s)he ends up back at home with a bag of toxic laundry.

Conduits were legally separate companies which bought assets from the parent bank and financed those purchases with an amount of equity and the remainder in the ABCP and longer-dated asset backed bond markets. Regulators treated these sales into the conduit as a true sale to a third party, so the parent only held regulatory capital for the much smaller equity investment and the minimal capital needed to provide a backstop line to protect the CP investors. As well as being the liquidity provider for the CP backup the parent might earn fees by providing other core services: maybe as the custodian or servicer of assets, the foreign exchange counterparty, or selling derivatives – so while the accountants, auditors and regulators allowed the banks to have off-balance sheet treatment – effectively saying that this investment structure was a separate legal and accounting entity to the sponsor bank, when you looked at a disaster scenario it was the 'parent' bank who would be the only one who could/would do something to rectify the situation. Thankfully, we know that that couldn't happen (!)

As the SIVs problems rippled, so did the more strained conduits forcing the parents or the parent's shareholders to take action which proved that these constructions may have been independent in a legal or accounting sense, but the risk apple hadn't fallen far from the banking tree.

Reputational risk is the effect that your actions have in the wider market, while perhaps the strict interpretation of a situation permits one course of action, the effect on client relationships hit home. Sponsors of SIVs, conduits, other investment products and hedge funds all had to consider the effect in the outside world if they stuck to the strict liability under the legal, accounting and regulatory rules and left the vehicle to founder, or did the founder have to ride to the rescue? A big question for this sector, which was being called 'Shadow Banking'. The lights were being turned up higher though.

The risk of loss strictly fell on the investors, but the bank had the reputational risk of bringing a dog to be sold in the market – in legality, the bank should just say CAVEAT EMPTOR! In return the investor says I'll never deal with you again you schmuck. And the sponsor gets a bad reputation in the market. It's another example of how you can't eliminate a risk, you can only change it into another kind of risk with which you are less uncomfortable.

Bear Stearns was one of the second tier of Wall Street firms – well known as debt traders and with a long history in the mortgage market. Its sporty reputation was counterbalanced by the iron control its CEO Ace Greenberg, the irreverent bridge-playing magician, exercised over the firm. Famous for forbidding the purchase of paper clips and internal mail envelopes (he repeatedly told staffers to use the ones sent in by clients), Ace had recently handed over day-to-day control and there were rumours that the firm was running too fast and senior management was playing too much golf, so the announcement (on 22 June 2007) that two of its real estate hedge funds were under pressure wasn't totally unexpected. What was odd was that senior management offered to support one directly through a huge secured loan but left the other freestanding. The second group of investors were irritated (which in US terms means considering class action).

And this is the second theme of our dance of financial death: contagion.

Everyone was active in toxic investments and only now did they all start to worry what exactly was inside the investment they had bought,

Banks had to keep growing business-generating revenues and squeezing profits out of existing business lines but without increasing the balance sheet. Investors, on the other hand, were just waking up to the smell of toxic assets. The problems were beginning to be recognised.

I'm told there is enough liquidity in the system to enable markets to correct.

President George W Bush, 9 August 1997

The third whammy (and if there's only one thing worse than a double whammy, it's a triple whammy) was when the risk mitigation started to crumble.

The banking world had been growing so fast that it looked for other ways to help spread their risks and to make structured investments more attractive to investors. One idea was using another well capitalised firm to guarantee some or all of the deal – institutions who were happy to interpose between the borrower and the lender promising to repay the lender if the borrower got into serious trouble and take a fee as their recompense. The investment risk was now on the guarantor firms rather than the underlying asset (or so we thought at the time).

There were a number of well trodden paths to achieve this result:

- **Fannie and Freddie:** in the US mortgage market there are a slew of institutions which were created out of the depths of the Great Depression to stimulate the economy. The two biggest are Fannie Mae (the affectionate nickname of the Federal National Mortgage Association or FNMA – try saying it out loud with an American accent) which was the brainchild of President Franklin D Roosevelt in 1938, and its sibling Freddie Mac (the Federal Home Loan Mortgage Corporation – I can't get the acronym to sound like Freddie either) which was born in 1978 to split Fannie's monopoly of buying mortgage loans of a specified standard size and structure from banks and mortgage companies and bundling them up into bonds to sell to the bond market. The underlying principle is that there's a large entity supporting the government's social policy of encouraging home ownership by being there to supply ready funds to commercial banks and mortgage lenders to ensure a regular and steady flow of liquidity to help people buy homes.

  These two behemoths in the US dollar markets were 'government-supported enterprises' – the USA supported the business with limited guarantees and some liquidity support but they were supposed to be freestanding commercial bodies with their own shareholders, boards and expense accounts. However, most players in the market assumed that Uncle Sam couldn't let them go pop, regardless of the legalities (just like the commercial banks and their supposedly off-balance sheet conduits and sivs!) and as the two competitors amassed well over half of the mortgages in the USA, it looked like a classic 'too big to fail' bet.

- **Monoline wraps:** in the USA many local municipalities and utilities issue 'municipal bonds' to finance capital projects (new schools, road works etc.) to be repaid over time out of the local rates or taxes. Investors found it very difficult to assess the credit of a village in Palinville, Alaska, or a school board in New Obama, Illinois; so a specialist group of insurers came into being. These 'monolines' (so called from the one specialist business they did) 'wrapped' or guaranteed the municipal issuer using their own Triple A rating strength to redefine the risk profile. In return the monoline got paid an insurance premium which they invested in solid, secure investments to meet any future claims

  By analogy, the securitisation engineers got the monolines into a new line of business (bi-lines?) and huge swathes of this new ABS market and project finance and loads of guff was insured. Over US$2,400bn of guff in fact. (And I forgot to mention that they widened their investment pools too and so took pressure on both sides of the equation.)

- **Credit default swaps** (the infamous CDS): the initial idea of this derivative was simple – if United Widgets goes bust a holder of UW's bonds faces a loss – this CDS contract allows him (the 'buyer of protection') to pay a regular premium to the 'seller of protection' (typically a derivatives bank or a hedge fund) and on the day of default, if the buyer 'delivers' the bonds to the seller, he receives a cash payment equal to the 'insured' amount.

The market took off exponentially, using these mitigation techniques with abandon and dragging billions of capital into new investments and so, naturally, the quality of the underwriting declined. An old and cynical risk colleague warned years ago that you never eliminate risk – you merely recharacterise it into a risk you prefer to take (or hadn't noticed). Insurance is a prime example – we'll leave to one side the fine print aspects of insurance cover – the warm-hearted loss adjustor, Santa Claus and the Tooth Fairy – one day we'll all be old enough to recognise these as figments of our imagination.

As long as you assess the contractual small print, insurance is great – but what happens if your insurer can't pay you? So when it comes to taking – forcibly or otherwise – a long hard look at your own books, you see that the banks had problems on both sides of the equation

Assets	Funding Liabilities
Toxic assets • Structured mortgage products – how do we know what they are worth? • Old sivs/conduits/opaque guff now on balance sheet with no sign of any buyers in the market. • Exposures to insurers/counterparties now in trouble. • Repossessed collateral with no resale market.	**Retail deposits** • If you're lucky enough to have them! General reduction worldwide as retail customers reduce levels deposited to keep within deposit insurance limits. • Big outflows linked to negative press reports. • Interest rates falling as central banks cut official rates to stimulate the economy (to the cost of savers and pensioners).
Difficult assets • Highly leveraged loans which were underwritten expecting to be sold into the wider syndication market (now closed) got stuck on the balance sheet. • Bridges – loans you didn't really want to make but which were done short term as you had the mandate to refinance in the bond market (also now closed).	**Wholesale Funding** • Competitor banks started to 'hoard' liquidity. Every bank knew (well not to the penny) its own asset side issues – so they were nervous about their rivals. The interbank market dried up. • Even secured financing – investors having pulled out of structured finance/asset backed – there is a 'flight to quality' where only the most

Assets	Funding Liabilities
• Structured Debt such as SIVs and conduits had to be brought on balance sheet wholly or partially to avoid reputational tarnish in the markets.	secure investments are purchased – the US Treasury Bond yields trade at or below 0%! It's just safer to have no return (and no capital loss) on something you can analyse and trade than any-thing complex.
Mark-to-Market • There is no market for much of this – we've moved from Mark-to-Market, through Mark-to-Model and past Mark-to-Myth. • Do the banks have sufficient capital to take these write-offs – if not then the bank faces **INSOLVENCY** (which is THE END)	**Market Liquidity** • If they can hold these assets at the new written down value, how can the banks fund them to their maturity and possible repayment? If the bank can access funding to the assets maturity, it won't take a loss – this is a case of **ILLIQUIDITY** (which is dangerous but not necessary terminal)

These problems moved quickly from being someone else's problem to becoming everybody's worry. The market, which relies on trust, started to seize up.

Mr Merdle had killed himself... and appalling whispers [began] to circulate, East, West, North, South. At first they were faint, and went no further than a doubt whether Mr Merdle's wealth would be found to be as vast as had been supposed; whether there might not be a temporary difficulty in 'realising' it; whether there might not even be a temporary suspension (say a month or so), on the part of [his] wonderful Bank. As the whispers became louder, which they did from that time every minute, they became more threatening. He had sprung from nothing, by no natural growth or process that any one could account for; he had been, after all, a low, ignorant fellow; he had been a down-looking man, and no one had ever been able to catch his eye; he had been taken up by all sorts of people in quite an unaccountable manner; he had never had any money of his own, his ventures had been utterly reckless, and his expenditure had been most enormous. In steady progression, as the day declined, the talk rose in sound and purpose. ... Numbers of men in every profession and trade would be blighted by his insolvency; old people who had been in easy circumstances all their lives would have no place of repentance for their trust in him but the workhouse; legions of women and children would have their whole future desolated by the hand of this mighty scoundrel. ... So, the talk, lashed louder and higher by confirmation on confirmation, and by edition after edition of the evening papers, swelled into such a roar when night came, as might have brought one to believe that a solitary watcher on the gallery above the Dome of St Paul's would have perceived the night air to be laden with a heavy muttering of the name of Merdle, coupled with every form of execration.

Charles Dickens, Little Dorrit, 1857

So we are in the classic place again. Everyone is nervous of bank assets so won't lend, invest, finance or deposit. The banks, too, withdrew from the wholesale money market where pricing rocketed. As each institution started to look at its own assets, and the bad news there, they started to ask: if I've got into this mess and I think I'm smart – what appalling toxic waste must be on the books of the other banks (who aren't as clever as me!).

This loss of confidence in the liquid interbank market was the final straw for several players. The first wave forced a number of firms into the arms of saviours on a relatively voluntary basis, the logic being that stressed smaller players had a core business that could be sheltered within a bigger group until the market turned and then foot on the gas again and profits galore. You could call this the 'From SIN into SYNERGY' strategy. Good examples were JP Morgan Chase supporting and ultimately acquiring Bear; Bank of America buying Countrywide (which seemed like a good idea at the time) in the USA and Alliance and Leicester being taken over by Santander in the UK.

In the first nine months of 2008, there were still capital-raising options open (at a horrible price) either from existing shareholders (who probably still rue signing those cheques) or from private equity where Sovereign Wealth Funds and Berkshire Hathaway (still wealthier than many countries) positioned themselves to support future winners (or at least to make a killing out of a crisis).

Governments were active – almost hyper-active with ideas to bring liquidity and certainty back into the market – eventually the pressure on Freddie and Fannie grew too much and the US Government stepped in on 7 September 2008 with a 'conservatorship' (the cynics were right – Fannie and Freddie were supported by the government – some senior executives and bondholders took a hit, but the concern over systemic risk was the imperative driver for public policy now – if one of these two went down, it would take many market participants down too which was too scary a prospect). The US authorities were very busy (in an election year where it was pretty obvious that a regime change was going to happen in November) but the real change in sentiment was still round the corner. Now in these early September days, there was apprehension, but underneath it a feeling that the combination of market savvy and regulatory guidance would ensure an orderly procession of government money and 'shotgun weddings' so businesses would be shuttled round about with new ownership and a chance to rebuild capital to return to rude health. While that's comforting, there's still a reluctance to extend significant credit lines to fellow wholesale market participants.

No man is an island, entire of itself; every man is a piece of the continent, a part of the main.

If a clod be washed away by the sea, Europe is the less, as well as if a promontory were, as well as if a manor of thy friend's or of thine own were: any man's death diminishes me, because I am involved in mankind, and therefore never send to know for whom the bell tolls; it tolls for thee.

Dr John Donne, Sermons, 1624

The nub of all this was the question of what happened next. The world and his wife had been on a binge following a pretty simple recipe:

INVEST your wee bit capital

BUY a modest share in an investment

BORROW a bit to buy some more

Leverage those assets by borrowing more

Buy more

Buy yet more

Borrow more

Buy more

Borrow even more

Buy even more

And what next?

DOMINO: In August 2007, an announcement was made by BNP Paribas that it had to stop redemptions on three of its funds because it just didn't know where the values of the underlying subprime assets were. This started the question of just what these securities might be (let alone how to value them). Act I of the drama. Not the point of tragedy though.

If your asset value falls, what does that mean? If it is your home and you can pay your monthly mortgage bill: just sit tight and don't redecorate. If you've got a Rembrandt: look at it and enjoy the picture rather than the capital appreciation; drive your Ferrari, sail your boat, drink your wine, go and swim at your seaside home. Your asset may be worth less to another chap, but the utility to you is unchanged so why not keep it, use it and see what happens when the market recovers.

Assuming you can pay the bills when they fall due.

So much of the world, though, was built on those bills. Every financial institution had levered up – like a family borrowing on its credit card and only paying back the minimum payment – what's a five percent capital repayment – and anyway we make more on paper from the purchase than we spend in cash on the card interest – especially when we take out a new card with a balance transfer or a sweetheart zero per cent interest deal – that takes the waiting out of wanting. The realisation that asset values were falling and that many assets had something inside that didn't smell good caused the buyers to pause.

ANOTHER DOMINO: Summer 2007 saw the 'shadow banks' get unwanted glare. Lowly capitalised and with funding models predicated on cheap non-volatile money from the interbank market they soon came under intense pressure, experiencing a sea change in sentiment. If you can have a negative wave of liquidity, it certainly happened. SIV Lites then SIVs and the riskier bank conduits. Each of these guys found that their calls weren't returned. 'Repayment please on the due date' said the financing creditors (they were financing 'partners' the week before – a long time in politics as they say, but a long long time in the interbank market).

AND ANOTHER DOMINO: Then came the autumn and the mortgage banks who embraced the new leverage paradigm find out the old-fashioned truth. Some of them may well complain that they have been politically encouraged to expand home ownership, the wonderful economic world might well have implied that every middle-class family would have two properties, one to live in and one for holidays (or for letting out at a profit), but now we all knew that these assets were weak. Money back please.

The next shoe to fall is the collapse of Northern Rock, the UK mortgage lender in September 2007. Not, to be fair, the first to go to the wall, but the first to do it under the BBC's cameras. No one seemed to know what was in the play book – the UK's vaunted tripartite structure (where each of HM Treasury, Bank of England and Financial Services Agency had a role to play) seemed to dither. Try-partite. Without certainty, the people who saw the story on the TV news took a day off work and queued outside their bank to take their money out as fast as they could get it. Unprecedented. It looked like the opening day of the Harrods sale. But the tills were emptying, not filling.

AND ANOTHER DOMINO: Subprime everywhere – and the trend is clear – it's hard to assess your assets and hard to get funding. As the biggest banks in the world now warn on write-downs, the rating agencies look at the mono-lines who have a huge exposure in guaranteeing subprime deals, but also have themselves equally huge investments set aside as reserves to meet those claims: those investments also under stress. So they are being squeezed at both ends: a greater number of potential claims but a declining value of invested capital to meet them. Downgrades ahead.

Everyone's looking at writing down the assets on their balance sheet hand over fist and which is eating up capital. But they were missing the silent killer in the market. The assets need to be financed and if your deposits are stable or declining, and your capital is slip slidin' away then you are tied to the interbank market. All the money you borrowed in the interbank market needs to be refinanced as it matures. Ouch. If those banks won't lend you enough, you have to try and sell assets faster in a market where there are more sellers than buyers. Similarly, as capital is eroded, you have to reduce your own balance sheet which means lending less. The quickest way to do that is to stop putting large amounts out in the wholesale markets. As lenders and as borrowers in the interbank market, many banks were caught between this particular rock and a hard place.

The first quarter of 2008 saw flurries of central bank activity across the major financial centres, both to increase liquidity in the markets by inventive emergency lending to eligible institutions and by hacking away at the interest rate (if you can't stop folly, you can at least make it less ruinously expensive) and we see the first signs of 'banging heads together' as a few large pre-emptive mergers (really rescue purchases) were arranged. Even the biggest banks in the world had to write to their owners asking for new share capital in rights issues.

At this stage it looks as if the theory of mopping up is working.

THE BIG DOMINO'S COMING: early September 2008 and most of us are still here – somehow or other there's a momentary wow as Fannie and Freddie are 'taken into conservatorship' (sounds like they're in a glass case in a Washington museum waiting for Ben Stiller at midnight) but while this was bad news it was rationalised by the market as (a) we were sure this was coming one day, so what – and more importantly (b) we always new Washington would blink – we traded against these firms knowing the Uncle Sam would have to protect them and over the years guess what – we earned a higher return than by lending to them rather than directly to him, so most creditors of the Government supported agencies could put a reasonably brave face on it. After all, the US Government stepped up to the plate (again) and they looked as if they would gaily carry on doing so.

Now the rules, the expectations and the whole world changes in a blink.

No one realized the extent and magnitude of these problems, nor how the deterioration of mortgage-backed assets would infect other types of assets and threaten our entire system. In April 2006, Chairman Bernanke predicted that the housing market 'will most likely experience a gradual cooling rather than a sharp slowdown.' In March 2007, he stated 'the impact on the broader economy and financial markets of the problems in the subprime market seems likely to be contained.' Similarly, Secretary Paulson said in June 2007 that the crisis in the mortgage markets 'will not affect the economy overall,' echoing the views of the International Monetary Fund.

> Dick Fuld, ex-Lehman CEO in Congressional testimony,
> October 2008

DOMINO DAY: 15 September 2008 – Lehman Brothers goes under. One of the best known Wall Street firms goes bust. We were trading with them then the phones went dead. Boys and girls on the streets with brown boxes. Bankers with prepaid cafeteria cards hitting the chocolate vending machines to try and get something back. All gone. 128 years all gone. A dead Wall Street firm – the first time that a household name on Wall Street has been forced into insolvency since Drexel Burnham Lambert, and they were out-siders. There have been rumours that Lehman was going to fall over many times before, but no one, no one at all thought it could actually happen, in fact, no one though that the authorities would permit it.

Now every news station carried photographs of the golden youth of finance with their belongings in a cardboard box out on the pavement.

In Shakespeare's words:

> Golden lads and girls all must
> As chimney-sweepers come to dust

The shock was threefold:

- Lehman had a reputation of having bigger ambitions than its capital base – over the preceding 20 years at various points they were the firm people looked at and said 'what if' a Wall Street firm went bust – it would likely be them – but when it actually happened it was a big shock;

- They had been in talks with a Sovereign Wealth Fund about a major injection of equity but negotiated too hard and the South Koreans let the firm go South instead. And there was a roundtable meeting at the Fed (where a decade before, magic got worked out in the smoke-filled rooms to wind down Long Term Capital Management) – but not this time as Bank of America (touted as the saviour) walked off with Mother Merrill instead (allowing BofA to win the famed army of retail brokers – the Thundering Herd, and a hidden hot potato in terms of the huge bonuses Merrill was planning to pay);

- The government (in its last six weeks before the Presidential election) let them go... unlike the Bear Stearns deal where JP Morgan Chase agreed to the marriage but got a sweet dowry by way of US$30bn in non-recourse funding, this time there wasn't a penny on show from the authorities, so Barclays kept its hands in its pockets. Better to buy the people tomorrow than the whole firm today. Everyone asked 'why 'and most nervously: who's next?

Ladies and gentlemen. Welcome to the new world.

The bankruptcy looked more complex than brain surgery in the dark, the whole market seemed to be involved in calculating what was owed in the Lehman bankruptcy when the domino run carried on apace.

The next day saw the Treasury take control of the venerable insurer AIG, (sacking its ex Citibank CEO) and pumping in an emergency loan of US$85bn in return for a 79.9 per cent stake in its shares. AIG caused two problems: firstly, lots of retail investors and policyholders were at risk of loss if AIG folded. This was unlike Lehman directly so the theory went – though many small investors were hurt when money market funds (like Reserve Primary Fund) lost money on their Lehman investments and 'broke the buck' (which is slang for having an asset value lower than the total deposits – a rare and bad occurrence). The second problem was AIG's huge derivatives unit. Using the group's Triple A rating, AIG was a beloved derivatives counterparty and they created and wrote some of the most complex Over The Counter derivatives. When the agencies downgraded AIG's rating the insurer had to post collateral with counterparties within 24 hours, and in these markets couldn't find the necessary liquidity. Lehman's marking-to-market was bad – AIG's would be unbelievable. So the Treasury told the Fed to act under a little known 'catch all' clause in the legislation.

Which they did. (What they perhaps didn't expect was that US$75bn of that pot flowed straight to AIG's investment bank derivative counterparties who received 100 cents in every dollar owed to them as collateral – if AIG had gone down, they'd have received substantially less and their own existence would have been potentially imperilled).

So a broker/dealer goes down and an insurer is saved. Crazy days.

Now everyone is spooked. Where is my money safe? The interbank market looks like Beirut in the '70s. It's just not safe to go outside or to talk to anyone outside your family. Banks can no longer borrow for the typical three month period – lenders are keeping short, in case more problems turn out. Interbank rates climb to credit card levels, assets keep getting written down as sellers exceed buyers in almost all asset classes. The short-sellers (or shorters) are rumoured to be having a field day – as bank stocks fall every session, they sell shares they don't have, then buy them later and cheaper to settle the trade. Perfectly legal (although contentious) but regulators step in internationally to ban the practice to remove one destabilising element.

The last standing Wall Street firms – posh Morgan Stanley and sharp Goldman Sachs – become Bank holding companies. This is the final move beyond the partnerships they were only a few years ago, and this gives them rights to raise retail deposits and get direct help from the Fed (Mr Buffett even takes a share in Goldman).

Pain everywhere: the stressed mortgage banks take pain, smaller countries take huge pain (Iceland and Ireland become a morass of failing banks). Who is safe, or more crucially after Lehman, who won't be saved? No one seemed safe. Country by country recognised that even household names in the banking sector needed emergency help and over the following months, governments internationally moved to provide direct capital – partly, effectively or wholly nationalising many institutions and providing unprecedented access to funds to finance their ongoing traditional banking business.

Senator Everett Dirkson famously warned 'a billion here and a billion there, soon it adds up to real money' and a year after Lehman's failure there are troops of lawyers, litigators and administrators still working through the mass – or mess – of trades in a winding up that could take several years yet, and which has already garnered extraordinary fees which would be enough to float a small accountancy firm on the stockmarket – nice work if you can get it. The entire financial landscape looks like a bad day in North Korea – a discredited management with enough power to blow a hole in the world... Add together the intervention both public and private – and it comes to over three trillion US dollars, that's US$3,000 billion or US$3,000,000 million or US$3,000,000,000,000 – just count the nothings... there is an old astrophysics joke that there are a hundred billion stars in the cosmos – so when we talk of 'astronomical numbers' the financial crisis is literally astronomic in scale!

The IMF – from their plush vantage point in Washington DC and on first-class business travel round the nicest hotels in the world – thinks that there's more bad news to come with a peak at US$4.1 trillion, or looking at it historically, where the G20 nations in 1980 had an average government debt equal to 40 per cent of annual GDP in 1980, at the end of this phase that is likely to exceed 100 per cent in 2014.

Which domino is next? Is it me?

THE CURIOUS CASE OF THE DOG IN THE BOOMTIME

> The job of the Federal Reserve is to take away the punchbowl
> just as the party gets going.
>
> William McChesney Martin,
> Chairman of the Federal Reserve, 1951–70

The regulators' decision to let Lehman go is a moment of history. The irony in this crash is the millions of column inches written prior to it, the hours of earnest European politicians droning and the wide concern of accountants (and other boring functionaries) on how the rise of the hedge fund 'vulture' and the private equity 'locust' would drive the world to disaster. That's not quite how it happened, though. The argument that we needed comprehensive regulation of these firms looks a bit flimsy nowadays after the publicly quoted and highly regulated banks have panned us into depression and have cost their shareholders dearly and the taxpayers (or maybe even the grandchildren of taxpayers) even more dearly.

The central banks and regulators must feel pretty foolish. Many have managed to hide any mandatory expression of shame in the wave of obloquy that has hit the leading bankers, but there's an important question here: why didn't they intervene to stop it? A question literally asked from the highest to the lowest as HM the Queen asked Professor Luis Garicano on Royal Inspection of the London School of Economics in November 2008: 'How come nobody could foresee it?' Just as Tam Dalyell went down in history for asking the 'West Lothian Question', so HM hit the nail on the head with the 'Ordinary Queen on the Street Question'.

The combined intelligence of the UK great-and-the-good were spurred into action and held a symposium of 'experts' selected by the British Academy gathered at urgent pace to deliberate this portentous question (in June 2009), publishing their famous letter four weeks later.

It's an odd letter written in a combination of the language of the central banker and the academic economist, and couched in the formality that is expected upon addressing one's Sovereign. Which could be construed as a way of saying it's very waffley and seems more designed to exculpate the Establishment because the crunch and its enormity was just too large to envisage and then when it hit, too big for any leadership group to contain effectively. Sounds like they've not been inoculated against Collective Amnesia – especially as they promise to hold a 'Never Again' conference next so that, as they put it, HM will never have to ask her question again.

(But it will happen again, regardless of what they say!)

It's a question to ask the regulators: what happened and why? Firstly, it's a simple fact that accommodative economic policies from the Fed and the major central banks allowed a rapid acceleration of credit in the last few years. The benevolent wisdom of Chairman Greenspan looks rather optimistic these days.

Most central bankers told us over and over again that you couldn't predict bubbles – that so long as consumer inflation was kept in line by setting interest rates, everything was dandy. So while the cost of a 58-inch plasma TV screen, a microwave curry and a copy of *Hello* (or whatever was in the inflation basket) chugged along at below three per cent per annum, it didn't matter that houses, stocks, bonds, cars, yachts, jets, divorces, commodities, art, sculpture, school fees, philanthropy were all uniformly not just increasing in price but accelerating – a fact ascertainable by anyone on a real life high street or commuter train. By the simple fiat of saying that the asset price increase was not 'inflation' it didn't matter. Oh yes it did! Those assets sitting outside the narrow definition of inflation grew in value which allowed us all to realise profits by selling and using the cash to buy more, or at the temptation of the banks, raise loans against those – either way, the world was awash with cash. Too much money, in fact. However as all those dollars, pounds, roubles and renminbi yuans were spent on houses, Picassos, Monte Cristo cigars, yachts and financial investments rather than on bottles of milk and bars of chocolate, it was NOT inflationary under the new definition, so feel free to carry on bidding up those assets old boy.

The policy of not identifying or correcting bubbles appears mainly driven by Alan Greenspan's success in handling the aftermath of the October 1987 stock market crash and particularly in his mature years after the dot com bomb, in 'mopping up' the problems following the tech boom and its bust. You have seen the old description of the role of the central bank which heads this chapter: it was to 'take away the punchbowl when the party got rowdy' – that is to raise rates and reduce liquidity when inflation (or 'irrational exuberance') was a feature of the markets. What in fact happened was that the Fed could say, hand on heart, that the punchbowl was hardly being touched – that the level of punch consumption was well within the model of a gregarious but not rowdy party – but the reason none of the guests were quaffing the punch was because they were all in the back room buying crack cocaine and getting high on that instead. Who needs punch when you have subprime?

So the question becomes not how do we mop this up, but have we a big enough mop? From August 2007 through to today, the central banks and monetary authorities have been as active as the Sorcerer's Apprentice in conjuring mops:

- Direct injection of liquidity into the financial system

- Improved deposit guarantee insurance for retail customers

- Cutting interest rates by unprecedented levels and speeds until we are facing what Greenspan called 'the tyranny of zero'

- Secured lending facilities to regulated banks, secured on increasingly general classes of assets

- Insurance for toxic assets, at a heavy cost to the bank

- Currency swaps between major central banks to relieve pressure

- Nationalisation, partial nationalisation, effective nationalisation of all sorts of financial institutions

- Regulatory encouraged mergers or at least acquisitions of 'good bank' business, leaving 'bad banks' on the central bank's own huge balance sheet

- Quantitative Easing: the modern way to print money.

In huge marble offices in mighty skyscrapers across the globe, our regulators have been running faster and faster to clean up the after-effects of the bubble they said didn't exist. Mr Greenspan's answer to the BBC was that it was simply a case of

> human nature, unless somebody can find a way to change human nature, we will have more crises and none of them will look like this because no two crises have anything in common, except human nature.

This statement is wrong. It's time to challenge the 'big boy did it and ran away' theory of financial mania. It is like the curious case of the dog in the night time. Regulators are given teeth by their governments, but why didn't Alan – recognised as the big dog of central banking – bark?

There are repetitive links in the form of financial crises but regulators have to try and ascertain when a bubble is occurring. It seems obvious in the lessons of history that bubbles do exist so you cannot just ignore them, can you?

In a 2005 speech, Mr Greenspan opined that

> Although a 'bubble' in home prices for the nation as a whole does not appear likely, there do appear to be, at a minimum, signs of froth in some local markets where home prices seem to have risen to unsustainable levels.

I like the quotation marks around 'bubble' as if it is one of those clichés that you are embarrassed to write down. That's the analysis which contributed to this debacle.

When you see the face of the failed banker on your television news, or on the placard of some anti-capitalist demonstrator or see him criticised by some French or German politico, just remember that all these decisions – or substantially all – were taken with the regulators and the rating agencies sitting on the flight deck watching and noting every action.

The finest plans are always ruined by the littleness of those
who actually carry them out, for the Emperors can actually do
nothing.

Bertolt Brecht, *Mother Courage And Her Children*, 1939

Well, here we are. Using the old CAMEL model, how does the banking
sector look after Domino Day?

	Problem	Solution
Capital	Pure 'Tier One' ordinary Share capital appeared awfully expensive. Of course it should be, as it's the ultimate loss buffer. In winding up any company, the ordinary shareholder gets his money only after everyone else has been paid. He and the other shareholders then divide up what's left in proportion to their respective shareholdings. Losses (those actually incurred by default or those marked-to-market and so not yet cashed in) eroded total bank capital quicker than imagined.

Poorer quality capital had been included in regulatory classifications – the problem that hadn't been focused upon is that the bank has to repay | Massive injections of state support to many banks leaves them completely, partially or effectively nationalised.

Most other banks have raised ordinary capital from existing or new strategic shareholders and are agreeing to swap existing low-grade forms of capital into new ordinary shares.

Of course, the investors who held the core ordinary shares have been effectively wiped out by a combination of attrition (where the share price is a few per cent of its peak) and dilution (as new shareholders have stepped in taking large stakes in the bank's shares). |

	Problem	Solution
Capital cont...	preference shares (and other 'Tier Two') capital or go bust anyway!	Even banks without government shareholdings get a halo effect – as the government can't let any big bank go down. Or can it?
Assets	Millions of deals were done like buying tins at the supermarket – relying on the label without checking the contents. Huge hits were taken on 'toxic' assets mainly in the trading activities of the banks with some large credit losses – but there's pressure in the economy so other businesses will fail and create increasing loan losses – the 'real economy' losses, losing capital for the banks and reducing the amount they can lend to stimulate economic growth.	If this were a political scandal (which in some ways it is) then we'd have politicians at the stump calling for 'back to basics'. If banks stop lending then we face a real re-run of the Hoover years (which truly sucked), so we need them to continue to support solid enterprises. That's difficult when confidence is low and many businesses are scaling back, when any more loan losses would be highly politically visible and when deposit rates are too low to encourage retail deposits for core lending.
Management	As popular as a porcupine in a nudist colony. They thought that in facing economic stress, they could be like Evel Knievel and, by speeding up, carry over the yawning chasm.	All change, save for a few who are working a very long notice period and a couple who escape into other sectors. But there look to be a lot of the same old faces – same old schools or

	Problem	Solution
Manage-ment cont...	They turned out to be Eddie the Eagle. Thanks guys (and the very few girls...)	same old MBA courses or consulting firms. Many who presided over truly appalling decisions are vilified (pass me some rotten tomatoes and I'll join in) but some who made similar decisions but who were lucky are still on the Exec Floor. Some have even been employed by other banks. Hmmm.
Earnings	Remember them? Hold that thought in your heart for a few years... Record results were demanded every quarter time after time. That is simply too good to be true.	Pass the red ink Alice... Though deep in the heart of many banks, the real utility banking businesses are still profitable and are rapidly being recast as the focus for future strategy. Also customer-facing investment banking (like hedging interest rates and FX) are doing well with volatility and fewer competitors allowing wider spreads.
Liquidity	At the real dark point of the crisis I asked a money market dealer friend 'how's the market today' – 'there is no market' was his sombre reply.	Government and central banks have followed the approach that liquidity in the market is like muck on the farm – you can't get enough and you can't spread it too far.

	Problem	Solution
Liquidity cont...	If banks weren't wanting to lend to each other it's hardly surprising that the punters were queuing to withdraw their readies and take them home to Mattress Bank.	There seems an irony in rescuing the banks who created too much cheap lending by creating too much cheap money from the Governmental printing presses – I know that there is some qualitative distinction between Zimbabwe rolling out limitless Zim Dollar notes and the Bank of England's Quantitative Easing (which sounds more like a cure for constipation... which it could well be). Every central bank exerts itself to provide emergency funding, so there's a wall of liquidity there – if we can just use it wisely.

'We shouldn't try to protect every single institution. The ordinary course of financial changes has winners and losers', as Greenspan was quoted saying once. Well, we tried that with Lehman and I can't honestly say I hope it's an experiment we try again. Yes, it's nice to see hubris meet nemesis but not so much fun when the audience gets caught up in the catharsis.

The scale, number and size of global official initiatives were bewildering. Lots of people, lots of ideas. That's a book that needs to be written in a couple of years as the picture is still far from clear. It was almost as if a chink of remembrance through the Collective Amnesia had the Fed and its fellows go up into the lumber room and find the dusty old suitcase full of market crisis remedies. They blew the dust off and had a good look.

As central banks are, in fact, still banks, the most straightforward approach to reverse the tight liquidity was to extend the 'window' concept. This is where any regulated bank can wander up to the central bank's lending department and, by depositing security of an agreed quality, borrow against it at an interest rate that's a wee bit punitive. In non-crisis times, there's a bit of a stigma in accessing the window and that could start rumours, but in these times trying men's souls, it's a good option. Especially if we widen the eligible collateral and make the interest rate attractive. Out of the window came a bewildering range of differing schemes: SLS, Term Securities Lending (TSL), TAF, TALF, TARP, CPP and others. This is a well tried (though not always totally successful) approach. Professor Kindleberger traces the prototype to the UK authorities in response to the crisis of 1763 (and those of 1793, 1799, and 1811, etc., so it wasn't a life-changing success at first). This operated in parallel with monetary coordination to lower official interest rates (though commercial interbank rates remained higher).

Capital support is rather more tricky. Not every bank could raise additional shareholder capital (from the existing shareholders or by bringing in a new strategic partner) to recapitalise to face the new world and its expectations. We saw brokered mergers – often with official assistance to make it happen where loan facilities would be made available to the acquirer, or by splitting the institution into saleable bits – often selling the customer deposit base (thus avoiding a charge to the public purse in terms of deposit guarantee) and nationalising the difficult assets. Political pressures were seen too: whether in the US Treasury's firm line with Bank of America when it was doing its due diligence on Merrill, or in the UK when Lloyds and HBOS were introduced as partners at a cocktail party (with relatively less due diligence all round).

That took us in to partial or whole nationalisation to the point that in terms of liquidity and capital support, we the taxpayers of the world own a significant proportion of the global financial market, at a value significantly below its peak two years ago.

> But don't you feel that City money is very chancy? It comes
> and goes so quick.

> Anthony Trollope, *Last Chronicle of Barset*, 1867

The really terrifying thing about the credit crunch – this one in particular given that it has been exported (all freight paid) from the USA into the UK and thence to virtually every banking system in the world (The Vatican and Andorra seem to be hanging on in there...) – is that as much as you might revile banks and their managers when people are nervous about placing deposits with them, they have to cut back or even stop lending and so commercial credit dries up for everyone be they Texaco or Mr Onions with a fruit and vegetable stall in the local market, and that constriction impacts the real economy.

Hence the priority to get the banks into a steady state, which is sometimes seen by the public as an unfair rescue. The good news for the public is that the totals involved (let alone the structures and jargon of how the support works) have become so huge – it could end up at more than US$5 trillion or about an eighth of the entire world economy – that they don't register in anyone's brain any more, we just don't have enough nothings in our imagination...

Not Game Over, just Hangover.

Retailers have tried to capture the mood – with some sale tickets reduced by over 75 per cent (a bit like bank shares now worth some 10 per cent of their peak – if 'worth' is a concept that has any value at the moment).

How can we teach our children what has happened? Maybe the big toy companies could help with:

- Bail Me Out Elmo – giggles all the way to the bank

- Cluedo – who killed Dr Lehman on Wall Street with the CDO?

- New Financial Monopoly – Go the Treasury, go directly to Treasury, do not collect your US$200m bonuses

- Cowboy Outfits – ten a penny along Wall Street

- Money Scrabble – making up jargon as you go along.

- My Little Bonus – a little, cheap plastic replica that you can cherish until you are old enough to have a real one

- Wonga Jenga – keep pulling away the bricks until the whole edifice falls over

- Pick Up Stacks – collect as many dollar bills from the pile on the floor without disturbing the shareholders.

All these wonderful products will be in the shops well before Christmas (assuming the manufacturer can get his bank facility agreed to increase production).

Turning and turning in the widening gyre
The falcon cannot hear the falconer;
Things fall apart; the centre cannot hold;
Mere anarchy is loosed upon the world,
The blood-dimmed tide is loosed, and everywhere
The ceremony of innocence is drowned;
The best lack all conviction, while the worst
Are full of passionate intensity.

WB Yeats, *The Second Coming*, 1920

I guess we all wait patiently for five years and see what happens... a bit like the boom years in fact. Joe Public's just along for the ride. Then the seeds of the next banking failures will be sown. To be honest, the first brown tendrils of the next crunch can be seen today.

This may be the biggest financial crisis ever – but it's not the first and it's certainly not the last.

How can we adults get to grips with the fiasco? As I said at the beginning of this book, there is nothing particularly new in the bad news on the markets this time – except that every kind of previous folly seems to have been undertaken imprudently, recklessly and all at once. Add the sheer size of the numbers and that's why we are here today.

We forgot to look at the lessons we have learned from in the past. Collective Amnesia.

The genuine concern must be – have the banks learned from this? Have the regulators, major shareholders, depositors – has anyone learned from this? Or has the concerted input of capital and liquidity merely stabilised a market that is bursting to return to 'Business as Normal'?

There are a lot of potentially negative cultural and strategic straws in the wind following some institutions' relatively robust profitability in the first half of 2009. Look closely and you'll see platforms building in investment banking as the acquirers of Lehman's businesses (and people) look to springboard into the first division of investment banking. Look at the boom in hiring bankers in certain fields – in New York, contracts were being signed with guaranteed bonuses in the first year – until the G20 fired a warning shot againsst the practice? Some long-term shareholders who stepped in to assist in the dark of the crises have cashed in handsomely already, not all management was sacked – some remain at the top (perhaps earning a measly US$1 this year (don't cry too hard, try and average out the last five years' credit in their bank accounts) while some who were fired (or at least 'got resigned') are popping up in other industries as gurus.

Banking is a relatively simple trade – the ways you can lose money are relatively few and they've been tested many times before.

Let's walk through the ten 'laws' of good banking – building on our case studies and on the discussion of what a bank is supposed to do and how that has just got messed up. Let us all try and remember the ways that a bank (or its shareholders!) can lose a packet and then see where that has happened in the past. Maybe, just maybe, this will be the time when the penny drops. Certainly a penny is as much cash as is available today!

As a dog returneth to his vomit, so a fool returneth to his folly.

Proverbs xxvi, 11

Part III
The Ten Laws of Banking and how they got broke

I sincerely believe that banking establishments are more dangerous than standing armies. If the American people ever allow private banks to control the issue of their currency, first by inflation, then by deflation, the banks and corporations that will grow up will deprive the people of all property until their children wake-up homeless on the continent their fathers conquered. The principle of spending money to be paid by posterity under the name of funding is but swindling futurity on a large scale

President Thomas Jefferson to John Taylor, 1816

Taking our mythical goldsmith Cosimo, and extrapolating his business to today, you can see that the elementary principles of running a bank are relatively straightforward: look after your depositors and you'll have quality liquidity; analyse your borrowers carefully and you'll make profitable loans; and treat the staff and shareholders fairly in terms of their relative share of the net interest income. Do all that and you too could be a Medici or a Morgan!

While banking does have its national characteristics, and there are structural differences between the three species of banks (utility, mortgage and investment), the basic ways to muck up the business are pretty similar for each. You might cynically believe that there are only two rules in banking:

- Never give a sucker an even break

- Heads I win, tails you lose

However, it is much more complicated than that. Just as acronyms need three letters to pass the jargon test, laws need to be ten in number to attract your attention. So here, in no particular order, are the ten laws of banking that you break at your peril (or at least at your stakeholders' peril in terms of their wealth and health... if you are a CEO reading this).

Commercial credit is the creation of modern times and belongs in its highest perfection only to the most enlightened and best governed nations. Credit is the vital air of the system of modern commerce. It has done more — a thousand times more — to enrich nations than all the mines of the world.

Daniel Webster, US Senator, 1834

FIRST LAW OF BANKING

CASH IS SANITY, ACCOUNTING IS VANITY

> It has been my experience that competency in mathematics,
> both in numerical manipulations and in understanding its
> conceptual foundations, enhances a person's ability to handle
> the more ambiguous and qualitative relationships that
> dominate our day-to-day financial decision-making.

> Alan Greenspan, Federal Reserve Testimony, September 2000

Banking is about numbers.

Many vocal critics of the current banking crunch pour scorn on the accountants (as it makes a refreshing change to try and find a new scapegoat...) and their quest to capture the essence of a bank in the cold clinical numbers of its formal financial reports and accounts. I recall the story of an insane cartographer who endeavoured to create the perfect ideal map. He went mad on realising the only way to accomplish his design was to draw a map as large as the world itself.

Hence, for every accounting innovation there is an unintended consequence. And there's good evidence that some sensible thoughts on making banking finance easier to understand actually exacerbated the crisis. Under the rather beguiling title of *fair value accounting* (and what could be fairer than that?), the debate started over the differing treatment for investment banks' and commercial banks' assets. While this sounds a bit arcane, unlike arguments over the offside rule, these changes were to have a profound effect on what happened on and off the field of finance.

Imagine a company which has raised money – let's call it Amalgamated Smokestack and Asbestos Inc. It has issued a five-year bond for US$100 through the famous investment bank Goldmines and has arranged a five-year term loan, also of US$100 through the well known commercial bank, Banca Rupta of Italy.

Unfortunately, one week later AmSmoke announces that a class action lawsuit has been launched against it. The price of its shares and bonds drops sharply as investors express their concern about the long-term economic effect of this development on the company, even though AmSmoke continues to pay the interest coupon (in full and on time) to investors, and let's assume that the bonds trade at US$90. Goldmines hadn't had a chance to sell the bond in the market and it is still holding the whole issue on its own balance sheet and has to record that US$90 as the value of the bonds on its balance sheet, taking a mark-to-market loss of US$10 through its profit and loss account (even though it hasn't lost a cent in cash).

Just across the road, Banca Rupta is a bit concerned by the news, but as of today AmSmoke has paid its interest bill in full and is in compliance with all the terms and conditions of its loan. So on the bank balance sheet, the loan remains at US$100, with no hit to profits. As the old banking saying goes, 'a rolling loan gathers no loss'. The loan was valued by the bank's accountants at the outstanding amount due to the bank, not the current market value for selling the loan to another bank. So the bond and the loan are treated differently, even though the economic effect of both look pretty much the same. This anomaly became more important after the law was widened to allow investment banks and commercial banks greater freedom to operate in each other's niches. For the first time, investment banks used their balance sheets to make loans to good clients to emphasise relationships and win new mandates.

It does seem a trifle unfair, so the accounting regulations changed. While credits 'held to maturity' would remain at cost in the balance sheet (subject to tests), most assets would now be marked-to-market (which involves obtaining a new, independent market price for the security at given specified dates). Now this is a great idea and is a perfect solution in wide deep markets where many players buy and sell commodities in an agreed standard – barrels of oil, bushels of apples, gallons of milk. So, too, in finance where foreign exchange, government bonds and shares are all openly traded, which allows an observer to define 'the market price' by polling a cross-section of dealers and traders in the recognised market for these kinds of instrument.

The system is less effective for bespoke or peculiar transactions. Over recent years, financial innovation has spawned myriad new investments where (if anybody does at all) only the original creators really understand the detailed mechanics (and even they'd forgotten – or lost track as others bolted on other ideas and variations – the 'bells and whistles' that were sounding on the Casey Jones index as it sped south). As no independent market existed, the practice of 'mark-to-model' was created. Or 'mark-to-myth' as it became known. This was where the bank and its accountants would agree a mathematical calculation based on observable data to create a methodology of measurement. A bit like saying:

This is twice as risky as US Triple A debt

US Triple A has fallen 20 per cent overnight

Therefore: we will write down the bonds by twice that or 40 per cent.

(Or you could just double it and take away the first number you thought of).

Of course those models are only as good as the assumptions built in, and, under stress, many buckled. Oftentimes a model would be certified as having a 98 per cent 'confidence level', meaning that its outputs would give an intelligent answer virtually all the time. This was a great solace to the auditors. However, looking at it the other way, that confidence level means that in the 200 trading days in a year, up to four days were off the radar. In good markets, with benign activity, this ran smoothly, but as markets fell into turmoil the models melted too.

And that's the overarching problem with models. They are an approximation, a representation and above all a mathematical simplification of the real world with its messes, hormones, jokes, wrath and blight. When you start and your model's 99 per cent right, there will be the odd few times the one per cent we ignore turns up, but it's a tiny bit on the side and you can ignore it. What happens when you are doing hundreds of trades a day based on the model. If it's 99 per cent right then equally it's one per cent wrong. Add all those one per cents together and they begin to add up! And of course, the one per cent risk isn't capped – it just doesn't fit in the model, so when it does occur the model can't cope, it could be a wee bit out or a total meltdown.

The final problem is what happens if there is just no real market? If a fair market price is defined typically as a 'willing buyer' and a 'willing seller' (i.e. neither has his back against the wall or his banker's hand around his throat) acting independently (at arm's length). What happens if you have a bank that needs to mark its loans to market? The loans are all paid up to date, the economy may have tanked, but the borrowers are still paying their way under each loan contract. The bank is not a 'willing seller' at any old price and has the capital to hold the loans. But there are no buyers – everyone's appetite for this stuff is full except for some opportunistic vultures who will offer to take the loan off your hands for a fraction of its worth. (Please note that 'opportunistic vultures' is rarely a fund management category found in the weekly listings of fund prices – but you'll guess who these guys are). What, then, is the real price?

This is exactly the dilemma many banks find themselves in today. They say the market is not truly open, so how can there be a 'market price'?

Of course, a canny bank can sometimes use this to its advantage. We've seen US and UK banks actually increase their profits as their credit rating has been cut. 'How?' I hear the cry. Simple – if you are an accountant that is. If the bank's own credit rating is marked down, then it's very likely the value of the bonds that the bank has issued fall in the market – so you have a mark-to-market gain – if you had to buy back those issued bonds today it would cost you less than yesterday, so add that to your P&L! The fact that an honourable, properly managed bank will pay its obligations in full is neither here nor there.

There are numerous examples of how accounting treatment ends up driving the reality of the company's business rather than merely describing its performance.

Enron's use of special-purpose entities was an egregious flaunting of common sense. Tech companies inflated sales revenues by booking deals agreed with clients but not yet contractually in place, equipment was tucked away off-balance sheet in leasing deals which were tailored to meet the exact mathematical accounting rules rather than common sense. Shadow banking (whether the SIVs or the conduits) rely on the arbitrage between what the regulators permit and what the accountants allow. Complexity inside the accounting rules means that even with increasing disclosure in reports and accounts and public filings, the context is so immensely technical that general investors (and I guess many bankers) are frozen out. So it makes sense to try and focus on the cashflows that the company can create – you can manipulate the accounting treatment but the amount of cash in the deposit account is hard to massage. If the cash is growing then that's a good sign.

Hence the joy of the good old commercial banks – when you hold the company's bank accounts, look at the cash balances. I'd rather see a sound credit balance than a statement of non-cash profit!

> If it looks like a duck, quacks like a duck and walks like a
> duck – then it's probably a duck.
>
> The Duck Test (traditional)

SECOND LAW OF BANKING

YOU CAN'T MAKE RISK DISAPPEAR

You can only change it into a risk with which you are happier
(or had not noticed, or had forgotten about)

> As we know, there are known knowns; there are things we
> know we know. We also know there are known unknowns;
> that is to say we know there are some things we do not know.
> But there are also unknown unknowns – the ones we don't
> know we don't know.
>
> Donald Rumsfeld, US Secretary of State, February 2002

If I had a pound for every time I'd heard a banker saying that something's no longer a risk because he's bought protection, I might just about have enough money to pay back their bad debts. There was an advert for one of the accounting firms some years ago showing a little guy on a desert island with a fishing rod with a big hook and a worm. What we could see that he couldn't was that he was standing, not on an island, but on the back of a sea monster who was hungrily eyeing up the bait with his big sharp teeth hidden under water...

Think about your own life. We face risk day in day out. A simple example is your home. You will have an insurance policy covering the physical building. So you have no risk have you?

Well, the insurance company could go bust – and have no money to settle your claim; there are formal obligations you have to follow – perhaps advising the company if you're absent from the property for more than 30 days – so when you come home from the six-month Caribbean cruise to find the mansion burned to ashes, you've broken the policy undertakings and may not get paid; if you do get paid, it will probably be the agreed 'replacement value', which, firstly, you won't see because it may all be used to pay out your mortgage first. So if you've lost credit status too, you are pretty much stuffed. And the rebuilding value may not be enough, for example in a boom when labour and materials are at a cyclical high.

So yes, you've covered off the risk of your house burning down, but there are little risks there in the shadows. Of course, our minds tell us – as does experience – that few people's houses burn down so the insurance risks only come into play if the big event (the fire) happens. And as we feel comfortable that it won't happen, then who cares? We could take the time, with a bright reading lamp and our sharpest bifocals, to read the thousands of policy words – maybe even understand them – but time is short, the risk of mishap seems far away and I had the sports pages to finish before falling asleep in my chair. I am a typical investor!

By extension this is one of the key elements of this current crunch.

The creation of toxic assets – not marketed under that name of course – but the philosophies of *'slice and dice'* and *'pump and dump'* were both predicated on the concept that it was 'safer' to have 100 shares of one per cent of each loan rather than holding one single whole loan. Diversification and correlation were the key words which waived away the risk and allowed us to look at these structures as if they were our insurance against loss.

The market downturn was like the house fire – no one believed that the entire market would tank – that every one of the 100 loans would stink – any more than we expected to see our home burning like Manderley against the sunrise.

(It's a little known fact that the whole global insurance industry pays out more in insurance claims annually than it gathers in in premiums – it makes its profits by investing the premiums to earn investment income; that yield is of course increased if the insurer can slow down pay-outs to policyholders.)

Bankers often joke about adding the 'gold and hostages' clause to borrowing documents, but even these mitigants are not perfect – gold's market price is volatile and hostages need to be fed...

Nothing is certain save Death and Taxes.

Benjamin Franklin, 1789

THIRD LAW OF BANKING

TRUST THE FOLLOWING FORMULA: $3 + 3 + 3 < 10$

(If your net interest margin is three per cent, you have no more than three martinis at lunch and you leave the office by 3pm then your golf handicap will remain in single figures during your long and happy banking career and a well-deserved golden retirement)

I've often thought that there was very little wit wanted to make a fortune in the City

Anthony Trollope, *The Prime Minister*, 1876

There was a time (which I can just remember growing up in provincial Scotland and even in my days as a graduate trainee in London) where every bank branch was run by a senior banker with great personal authority not only in the management of the physical branch and its personnel but crucially in terms of lending. The bank manager was almost the ambassador (or colonial governor-general) of the bank's head office (the analogy is a good one – and both offices have diminished as communication has moved to being nearly instantaneous – nowadays we prefer to email monkey@bigbank.com rather than arrange an appointment in two weeks' time to talk to Mr Organ-Grinder round the corner).

Like all golden days reminiscences, this one has its weaknesses – any British reader will remember Captain Mainwaring of Dad's Army and his team of Sergeant Wilson and Private Pike, respectively the manager, accountant and cashier of the local bank branch, as being rather less effective as bankers than as volunteer defence troops (and that's saying something). Traditionally, the big banks rotated managers on a three- to five-year cycle and after a period of a business grower, a more conservative man (for in those dark days they all were men – still a bit of an issue of course) would be employed to tamp down the loan book, to weed out the errors and to ensure that the foundation remained strong enough for the day he received his next promotion, vacating the leather chair and big oak desk for the next manager to grow the book again.

This law has a fair bit of tongue in its cheek – but there are some biting points too.

- Net interest margin – the best deposits you can get are from the public. Treat them well (and don't fall in the trap of fêting only the borrowers – your depositors are crucial too).

- Golf – (in which I must say I have no ability at whatsoever) is a bit of a banking fetish, but worthy of thought on two levels: the banker who knows the chairman of his borrower and all the senior team will know them inside and outside the meeting room – more chance to understand the people making the real decisions. The relationship banker from Banzai Bank who meets the assistant treasurer at head office for 50 minutes once a year to discuss the report and accounts only buys the received story. (Mind you, it can be taken too far – in 2007 a number of Wall Street executives were tracked online as they recorded their golf scores on a handicap website – they should have been back at the ranch stomping on those fires!). Most of them have a lot more golfing time these days.

- The Martinis – well, that has changed. Twenty years ago, whether in the client dining room of the famous old City pubs (such as the Jampot off Lombard Street in London or Henry's on Hanover Square in New York), the end of the morning session was enthusiastically celebrated in alcohol. Then after Big Bang, the tone changed as dry US bankers and traders took advantage of the new freedom in the market to set up shop – it was a level marketplace when everyone was tipsy, but to have a few sober dealers was a problem! For the purposes of the restatement of this law, we could substitute the martinis for something fattening – maybe a lunch of 3,000 calories?

Successful deployment of bank capital (which is, after all, mainly other people's money) is aided when there is one central person in the bank who 'owns' the customer relationship and who is recognised as such inside and outside the bank (subject to challenge and governance of course). This is supported by an effective and experienced credit department who will have direct experience of the borrower, its sector and the economic cycle in which it operates.

It also depends on the institution having a credit approval process that absorbs and remembers trends across the boom and the bust. When you fall off a bicycle, you are meant to get back on straight away and start pedalling like billy-o, but never to forget why you fell off. Banking cycles seem to be treated in the opposite manner! Keynes made mention of the seeds of the next recession starting when the last banker who made the loans in the last recession retired, and there is a lot of truth in that. Even Alan Greenspan admitted in 2001 that 'the worst loans are made at the top of the business cycle' – certainly there seems to be what is called a 'procyclicity' in the bank's behaviour – with increasing lending towards the end of the economic boom, then a sudden reversal in lending appetite as the economy falters (when the best result for the economy is probably the opposite – a slowdown of loan capital chasing up the market and a stable appetite to lend to creditworthy enterprises in the bust).

This isn't a formal paper, so I won't mention Berger and Udall's paper 'The Institutional Memory Hypothesis and the Procyclicity Of Bank Lending Behaviour' (BIS Working papers No 125, January 2003) which brings a lot of force behind the argument that 'the capacity for loan departments to identify risk and identify potential future problems deteriorates as time passes since their last 'learning experience' with problem loans'. Broadly speaking, as the boom takes its turn, lending bankers become more confident and experienced in the growing market (typically those with experience of the last bust will have been sacked last time round – either directly in loss-making departments or indirectly as the bank reallocates personnel from loan creation to loan management) while a similar erosion occurs in the credit officers or committees deliberating on the transaction. Then comes the crash and inflexibility becomes the philosophy of the day.

Of all the lying things a liar can tell you, 'this time is different' is the most readily believed.

Or, in family terms, your Mum tells you not to climb the tree, for if you fall it will hurt. One of two outcomes – you are a good lad and believe Mamma, thus preserving the knees of your trousers and avoiding bruises, or you climb, fall, take £10 damage out your trousers, get a good whacking from the maternal parent and get sent to bed and told not to climb trees any more.

If Mum's not on duty, and you and your mates are in the boughs, then you can be sure that testosterone flows upwards, so a lot of climbing and falling is set to happen. That is part of the human condition, along with the ability to forget about any unpleasant downsides in falling out the tree. So it is both wrong and highly irritating to hear commentators proclaim that this mess we are now in (a) couldn't have been predicted and (b) is unique as nothing like this has ever happened before.

That shows an extraordinary blindness – as we have seen in the Case Studies, it has happened before. We just assumed that it wouldn't happen again.

We had a benign environment for over a decade. Mummy (in the form of the central bankers) even started inventing new economic terms to describe the wonder world we lived in – NICE (Non Inflationary and Constant Expansion) or the Goldilocks economy (not too hot, not too cold) or the one I liked least: THE GREAT MODERATION. But even with Alan Greenspan as cheerleader, the bears come home to catch Goldilocks – you should always believe in the bears, my children... not least because they have very sharp teeth and claws.

Of course it's happened before – one of the great Aristotelian philosophies is that all art is the product of the mechanical repeat of human nature against events – no US President ever reads Gibbon about the fall of monolith empires, no more than bank CEOs look at last time their sector was seen round the bankruptcy courts because *nous avons changer tous céla.*

(Except we haven't.) That's why the Case Studies are often seen as events without parallel, or tragedies without equal, except for the fact the underlying blight in each has been repeated generationally throughout the financial markets. We must remember and from that remembrance we must learn. That is difficult if there are no experienced bankers to hand. And I bet that's true in other industries too.

And once banks have built up confidence and thence capital, and when real businesses are tired of using their own equity to capture a share in the growing economy and when international capital flows again into financial institutions and when competition builds, and asset prices rise, then, life is a cabaret, old chum, so come to the cabaret...

Ils n'ont rien appris, ni rien oublié.

Tallyrand (on the Bourbon Kings of France –
who learnt nothing and forgot nothing
from the Revolution), 1796

FOURTH LAW OF BANKING

GIVING A BANKER CAPITAL IS LIKE GIVING A DRUNK A GALLON OF BEER

You know what's going to happen, but you don't know against which wall (Sibley's Law)

'They breathe profits; they eat the interest on money. If they don't get it, they die the way you die without air... We're sorry. It's not us. It's the monster. The bank isn't like a man.'

'Yes, but the bank is only made of men.' 'No, you're wrong there—quite wrong there. The bank is something else than men. It happens that every man in a bank hates what the bank does, and yet the bank does it. The bank is something more than men, I tell you. It's the monster. Men made it, but they can't control it.'

John Steinbeck, *The Grapes of Wrath*, 1939

This is a favourite aphorism of the great financial columnist Christopher Fildes who dubs it 'Sibley's Law'. It is an important truth about bankers, but like all clever proverbs, it cuts two ways.

Who is the stupid one: the banker for wasting the money (again) or the investor for giving it to him (yet again)?

After the event, of course, it was easy to put the blame on the reckless activity of the banks or the timidity of the regulators!

This recycling – whether by the German Landesbanken (the large regional wholesale banks who until very recently used the German Triple A guarantee to borrow at fine rates in the open market and lend on very aggressive terms to non-German companies) in the 1990s or the Japanese banks (with the profits from the Japanese boom years) in the 1980s – was prodigious. So today, with similar ferocity, the wall of money rolled until it became a wall more of Jericho.

Two overlapping cycles explain Mr Sibley's oft proven proposition.

1   There are many traditional banking products which are like a utility in nature – the financial plumbing of the modern world. Some are obvious – the payment systems, bank charges, the spread between the wholesale and the retail price for foreign exchange or fixed rate mortgages.

Some are less obvious – a good example being the float – all that money which leaves your account at bank X on Monday but isn't credited to your friend's account at bank Y until Thursday

An extended example of this is to be seen in the economics of the issuance of travellers cheques. Thomas Cook and AmEx were the greatest beneficiaries here with many billions of dollars in travellers' cheques paid for upfront – you make a fair bit of money on the holidaymakers who will spend or return the currency cheques within a few weeks, but a great volume lies under mattresses or in safety deposit vaults as an emergency store of value that is never (or rarely) encashed. The issuers invest the initial sale proceeds of their travellers' cheques (an invention of a Scottish bank, by the way...) against the day of repurchase and make a tidy investment income).

In general, there are big barriers to entry to a competitor wanting to encroach in these areas, and the existing big banks in each country tend to enjoy their oligopolies (in fact, in the USA until the 1980s it was illegal for a bank to open branches across the border in a different state!).

These 'clearing banks' diversify their income into riskier areas – lending long-term money to companies or to buy-outs, or underwriting bonds or trading in currencies, interest rates and commodities.

This is when outsiders get interested.

You'll laugh when I say this, but on average there is too much capital in the banking system over the cycle.

New competitors come into the market typically poaching staff from the incumbents and in a new market tend to compete on price. There are innovations – a good example being successful product in one market which can be rebuilt in a different market – but the broad trend is:

- Decreasing price
- Longer period of repayment
- Weakening structure
- Doing it with weaker credits

2 The second effect is size. To maintain the size of the bonus
pool and the dividend (in fact, it's probably calculated
only on the first of these...) absolute levels of revenue need
to grow.

Initially, banks will look to develop the relationship with the
client into new areas. Quite logically, if the margin on lending
is declining we can compensate for that by selling something
else that (a) the competition doesn't have and (b) that makes a
good profit. The phrase often heard (in the boom at least) is
that the participation in the low-yielding loan is the 'ticket to
the dance' – without that there's no chance at all of dancing
with the pretty girl.

Of course, the competitors think likewise and will develop
rival product teams (at some considerable expense, buying
personnel from existing banks – the first wave being bankers
who are looking to head a business and make a fortune, the
second wave are the deputies who fear that their chance will
never come in the home organisation and the final wave is just
about anyone at all from a reputable bank).

The ticket to the dance now only gets us into the hall – there's competition
inside too. Strictly Come Banking.

By now the leading banks to a company or industry are probably making
(just) enough return on their best clients, but many 'relationship' banks
find it hard to grow the 'ancillary' income out from their utility functions
(e.g. cross-border payments, processing payroll, local transactions) but
still we need to grow the top line. This means moving down the credit
curve – by introducing concepts developed for large companies into the
smaller corporate clients who will pay more (as the credit is weaker).

Of course, as more 'chase yield down the curve' then the pricing and structure in those markets decline too. Yet the engine of growth needs feeding
more than an obese high-school kid. When it goes 'pop' you can see the
effect – a general reduction of capital reflecting actual or potential losses
causing foreign players to repatriate capital by closing international businesses while local markets see consolidation. The quantum of competitive
capital declines, the number of players declines and rational pricing comes
in as the depositors expect more (probably frustrated by the policy makers
who reduce interest rates, but there we go, more borrowers vote than savers
as a rule...) and the cycle – the dance to the music of money – starts again.

It reminds me of the waspish rhyme from Hillare Belloc:

> The accursed power which stands on Privilege
>
> (And goes with Women, and Champagne, and Bridge)
>
> Broke and Democracy resumed her reign:
>
> (Which goes with Bridge, and Women, and Champagne).

The classic quote this time round was from Chuck Prince, the lawyer who headed Citigroup (I know, a lawyer running possibly the biggest and most complex banking group in the world – I bet there are no successful law firms headed by ex-bankers). One of the interesting features of the composition of boardrooms in financial companies was that in their desire to widen the selection list from the 'good old boy' bankers – who accountants and governance experts claimed were naturally predisposed to nod along with the management rather than in calling them to account – they forbade the grey-haired and experienced and instead found captains of other industries who, by-and-large, went down with the ship). Counsellor Prince was infamously quoted (in July 2007):

> 'As long as the music is playing, you've got to get up and dance,' he told *The Financial Times* on Monday, adding, 'We're still dancing.'

Chuck (who was soon to be a verb rather than a noun) has a lot of spare time to dance now.

Sibley's Law conquers all. Just don't give those banks too much capital! You know what will happen next.

Shareholder question:	'Why did you lend so much on real estate?'
CEO Reply:	'We made a mistake.'
Shareholder reply:	'If you make two mistakes they send you back a grade.'

Citibank AGM, 1990

FIFTH LAW OF BANKING

ALWAYS HAVE TWO WAYS OUT

The pound of flesh which I demand of him is dearly bought,
'tis mine, and I will have it.

William Shakespeare, *The Merchant of Venice*, 1596/98

When Napoleon threatened to cross the Channel and invade England in
the early 1800s, the venerable Bank of England resolved to guard its own
gold reserves with a volunteer regiment raised from the bank's clerks. They
had a natty uniform with a plumed hat and a standard proudly bearing the
bank's seal of Britannia and the motto:

NO ADVANCE WITHOUT SECURITY

This encapsulates the fundamental safeguard in all banking transactions
(the one, it used to be said, which differentiates between a 'lender' and a
'banker' – the lender merely happily hands over the loan proceeds, while
the banker is the one to analyse and estimate the borrower's business and
cash flow). The wise banker knows that there are margins of error in all
commercial life, so you need to have a plan B. Being an old fashioned
banker, while I ignore the airline safety demonstration (if we get into that
mess, sticking my head between my knees is only going to preserve my
dental records...) I will check where the nearest exit is.

If you are lending to a company to build a new factory building, you will
have your primary source of repayment of your loan out of the increased
production generated by the factory (as a part of the overall revenues generated by your borrower in his existing business). As a secondary source
you will take a mortgage over the factory (so that you can sell it to recoup
your loan if the cash flow doesn't materialise) or perhaps take rights over
the other parts of the business (by guarantees or by mortgages) or perhaps
by taking the personal guarantee of the owner/shareholder (potentially
backed by cash or his/her home). You might even find a banker who wants
all of the above! (It is now unconventional to demand hostages to be delivered to the bank headquarters but I have a feeling it will come at least
metaphorically back into fashion any time now.)

The key to taking security is to find a source of repayment that is independent of the primary source of repayment. If the new production fails to
sell in the depression that affects that whole industry and your secondary
security is a second or third factory, then the value of the other factories

will be lower in the difficult markets too. A typical error is to have the owner give a guarantee without adequate tangible and liquid backing. Imagine if all or most of his wealth is in the shares of the company that's trading badly and so unable to pay him dividends or they are trading at a depressed value in the capital markets so he can't even sell some of his shares to meet his obligation to you. (Think of some of the recent the Russian oligarchs.)

So you need other tangible protection. In the world of small and medium-sized enterprises the banking tradition was to take a second mortgage over the chief executive's family home, which is good unless we are in a wide recession like today or if there's a correlation with the main business. If you have the deeds to a builder's own home as your security/second way out, if his house building business can't sell houses, then the likelihood of selling his house may well be impinged. Two ways out – and distinct risks.

A lot of what is now called 'toxic' debt has this sort of issues. The capital value of the bond was determined on the cash flowing out of the underlying instruments (be they credit cards, home loans or whatever) – when defaults rise, the cash flow falls and the capital value declines too. The theory was that by having a wide spread inside the bond the diversification effect would act a bit like a second way out – because the structurers and rocket scientists told us that it was well nigh impossible that everyone should be affected by a global credit pandemic. All our piggy banks caught swine flu and reacted the same way, proving it's a very narrow gap between having one way out and having no way out at all.

If the business plan does not go to plan, the banker has to have alternative cash generators to see him free and clear.

There is a route that many rely on as a 'get out of jail free' card, whereby another way to get repaid as a banker is to be refinanced – where another lender is happy to approve a new loan and replace yours (or, you yourself might be pleased to extend the terms).

In hard markets, however, all these cash-lined avenues can be pressured (especially refinance) and so the bright guy is the fellow who thought the unthinkable on day one and tested and evaluated each repayment source, taking several to ensure that he was repaid in full.

When the loan is a simple contract between one banker and one borrower, this is a relatively straightforward process and, to some extent, if you make a mess of it, tough luck. As the world became bigger and bigger, banks were reluctant to hold the whole loan on their own books, and looked for ways to share the loan (or load).

The first structure to achieve this was the syndicated loan, which remains a big (not quite as big as before) sector in banking. Here one bank (or a small group of banks) negotiates terms with the borrower with a view to selling participations to other banks. Sometimes these large banks will make a committed underwritten loan themselves or, in a cheaper route, they will find new players 'on a best efforts basis'. The Arranger Banks (who receive escalating titles – Mandated Lead Arranger being the current gold medal) make extra fees for organising the facility (terms, documents, monitoring it, paying the money away and in finding other banks to take part) while those participants (who also receive fancy titles formally but are usually called 'the stuffees' – not a badge of distinction and never ever used to describe your firm) get access to borrowers with whom they would not otherwise get to deal.

In good times, the stuffees receive an Information Memorandum with data on the borrower (and maybe a town hall meeting with the company's senior managers) and are given a couple of weeks to make up their minds. So as you can imagine, the level of analysis can be quite attenuated. I knew a bank in the late 1980s whose assessment was solely on who the lead arranger was – if one of the UK clearers was arranging the deal they would take 10 per cent of it. They took a horrible cold bath in the early 1990s as this strategy ensured that they had one-tenth of all the pain in every bad deal in the UK. As loans became more commoditised and stuffees started to analyse deals based on credit rating versus yield, there was a concern that the institutions furthest away from the borrower (and potentially less able to assess the risk in detail) were in aggregate holding the bulk of the risk.

Certainly, many remember going to creditors' meetings of failed or failing companies in the early 1990s and finding that over half the people in the room were Japanese bankers (or representatives thereof) who had bought the loans in the secondary market, often with little idea of the industry involved. When a company is in trouble the project to try and save it ('the work out' as it is known) is usually given a code name. One memorable meeting saw a senior stuffee banker asked what the legal implications were from changing the company's name from X plc to 'Project Flamingo'. The question – like the company – hardly had a leg to stand on.

This became a mantra in the recent boom – whether through syndication of loans or bonds, or securitisation or whatever, the bigger banks lived by 'originate and distribute'. No longer were the Lead Arrangers expected to hold the largest participation in their deals – they would often sign up for an initial commitment which they would sell before the champagne was drunk at the closing lunch. This gained momentum as not only other banks but also hedge funds and insurers started to express an interest in investing in bank facilities, to the extent that many were structured with a specific 'B Loan' which was designed to look more like traditional bond to meet the requirements of non-bank lenders. As the originating house was not anticipating holding a material stake in the deal, its own assessment standards were changed – 'is this an OK deal to hold for 30 days until we sell it down?' was the question rather than 'will this company repay us in full over five years?'. This had two serious consequences: (i) the arranger was less concerned about the detailed structure and protections – if it met the market price it would sell – so this encouraged a lessening of credit analysis and structuring and (ii) the borrowers knew that monitoring of the facility would be weaker – in areas such as subprime, so long as the underlying mortgage met the criteria at face value, then that would be OK, the fact that it had a 'teaser rate' (a low initial rate to encourage the borrower which became a much higher rate after a short time) or similar surprises and that the underlying borrower had no way to service the loan often wasn't captured.

Of course, this strategy, which as it grew became known as Pump and Dump, came a cropper when the stuffees were full and could not take more and all of those short-term underwritings became long term loans on the balance sheet. The sausage machine ground to a halt faster than the abattoir could slow down killing the pigs.

Always have two ways out. Especially if you are one of the pigs.

> To expect the unexpected shows a thoroughly modern
> intellect.

> Oscar Wilde, *An Ideal Husband*, 1895

SIXTH LAW OF BANKING

THE EASIEST WAY TO BUY A SMALL BANK IS TO BUY A BIG ONE AND WAIT FOR THE PROBLEMS

> Bank failures are caused by depositors who don't deposit enough money to cover losses due to mismanagement.
>
> Dan Quayle, Vice President USA, 1989–93

Reading some of the recent articles on the banking crisis, you'd think that banks never went bust. Au contraire. All over the world regulated banks fail every year. Now it is fair to say that it is unusual to see this happen in Britain (or is it – what about the Secondary Banking Crisis in 1973 or BCCI or Barings more recently, or the collapse of the small lenders in the '90s?) Just as this was going to press, PWC's banking insolvency team announced the completion of the winding up of a UK bank, Israel British Bank, which had gone under owing £34million in 1974.

In the USA even the largest banks (or perhaps especially the largest banks) have faced near-death experiences. Continental Illinois (which, at its peak, was the seventh largest in the USA by balance sheet and the largest corporate lender overall) had an overextended concentration of loans to 'Less Developed Countries' in 1984 and because the laws of Illinois prevented it from having any branches other than its head office in Downtown Chicago, the substantially correct rumours caused the interbank market to dry up. So when the day came that it could not renew its wholesale loans from other banks to finance its own book, the rumours successfully toppled the bank. A few years later, Bank of America, then the biggest bank in the world, ran aground in a very similar manner (with a global franchise of poor loans) but there, a vastly loyal (and perhaps stupid) depositor base in its home state of California stuck doggedly with the new management until the BofA eagle flew high again (and until recently, when, some years after being taken over by NationsBank of North Carolina, a controversial acquisition of Merrill Lynch – possibly with the Treasury's shotgun pointing at the CEO – has brought them back in the headlines). In the past even Citibank has had to operate for a number of years under strict regulatory oversight in the early 1990s on the back of a combination of real estate and emerging markets problems. Of course, depositors can be fickle. One of the final nails in the coffin of Bank of New England (the largest Boston bank and one of the most aggressive real estate lenders) was when ordinary depositors – the canny folk of Massachusetts – withdrew the best part of US$1bn through the ATM network on the weekend of 4/5 January 1991.

The banking crisis that shows the USA at its best and at its worst was the huge train wreck from 1978 through to 1988 – known in the history books as the great S&L Crisis – which effectively wiped out a whole tier of the US banking system. The Savings & Loans Associations (the S&Ls or 'thrifts' as they were usually nicknamed when they were popular). were supposed to be a fairly simple banking model – lending to local families to buy their own homes – but it cost the US taxpayer US$150bn to bail out 1,320 failed S&Ls. (During the same period, 1,650 banks also failed with a mere cost of US$37bn.)

You will remember from President Jackson's memorable attack on banks that US public policy on banking was always slightly schizophrenic. As well as the fabled Glass Stegall Act separating investment banking and real banking, commercial banks were tightly controlled and until the 1980s, it was even against the law to open branches across state boundaries, and within states there were severe restrictions on what business branches could do with each other. There was a local political appeal in having local banks rooted in the community – a sort of 'states rights' in the financial sphere – including both full-service commercial banks and the thrifts with their simple banking model that could only take deposits and make mortgage home loans. No Wizards of Oz could then leach valuable deposit capital out of rural America and splurge it on Wall Street whims and their city-slicker chums.

There were in the region of twenty thousand independent regulated entities in the US banking market in 1978 (and almost as many regulators...). Many of the localised thrifts found it hard in the economy then prevailing. Firstly, as mutual societies with no shareholders or access to the stock-market, they could only fund themselves through deposits. Another arm of public policy had decreed (for reasons that still elude me) that it should be illegal for any bank or thrift to pay interest on deposit accounts that were repayable on demand or pay a yield greater than the maximum interest rates for term deposits set by the authorities. This prohibition did not extent to the money market funds, so naturally there was significant outflow from the regulated sector in one of the first of a set of scenarios that bankers fear – 'disintermediation' (i.e. becoming irrelevant, thus poorer, no holidays, children out of private school, etc.). This was biting particularly hard in the Carter years as short-term interest rates were on the rise to record levels, yet most of the mortgage loans were fixed at long-term rates, which were up to one per cent lower than current market – a huge squeeze on S&L profitability.

Government in its wisdom looked down at the problem and saw that thrifts were making fewer loans because they said that their profits were too low. The administration thought that if it reorganised the thrifts to increase profitability then home loans, and the socially beneficial effects of home ownership would expand.

The snappily entitled Depository Institutions Deregulation and Monetary Control Act (or DIDMCA – oddly no legislators offered to put their name to this one) allowed the thrifts to expand beyond a de minimums level of 'ADC' loans – for Acquisition, Development and Construction of real estate – for those of you who don't know that's the riskiest part of real estate lending! As a bolt-on, the Congress increased Federal Deposit Insurance from US$40k to US$100k. This emphasised the problem of moral hazard – where the bank managers know that, if their bank goes bust, the government will bail out the depositors.

In parallel, the regulator started to wind down the amount of capital that had to be held (from a low six per cent of capital down to three per cent, but with changes in definitions that actually meant many lending institutions had to have effectively zip to their name), all with the laudable aim of stimulating growth.

Finally, the old rules, which insisted that the local thrift be owned by at least 400 depositors of whom 125 had to be local residents and where no single person could own more than 10 per cent of the thrift, were 'simplified' so that a single individual could own the whole thrift (and not only that, the new owner need not pay cash, but could use real estate as consideration for the purchase). As the Tax Code had been rewritten in 1981 to allow very juicy tax breaks for individuals developing real estate, the perfect storm was created – the ideal financial solution for a thrift was to find a land-rich property developer (usually with no banking expertise) to acquire the whole business in a land for shares swap and then start financing his and his friends' development portfolio (while adding in some other riskier ventures too). The final joy was that any goodwill on acquisition would be counted as regulatory capital. Shades of the Ayr Bank.

Initially the regulators thought that they had cracked the problem. The combination of lower interest rates in 1983 on top of the deregulation allowed many regional S&Ls to announce profits for the first time – but the overall sector was far from healthy as one in three thrifts still posted losses and one in 10 would have been defined as insolvent if the same rules as those that apply to banks had been used. But these seemed technical issues that would be ridden out in the economic cycle. Certainly the thrifts were doing their bit to grow the economy: from the passing of Garn St Germain (which sounds more like a Parisian train station than an Act of Congress), the ambitious thrifts in the booming economies of Texas and California tripled in size in the years up to 1986 – with the engine of growth being commercial development.

It was a one-way street. The entrepreneurial thrifts could offer huge interest rates to depositors (including large wodges controlled by brokers who collected individual depositors and then shopped the hot money round the system) as the government deposit guarantee meant that the depositors would be made whole even if the risky loans went bad. Most Mom and Pop investors didn't see any need to change the system – *laissez les bon temps rouler*! On the asset side, growth in home ownership in the south, and California in particular, aligned with an open chequebook policy on real estate, built great arrangement fees and interest receipts – another new regulation tried to capture declining asset quality by using a regulated, eight point grading system where loan loss reserves had to build up after notch 4 ('Other Assets Especially Mentioned' in the quaint phrase) – however, so long as the credit department waived any problems and the thrift borrower was less than 90 days in arrears, he stayed below 'notch 4' and was legally was a good customer.

The chief regulator for S&Ls changed in 1983 and the new guy was unhappy at the state of things and so started a long-fought claw-back of the freedoms given away by his predecessors. Politicians, entrepreneurs, even the courts slowed down the reversal of policy until the first cracks appeared – Empire Savings of Mesquite Texas went under in early 1984 (a us$300m hit to the deposit fund – start counting for the numbers are going to go one way from here) with over a hundred people facing criminal charges for fraud. The whole of Ohio's S&L industry fell over in March 1985 with Maryland's close behind – these States had run out of money to support their thrifts and after a run of runs, Washington in the summer found it had less than us$5bn in its coffers to meet a forecast demand (woefully small) of us$20bn!

So 1986 was a difficult year – there wasn't enough cash to close all the dodgy thrifts and there wasn't the regulatory control in place (though to be fair they were trying hard). The war became political, with Congressmen and Senators from the growth states being particularly active. (Did I mention that many of them had received substantial financial campaign donations from the thrifts – a bit like the 10 years to 2008 which saw the subprime lenders in the US spend over US$380m in lobbying and campaign contribution – money talks… and usually it talks loudest to power with one particular thrift boss, Charles Keating, doing an awful lot of talking.)

Keating was the archtype of the new industry and his belief that the regulators were harsh and arbitrary was repeatedly echoed by five senators – including to a more limited extent John Glenn and the recent Presidential candidate John McCain (I can't recall Keating being mentioned when he flew to Washington around the time of Lehman's failure). He was big in everything he achieved, including the cost of the bailout. The Lincoln Savings & Loan collapse was a particularly messy one. Keating's holding company, American Continental, was suffering heavily because of losses on its real estate business, and raised cash through Lincoln who offered customers (mainly retired people) an opportunity to invest in a higher yielding bond from AC (forgetting to tell them that if they moved their deposits out of Lincoln into AC, they would lose the Federal Deposit Guarantee). The total cost of this one group's clean up was the best part of US$4bn (which seems a derisory amount of cash now but was shocking way back then), Keating went through several court proceedings including being sentenced by a judge who quoted Woodie Guthrie (that's a new one from the Bench): 'more people have suffered from the point of a fountain pen than a gun'.

But I'm ahead of myself. This political wrangling effectively killed the restructure of the deposit fund (there was a token gesture in August when an additional US$10.8bn was added to the deposit guarantee fund – though anticipated losses were in the region of US$40bn) until GHW Bush was elected and launched comprehensive measures to cap the issues in legislation. In a series of drastic changes the old deposit scheme (or the three cents left therein) was closed and the FDIC, which guaranteed bank deposits, took over. Similarly, the old regulator was canned and a new office created with the remit to enforce standards equivalent to those used for banks. The final leg of the tripod was the creation of the huge Resolution Trust Corporation ('RTC') a big bad bank.

There was a great political firestorm and it was recognised that direct intervention was required if only to slow down the claims on the government deposit guarantee which clicked in if a thrift fell over. The Bush Senior team put together a suggestion that looked market centred. The RTC was a brand new institution mandated to take over failing S&Ls before their formal collapse and to dispose of the valuable assets promptly for a higher return than could be expected through a liquidation process. This was sold as a mandate to reduce the cost to the Taxpayer.

This was truly a jumbo task – and in fact RTC seized 747 thrifts with assets of over US$400bn in total and restructured the businesses to be sold to new investors. The total cost to the USA is usually estimated at US$125–140bn but it did keep the system on track until it was folded into the FDIC in 1995. Many commentators see parallels both in the cause and the remedy when compared with today.

The causes of the S&L crises were centred on:

- A relaxing of capital standards in a period of rapid economic growth

- Entrepreneurial bank leaders without any actual banking experience

- Underpaid/overstretched/unpopular regulators with overlapping mandates and little active political support.

Sound familiar?

Looking at the Japanese banking crisis (which started in the early) '90s and is still in some ways unresolved) you can see the argument against government timidity in Japan's 'lost decade'. Zombie Borrowers (with no sensible economic prospect of recovery, let alone of being able to service the debt mountain they had incurred) were kept limping on so that the Zombie Banks (Loan of the Dead) could stay in business – which was necessary given their huge cross shareholdings in the less challenged companies in Japanese industry and commerce. Tokyo's financial officialdom were nowhere to be seen – it took them to the end of the decade to slash interest rates to zero amidst structurally entrenched deflation.

On the other hand the Nordic governments received great praise for the forceful handling of their several collapses in the 1990s. Sweden, in particular, in 1992, had seen a relaxation of regulatory standards and its strong economy turn into a real estate maelstrom which was in the process of bursting with a catastrophic outlook for all the country's major banks. The Swedish economy was failing, the Swedish krone was attacked and the central bank raised rates to defend the exchange rate, piling on economic distress at home. With some banks teetering, the government announced a platform of support.

In return for a government guarantee of all bank depositors and bank creditors, the government forced the banks to come clean on the loan book, writing it down to the harsh realities of the prevailing market, and for the existing shareholders to take the pain, losing all or nearly all of their investments. The state then offered to recapitalise banks under a new state agency while providing a second body to control the orderly disposition of the banks' impaired real estate collateral.

The total programme resulted in a gross cost to the government of about four per cent of the country's GDP, but adding back the returns on the equity stakes taken as recompense, the Swedes say the net cost was more like two per cent (although it's not all worked through the system yet as they hoped – 19.9 per cent of Nordea remains in government hands and might take some time to sell). That being said, I don't think we're going to get off the hook this time this quickly or at this cost.

As we watch the entire banking systems of Iceland and Ireland effectively collapse, along with the effective nationalisation of several large British and US institutions, there seem to be so many different 'solutions' and schemes – partly because the public's desire to see action is a strong political driver. At the moment, Swedish cooking seems in fashion to some extent but the major regulators seem to be adopting another Nordic cuisine: the *smorgasbord* with a bit of everything at once.

Gordon Brown has a great reverence for Adam Smith, so maybe this passage from *The Wealth Of Nations* resonates when he looks at the bank stakes the UK government came to own on his watch:

> The state cannot be very great of which the sovereign has
> leisure to carry on the trade of a wine merchant or apothecary.
> The profit of a public bank has been a source of revenue to
> more considerable states... A revenue of this kind has even by
> some people been thought not below the attention of so great
> an empire as that of Great Britain... But whether such a
> government as that of England; which, whatever may be its
> virtues, has never been famous for good economy; which in
> time of peace, has generally conducted itself with the slothful
> and negligent profusion that is perhaps natural to monarchies;
> and in time of war has constantly acted with all the thought-
> less extravagance that democracies are apt to fall into; could
> be trusted with the management of such a project must at
> least be a deal more doubtful.

Adam Smith, *The Wealth Of Nations*, 1776

THE BONUS POOL DOES NOT REWARD BEHAVIOUR
– IT SETS IT

> This disposition to admire, and almost to worship, the rich and
> the powerful ... is ... the greatest and most universal of the cor-
> ruption of our moral sentiments. That wealth and greatness are
> often regarded with the respect and admiration which are due
> only to wisdom and virtue; and that the contempt, of which vice
> and folly are the only prober objects, is most unjustly bestowed
> upon poverty and weakness, has been the complaint of moral-
> ists in all ages.

> Adam Smith, *The Theory Of Moral Sentiments*, 1759

Bonuses. Bankers' bonuses. Huge bonuses. Immense bonuses. Vast wads
of cash. Quite literally the 64 million dollar question today.

Despite the horrendous financial crash, it looks as if the best part of half
of the remaining global banking revenues will be distributed in the pay
packets of bankers worldwide. At a time of immense explicit or implicit
governmental support, there is significant concern from taxpayers, lawmakers and regulators about the apparent unfairness of institutions saved
from the brink of bankruptcy paying bonuses as big as usual. Everywhere
is the echo of Balzac's proverb: 'behind every great fortune lies a crime'.

On the other side, the concerns from the denizens of the City are that a
wholesale change in bonus culture would put the competitiveness of their
bank or their market in jeopardy to the detriment of the country's economic recovery (and make them quite a bit poorer, too). On their lips
would be the mantra 'Is the workman not worth his hire?'

More words have been written on bankers' bonuses than there are dollar
bills dished out on Goldman's payday (and that's an awful lot!). Why are
bonuses so important in the banking world – and more importantly, are
they a cause of the recent crunch or merely an unpalatable effect of how
the money machine functions?

The first question is very basic. Why do we need bonuses at all? The answer
is linked to one of the oldest problems faced by owners and investors in
all industries: the simple fact that no one on Earth will look after your
interests as well as you will yourself. It's called the agency problem and is
a very old conundrum. The Gospel According to St Matthew (xxv, 14–30)
tells us of a rich business man who was heading off on a business trip who

called his servants and entrusted to them his property; to one he gave five talents, to another two, to another one, to each according to his ability. Then he went away.

He who had received the five talents went at once and traded with them; and he made five talents more. So also, he who had the two talents made two talents more. But he who had received the one talent went and dug in the ground and hid his master's money.

Now after a long time the master of those servants came and settled accounts with them. And he who had received the five talents came forward, bringing five talents more, saying, 'Master, you delivered to me five talents; here I have made five talents more.' His master said to him, 'Well done, good and faithful servant; you have been faithful over a little, I will set you over much; enter into the joy of your master.' And he also who had the two talents came forward, saying, 'Master, you delivered to me two talents; here I have made two talents more.' His master said to him, 'Well done, good and faithful servant; you have been faithful over a little, I will set you over much; enter into the joy of your master.'

He also who had received the one talent came forward, saying, 'Master, I knew you to be a hard man, reaping where you did not sow, and gathering where you did not winnow; so I was afraid, and I went and hid your talent in the ground. Here you have what is yours.'

But his master answered him, 'You wicked and slothful servant! You knew that I reap where I have not sowed, and gather where I have not winnowed? Then you ought to have invested my money with the bankers, and at my coming I should have received what was my own with interest. So take the talent from him, and give it to him who has the ten talents. For to every one who has will more be given, and he will have abundance; but from him who has not, even what he has will be taken away. And cast the worthless servant into the outer darkness; there men will weep and gnash their teeth.

Or take a modern example. Peter Plank is 60 with an 18-year-old son. Peter's father was a farmer and had many woods on his land. When Peter's day came and he inherited the farm, he branched out into the lumber business, building a profitable and sustainable sawmill which he wants to pass on to his son in 10 years' time. It's hard work, though, and he's not the stripling he used to be, so he needs to hire a manager for the years until the son takes over.

But the best person to look after your interests is you yourself. How do you align a third party's interests to yours to ensure that you are both working together to make one of you as rich as possible?

If the new manager is paid a fixed amount in salary, regardless of the business outcome, then he probably won't be motivated to work harder if called upon. On the other hand, if you offer to pay him a higher overtime rate, then the job will always take that little longer to do (except on Thursdays which is bowling night).

The obvious plan is to offer him a bonus if he exceeds certain targets (nowadays set by reference to specific, measureable, jargonful benchmarks bought from an expensive HR consultant). But it's not that easy. How do you set the target to achievve the maximum potential out of your employee. If it's to produce 1,000 planks each and every day, then he might do that daily volume but sell at a loss, or pile them up in the back lot to rot – either of which means that while he's beaten his target, you don't have the cash to pay him. Or, if he's rewarded on the basis of the current year only, he may put off planting new trees for the future (which he's not going to be around to share) and devote his attention to short term activities which (unlike the trees) will bear fruit in this specific year. The agency problem has now bumped into the law of unintended consequences! In fact this is another example of Goodhart's law: 'any observed statistical regularity will tend to collapse once pressure is placed upon it for control purposes', the very act of choosing a bonus target means that the employee's focus will be on that one indicator, distorting its usefulness while often ignoring other important metrics in the business model.

The key to success is to align the agent's targets and rewards with the principal's desired financial and operational results as closely as possible. So, in many ways, the only way to eliminate the agency problem is by eliminating the agency role – take on, not a new employee, but a new partner. Now that he shares directly and proportionally in the rewards of the whole business, he should (if you have found the right guy) see life the same way as you do.

In the old days of merchant banking, the clerks' room at Hambros was reputed to have had a family tree on the wall with the names of the unmarried daughters underlined in red. A bit of a drastic way to align owners and managers, but at least it was easily understood.

Which brings us neatly to our financial world. Here, bonuses come in bigger packets than The Plant & Son Lumber Company can pay, but the problems are just the same. The bank's Foreign Exchange dealer who achieved his profit target for the year to December on 4 September probably won't touch another FX trade until January unless he has to. Conversely, being shy of target in December with a few weeks to go could equally cause him to take a few extra risks to make up the slack. The advisor who has had a bad year could either push his big deal through to conclusion late in the year so the fee counts for this year's bonus targets, or if it's not big enough to take him over the line and guarantee a good bonus, he'll slow it into January so as not to waste it on a lost cause, but prime the following year with a good start. (Legend has it that one banker who was adept at collecting fees from clients in November/December in the form of cheques which he handed over to the accountants a few weeks later in the New Year towards the following year's bonus went on to become a senior compliance officer.) Sometimes the effect can be destructive to the business – given the choice of working on a small deal which will bring revenues to your bonus pool or being a 'good citizen' and helping close a huge deal for a different branch in another country (where you'll get a pat on the back but for which your boss sees no green-backs) – what do you do? Go figure.

We'll leave the politics of how to set targets (hope that you can look your boss in the eye and then under-promise and over-deliver seems to be the favourite solution all the way up the line). How do we align our employees to a set of objectives that drives them to work in both their interests and ours and (with a little help from the Invisible Hand of Jupiter – or Maradona's Hand of God, perhaps) delivers a result that benefits the holders of the equity too? Who wins in the trussle? The old management favoured the policy of 'dog eat dog' – with the new management, it's the other way round now.

So what are we trying to achieve in awarding bonuses? Let's look back for a minute at where we started from.

Bonuses started out as an eminently sensible idea. It seems ironic now, but the word comes from the Latin for 'a good guy'. The first kind of bonus paid was the distribution of partnership profits to the partners who had risked their own capital in the year's business. You put in money and effort, and you get money out. The second type of bonus came in relatively modest amounts given to employees, either a fixed amount at Christmas (some-times in the form of a turkey but in the real world, I bet a clerk like Bob Cratchit would rather have shared in Scrooge's cash) or perhaps an extra month's wages for sterling efforts. The third form of bonus compensation was linked to traders. These guys were employed on a smaller basic wage than banking employees as their productivity was harder to predict. In return they received a bigger bonus but only if they outperformed their targets and of course they ran the real risk of redundancy if they failed. (There were also 'half commission men' who received almost no basic pay but took a share of the profit on every deal that they closed). To compensate, the traders' bonuses were large, the argument went, because (like professional sportsmen) they would have a shorter career as they would 'burn out' after a few years. Tortoise bankers and hare traders.

Over time, as banks moved from the simple structure into combining traders and bankers and branches, these differing philosophies clashed. The sales culture came into bank branches, incentivising product sales over the till counters. Corporate bankers lost 'a job for life' and found their Gilt-edged pensions being eroded so demanded bonuses of a substantial percentage (or multiple) of salary instead. The traders, whose stressful lives had been simplified by technology, didn't burn out as quickly and sought to maintain a higher bonus pool than the bankers. This could be seen over time in the disparity of a measure called the cost-income ratio of the banks. Efficient retail banks would spend around 50 per cent of the income earned on costs (including pay and bonuses); at the other end of the spectrum it was not unusual to see investment and universal banks where that ratio was in the 90 per cents. All because of compensation. In the boom years, shareholders seemed comfortable with this pay bill as their dividends were increasing and especially because the capital value of their shareholding was skyrocketing. Now we shareholders (directly or through our governments) face a totally different economy. The world has changed and our bonus policy has to change with it.

Leaving aside the politics and outrage, the new philosophy for bonus policy going forward must be to align the interests of the managers/employees and the owners/shareholders more accurately over a longer timescale to reflect the risk.

The easiest way to achieve that aim is the partnership where everyone who is eligible to be paid a bonus is an owner with capital invested for the long term. I recall going onto the Goldman Sachs trading floor for the first time nearly twenty years ago when that company was still a true partnership and being shown a bank of ten desks. My host introduced me to the partner who was running that group who memorably explained that if any of the other nine lost money, his kids could have to leave college because of the personal financial impact it would have on him – he certainly watched those traders! It's a model that you'll still find and not just in the financial markets, the UK retailer John Lewis remains a partnership (and a highly successful business) to this day.

The problem with that is the limited ability that partnerships have to raise additional capital from outsiders to support growth (or losses) – bringing in new capital brings in another mouth to feed. And that's where the difficulty lies. So how can we recreate the ethos and economics of a small unlimited liability partnership within a huge multinational limited liability company quoted on a stock exchange?

Remuneration Consultants (who earn a handsome amount themselves) created various ways of replicating this ownership alignment. One problem in achieving this is that it is hard to get truly independent advice. You have a remuneration expert (directly or indirectly incentivised to keep raising the bar) talking to the remuneration committee of the Board which is made up of guys whose day job pay is in turn decided by similar committees, possibly including people whose monetary fate we are deciding today. That's why these bodies have become ReNumeration Committees – always re-numbering upwards.

Yes, safeguards can be built in – share options at a lower than market price, but which can only be exercised in three or five years' time – but in the US after the tech bust it was apparent how many share options were under water and where companies changed the rules to maintain 'motivation' by adjusting (in some cases quite illegally) the contracts to ensure that the bonuses were worth more (the shareholders, of course, didn't get their share price adjusted). Another good wheeze is to set benchmarks against a peer group. Here the secret is to pick your peer group wisely so they are easy to beat!

It has been heartening to read of senior financial CEOs (and even some major industrialists) who have waived bonuses and even pay – with some key industry leaders offering to work for US$1 per annum. The cynic in me thinks that after several years of stratospheric pay packets (in the 1970s the average US CEO earned some 40 times the average wage in his company, by 2000 it was 250 times and estimates now are around 450 times) working for nothing for the last couple of years of your career still averages out to be a pretty healthy wage in any case. It also brings to mind a huge motivational query. Once you are so rich and you have everything (palatial master house in capital city, country estate, beach cabana, BlackBerry, face lift and a bank balance that is so huge your broker returns your calls), then you are set for life – the next US$100m gets your kids the disease the Americans call affluenza and then after that you are working to ensure that your grandchildren are guaranteed to be some of the richest people on the planet... that's a lot of foresight for a guy whose life lives and dies on a quarterly cycle of quarterly earnings guidance to the analysts). After your first few hundred millions you, your kids and your future generations (even should your progeny be as many the stars of the sky or the sands of the shore) have their college, housing and country club set up. The lady in the call centre who lived off her salary each month probably doesn't see it that way at all. Nor the average bank employee who received a modest annual bonus and invested it in his employer's shares.

So who should bear the risk and reward? Partly this is one of the differentiators in looking at the three species of bank that we looked at.

The retail or utility bank traditionally had a primary responsibility to depositors. It was their money which topped up the shareholders' equity to make loans to the borrowers. The sanctity of preserving the depositors' capital was the over-riding principle. The staff were rewarded by longevity of employment, trust, social position and pension. Management and key employees would have professional qualifications akin to accountants and architects and would have the respect and recognition of local society as an important non-financial reward. The shareholders got a dividend annually of a constant and predictable nature, commensurate with the 'slow and steady' policies of a conservative, narrow bank who looked after 'the widows and orphans'. There is a good argument that would suggest that the creation of national governmental depositor guarantee schemes to protect the greater part of the savings of the small individuals took away that moral hazard or at least displaced the depositors from their prime relationship with banking management, but that's another story.

The utility banks, therefore, had policies which guaranteed a comfortable life and a very comfortable retirement after years of service. Totally driven by the long view.

The long-term banks – as either mutual societies (or state or national government entities in many countries) delivered a socialised return over the long term, recycling local deposits into socially worthwhile projects (whether housing or infrastructure). Naturally their pay and rations philosophy was driven by long term thoughts, too.

The Casino Banks – a term which captures the political flavour to much of the criticism of investment banking in this crisis – had duties of good execution to clients (out of reputation and prudence) and in the public markets, had to maintain the standards of the members-only clubs that were the stockmarkets in those days. As the partnership capital came from the traders themselves, so the partnership profits, and of course losses, followed back into the bank accounts of the principal traders as partners (i.e. owners) of the firm. While relatively large amounts were paid out in bonuses (strictly speaking, in profit sharing), the bulk of a principal's wealth was tied up in the partnership accounts while they were employed, and then would be released over a period – and that could be as long as a decade after retiring. When the old Wall Street firms sold out – firstly Sollys to Phillips Brothers (you'll have seen Phillips Bros, or Phibro as it is now called, at the centre of the bonus debate in the US) – the new owners had corporate bank structures, but the old Firm and the way its compensation bill (called the Comp) worked lived on as a hermit crab in the new shell. The only difference now was that it was paid to the bankers (no longer as partners, but as employees) in cash or equivalents rather than in a long-term capital allocation that was directly linked to the firm's future success. You will remember that the investment banking world sees from 60 per cent to 90 per cent of every penny made in revenues given to staff in compensation. The difference now is that in a limited liability company, the direct risk of loss of capital falls squarely on the shareholders (or increasingly the taxpayers) not the bankers, as the partnership link to losses has been broken, leaving only upside in the bonus pool.

So there is a great deal of heat involved in this subject. One US commentator, Pulitzer prize winner Connie Schultz, summed it up in a column in *The Plain Dealer* in April 2009:

> There has been much hand-wringing lately over the surge of
> 'populist rage.' Love that term: populist rage. What a fancy
> way to say the majority of working Americans are done being
> chumps at the hands of the privileged few...

So that principle of 'hang 'em all' strikes a popular (and populist) chord which is not helped by the defensive responses of the recipients of the bonus largesse. But there are important counterarguments against the No more/ Never again backlash.

What about the many people working in banks who (a) work hard in profitable departments and (b) have a bonus element in their package but have a basic salary much lower than the journalists, parliamentarians and businessmen critics of the banking sector? Banking pay is an important element in the debate about reconstructing the financial sector after this crash as we all agree that personal reward influences the amount of risk the firm or bank gets committed to by its employees, but it does seem to get a disproportionate attention when other fundamentals like liquidity and capital regulation are equally – in fact, more – important. It's just that the technical issues are boring and complex and so hard for politicians to wax lyrical about. Shame really. The simple fact is that, without capital and liquidity being available for the traders to run their books, they can't do big trades. And if the bank's risk management systems are up to scratch, the trader shouldn't be able to do small and very risky trades. So to that extent, there should be checks and balances on the bonus cheques and bank balances.

On the other hand, it's hard to see that some bank managements and their employees have learnt how to handle the situation. Partly this is out of concern that changes become a demotivating factor to the workforce, partly this is through the fear that there will be an uneven playing field so banks of some nations will be permitted to continue with huge payouts, meaning that banks more strictly regulated will lose talent. My favourite response to these issues was the bank who recently promised to reduce the bonus culture by cutting the potential bonuses by 25 per cent but by adding that same amount onto the employees' salaries. By any logic that's guaranteeing the bonus (and paying pension rights on it too). If the whole debate is about solving the agency problem in today's markets, then the worst solution is to increase the fixed amount of compensation that is earned – the drive must be to ensure that variable pay is truly variable and that it is aligned to longer term behaviours, which is behind the concept of 'clawback' that future bonuses should be forfeited if the business written deteriorates within a three year period. It's all back to that difficult balance of ownership and reward.

Overall, however, I can't think that any government or its electors want to keep the banks under substantive public ownership or support for one moment longer than it takes, so the banks have to build a team that can grow the banks organically out of this mess. That needs reward and incentive – transparent and open contractual packages, set to measurable long-term goals, paying out over time within some equitable framework to encourage and reward success.

And guess what, the government will get a good bit of that back in income taxes. A partnership balance between risk and reward – that's where this whole question started at the beginning of the chapter.

The problem at Salomon Brothers has been a compensation plan that was irrational in certain crucial respects.

Employees producing mediocre returns for their owners should expect their pay to reflect the shortfall.

Warren Buffett, 1991

EIGHTH LAW OF BANKING

EVERYONE HAS AN AXE TO GRIND

Once in the dear dead days beyond recall, an out-of-town visitor was being shown the wonders of the New York financial district. When the party arrived at the Battery, one of his guides indicated some handsome ships riding at anchor. He said, 'Look, those are the bankers' and brokers' yachts.' 'Where are the customers' yachts?' asked the naive visitor.

Fred Schwed Jr, Financial Commentator, 1940

There are no disinterested players in the financial markets. There are many uninteresting ones, but none are disinterested. The only person who has 100 per cent of your interests at heart is you – and that's only if you are smart and keep focused.

The temptation to outsource our decisions is almost overwhelming. If an average investment prospectus fills 60 pages of 8-point print to describe one single investment with the regulatory specifications on risks, rewards and reporting, imagine a complex collateralised debt obligation (or CDO), which is a structure aggregating maybe 100 different investments, that's 6,000 pages to read (and if possible understand). Add to that, the language of these prospectuses serve two purposes: (a) to meet the statutory and regulatory requirements about full and fair disclosure and (b) to avoid the issuing company and its directors (and highly paid advisors) getting their pants sued off if it all fails.

If you are wealthy enough then you may well have a private banker or an independent financial advisor or a chartered accountant who does this research for you and makes wise and sober recommendations on where to place your extensive wealth, allowing you both to live well by day on the yield and sleep well at night on the risk. For the rest of us (and actually, most of the professional advisors) reliance has to be placed on a quicker and less costly way to assess the risks underlying an investment.

For years this traffic cop role was played by the rating agencies (for bonds) and the research departments of investment banks and brokers (for shares).

The two biggest rating agencies are Moody's Investor Services and Standard & Poors followed by a third firm Fitch Ratings, and there are various smaller specialist organisations around the globe. Their function is to provide an objective assessment – based on public and non-public information from a company – of its ability to pay you, the investor, back in full and on time in terms of repayments of principal and interest.

While the rating scale is quite detailed, many investors are driven by one great divide – the difference between sheep of 'Investment Grade' (sometimes called 'blue chip') who are the strongest issuers and have historical rates of default that give great comfort (meaning that it is most likely that you as an investor will receive payment of your regular interest coupon and timely repayment of your investment) – and the goats of Non Investment Grade (also called NIG or Junk – the latter is a phrase not often used in the earshot of those so rated, the euphemism used is usually 'High Yield') who are riskier.

Ratings became increasingly important as some investors by law or regulation or through internal policies were debarred from investing in paper below certain limits, so in some respects they became the outsourced analytical groups for many bond investors.

In the current crunch, there have been a lot of spectacular downgrades, where agencies have had to review their analysis often in a rush and very often around structured bonds or securitisations. Many think that the small number of recognised large agencies has stifled competition and perhaps allowed a group-think mentality compounded by a business model where the companies whose issues are being rated pay the rating agency. That's certainly a conflict of interest! But the real fun has happened on the equity side.

In the Equities markets, the structure was more complex, with a direct potential conflict of interest. Most equity analysts were employed by the firms who brought the share issue to market, or who were trading or making markets in those equities.

This brings us to the concept of 'Chinese Walls' – and did they work. In the sorry saga of Robert Maxwell's career, two equity analysts dared to question the maestro's businesses, albeit in an oblique way. One report escaped the Captain's eye – a study called 'Maxwell: Unravelling Melmotte's Skein' which tied Capt'n Bob to the fictional Melmotte (old days indeed…) and the less subtle commentary (which cost the young analyst his job) – rather than 'buy' or 'sell' his recommendation was the caustic acrostic:

Cannot
Recommend
A
Purchase

The theory is simple. The analyst builds a financial model after discussions with the company, and runs various sensitivities and economic paradigms through it to forecast future dividend income. In the simple days, that would result in a Recommendation – Buy (which meant buy), Sell (which meant sell) and Hold (which meant, at the risk of being patronising, I'd hang onto what you have but would sit tight for now, neither buying nor selling).

Simplicity and honesty can do you no favours, however. When your wife asks you how she looks in her new jeans, when your sister shows you the picture of her baby, when your husband asks if his hairline is receding, when your CEO asks how his stock is rated – what can you say? Fat, ugly, bald and sell?

So the Sell word was sent to H*ll.

On the other hand, while we've not offended our loved ones, it's a bit hard on the outside public who are being told that Fat/Ugly/Bald/Broke are judgements that we are not going to use because these are just the stocks Joe Public wants to avoid. The potential conflict of interest is there: do you tell a 'warts and all' story and offend your investment banking client or do you 'sanitise' the story and risk selling a poor investment to your loyal retail investors?

There are three cunning ways to meet enough of the public expectation while not upsetting the client.

Silence is golden. Start the research coverage and then promise an annual update (but not every year) it just gets stuck at the back of the pile and never quite gets out. By the time it does lo-and-behold it's looking a bit Thinner/Prettier/Less bald (don't know how you achieve that – financial Rogaine or a wig...).

Breaking it gently. 'Hold' is a fairly elastic category. By definition everything we possibly think can fly is a Buy. Therefore, cynically, everything else should be a Sell (Hold is for wimps, like lunch). So by default we stop saying Sell and use Hold. For the few Holds we think should be held (those people we are really really trying to keep as buys but...) we could call 'Strong Hold'. The Hold becomes as good as Sell and weak Hold is 'Too late schmuck'.

Of course, the final way to get out of this bind is just to do your analysis – see how the stock looks and **call it a Buy anyway**, regardless.

The entertaining example of this (if you didn't own the stocks) was in the train wreck Broadway show where the New York Attorney General Eliot Spitzer (a man with feet of clay, although those were not the specific body parts which got him into trouble later) took Merrill Lynch's Internet

Research Group to court over alleged conflict of interest. Spitzer's investigation had been fuelled by an interesting statistic – Merrill's research list used five categories (from Buy down to Sell) but there had never been a four or five rating – not one single stock was on the Sell list. The AG's office noticed a marked discrepency between the public ratings and the description of stocks in internal e-mails.

Rating Grades	Public Definition	Internal Email Comments
1 BUY	20% or more price growth expected.	'this stock is a powder keg' (not a recommendation!). 'bad smell'. 'piece of junk'.
2 ACCUMULATE	10% to 20% or more price growth expected.	'six- month outlook is flat'. 'neutral'. 'such a piece of cr*p'. 'POS' (copraphilic abbreviation for 'piece of s**t'). 'no hopeful news to relate… we see nothing that will turn this around near term'.
3 NEUTRAL	Between 10% growth and 10% drop in price expected.	'nothing interesting in this company except banking fees'. (fundamentals [are] horrible).
4 REDUCE	10% to 20% or more price drop expected.	Silence.
5 SELL	20% or more price drop expected.	Embarrassed silence.

At the time Merrill's was not only a leading underwriter of equity issues, but a major retail brokerage, so the odd part of this equation is that to keep one department happy (investment banking) the research group were rating poor investments for sale into the famed Thundering Herd – the mass of retail brokers who were trusted across the USA by ordinary investors. Of course, the investment banking team were happy to share fees or at least credit the research team with being important helpers in building the pipeline of deals, so that couldn't particularly help the objectivity of their work.

The analysts' CVs were certainly marked as four or five in the subsequent re-rating. The firm and the office of the Attorney General hammered out a settlement involving increasing the independence of the analysts. But as we have seen, there are many conflicts in this world – so who should you believe?

Three guesses – your own analysis (or at the very least your own gut feeling).

> The financial world sustains a large, active well-rewarded community based on compelled but seemingly sophisticated ignorance.
>
> JK Galbraith, *The Economics of Innocent Fraud,* 2004

NINTH LAW OF BANKING

IF YOUR CUSTOMER OWES YOU £5 AND DEFAULTS – HE'S IN TROUBLE.

IF YOUR CUSTOMER OWES YOU £5 BILLION AND DEFAULTS – YOU'RE IN TROUBLE.

> There can be no freedom or beauty about a home life that depends on borrowing and debt.
>
> Ibsen, *The Doll's House*, 1879

Concentration Risk is not the percentage chance that the market will exhibit a bout of Collective Amnesia. It's the genuine concern that you end up with all your financial eggs in one basket – if it goes wrong then, it goes wrong big time.

There are more complex reasons, though, that this can occur. It's always easy to make money and to do business with existing clients, people and businesses you know well – maybe even as well as or better than the clients themselves. In an environment of annually increasing revenue targets from the bank head office, the way to make 115 per cent of last year's outturn (and to exceed it to make a nice fat bonus) means that these key clients are crucial. In the initial years they provide good lumpy transactions which bring in good revenues, but the higher that revenue line grows, it still has to grow by 15 per cent next year or no bonus. So by an initial process of innocent momentum – one account becomes vitally important to making your budget for the year – how can you beat the target if you don't sweat your best client?

Of course, there comes a point where innocent activity isn't enough. Complicity happens and we end up in the disaster cases like Enron and Parmalat. These are by far the exceptions.

This can also happen in whole sectors, and the best example I can think of is the recent bull run in the field of leveraged finance.

While one of the great inventions of capitalism (though not without its glitches) is the quoted company whose shares are traded publicly on a stockmarket, the model is not without its problems and potential inconveniences. The quoted company has to report its performance regularly (maybe as often as every 12/13 weeks) which could tempt it to go for the short-term fix to reach the target profits expected by the market (which is necessary to keep the share price up); the company might for example be tempted to keep earning cash flow out of inefficient divisions and rather than reforming them (and taking the costs of these actions as a one-off loss) or selling them to a new owner who would take those hard decisions, the report of profits to the market may include items which cause accounting losses but don't stop the cash flowing in (that can spook investors and cause the share price to fall) and perhaps most of all, as we've talked about, profits may be distorted if the directors' and managers' incentives are misaligned with those of the shareholders (be they long-term investors or short-term hustlers, the agency problem is real for everyone owning shares).

Of course, the rationale for turning your business into a public company and listing your stock is to raise outside capital to fund growth in your business and thus make bigger profits going forward. What if there were another way? This is the realm of private equity and the leveraged buyout (often called 'PE' and 'LBO').

The theory is quite simple. A private equity investor discovers a public company (or one of its divisions or subsidiaries) which is underperforming and offers to buy it from the current shareholders, relinquishing its stock-market listing. The company will be managed henceforth to maximise cash flow – there's no need to inform the outside market of the results and forecasts (though typically the PE investor has a very critical eye on reports and systems to observe the company's performance) while the management (either the existing management – management buy out – or MBO or new management parachuted in – an MBIn) will invest alongside the PE player so that they are directly incentivised on the same terms. This is a very different philosophy to the 'asset stripper', who buys up underperforming companies, sells any profitable businesses and assets and then remorselessly closes the unprofitable rump that is left.

But the thing that makes this magic happen is debt. The publicly quoted shares will be bought out with a bit of equity (from the PE investor or nowadays mainly from an investment fund arranged by the PE firm) and a lot of bank or bond borrowings. (At least that was the model until last year!). The economic theory behind this is interesting. The practical part of it is that equity holders get paid their dividends AFTER the profits have been calculated and taxes paid to the Government. For a company, the interest costs of borrowing are a cost to the Profit and Loss account. If you borrow, you reduce the amount of tax you pay.

As the new managers are adept at generating and managing cash flows, the banks created a product called the 'leveraged loan' where a significant debt burden would be taken on by the company which, although paying a high margin over the cost of funds, sheltered the potential to pay tax. The cash, remember, is king. These high-risk loans were (initially) set with strong projections for the lending banks who would make rules (or 'covenants') that could not be broken by the leveraged borrower. For example, excess cash would be 'swept up' and used to repay debt quicker, profits from disposals, ditto, and there would be restrictions in how much the company could remit to its new owners or commit to capital expenditure. The fundamental monitor of the new businesses success was called EBITDA (an accounting acronym which is quite simple:

E	Earnings	The company's profit for the period.
B	Before	Before the accountants deduct the following items from the profit & loss account.
I	Interest	All interest costs and fees paid to banks and financial creditors (so this wouldn't include penalty interest for late payment of a supplier, for example).
T	Taxes	The taxes due on the profit for the period that need to be paid before the shareholders receive a dividend.
D	Depreciation	When a company buys tools or plant or assets needed for the business, it would be a big hit to the profit if the whole cost of the item were charged against the profits on the day of purchase – for it has a useful life of some years, so it will generate profits over its life. Depreciation is the way accountants accrue (or spread) the cost of the asset over its working life. The cash is paid out on day one, of course, but the effect on annual profits is split (usually in equal periodic amounts) over the anticipated life.
A	Amortisation	Amortisation has two parts: (i) it's the equivalent of depreciation for intangible assets – contracts, patents etc and (ii) it's the instalments paid back on your financial debt.
(R)	Rentals	Occasionally, if a company is a big user of assets under true (or operating) leases, then the leasing rentals will be deducted too (this is called EBITDAR).

Many commentators call this a cash flow test, and it is and it isn't: it's a poor cash flow test as it doesn't fully capture what's happening in the businesses. To do that we also need to consider:

- **Working Capital**: which is quickly defined as the amount of cash you have tied up in your stock of goods and materials (or safely deposited in the bank), plus the money owed to you by people who've bought your products but haven't paid yet, less the amounts you owe your suppliers but haven't posted the cheque yet. Poor working capital management – typically not collecting from your customers quickly enough or piling up your stockroom depletes your cash flow, while the naughty tactic of waiting to the last minute to pay your suppliers can increase it.

- **Capital Expenditure**: To keep the business going, you will have to replace tools and refurbish buildings, shops or warehouses. To grow business you will need to increase productive capacity by acquiring more machinery or vans or other kit. The costs of these are 'capex', which can be a big cash item in many companies.

What EBITDA really captures is how much cash is available for the management to use to pay the bank its regular interest payment and to pay its debt back in instalments. This concept was also captured within the covenants with leverage being defined as the ratio between the total debt borrowed and the EBITDA. Typically the other measure is EBITDA divided by debt service (the cash needed to keep paying the bank debt interest and any repayments too). The big idea is that using these two tests (plus the other structural protections within a loan agreement) the bank can set a series of thresholds for the maximum amount borrowed and its serviceability based on the business case for the leveraged business. If the business does not perform to expectations (with a certain tolerance) it will breach one or both of these financial tests, forcing a refinancing or repayment.

Traditionally banks assessed how indebted a customer was by comparing the total amount of borrowings to the total equity in the company. This test, called 'gearing', typically held that owing a greater amount of debt that the sum invested by the shareholders made the company a risky proposition. Yet within a decade we had moved from being nervous of 100 per cent or 200 per cent gearing to being comfortable with companies taking on debt at two, three or up to seven times EBITDA. Why?

The practical answer from participants is that if you set the EBITDA tests correctly, there would always be cash to pay the bank, so what's the worry? A more complex and philosophical answer came from the economists. (I'll let you decide which is the more delusional.) For centuries everyone had felt comforted that the more shareholders' equity there was in a business (and hence the lower the amount of debt) the 'safer' that company was. Step forth Dr Franco Modigliani (Nobel laureate 1985 in Economics) and Dr Merton Miller (who won his prize in 1990). The Modigliani–Miller theorem set aside this conventional wisdom by 'proving' that the value of a business is not affected by the proportion of equity to debt employed. In non-technical hands, this was a free pass to the world of unlimited leverage.

(To be fair to the two Doctor Ms, they had a shopping list of assumptions – a world without taxes, free bankruptcy, and of course the ubiquitous, but fictitious, Efficient Market – so while it makes good reading for a mathe-matician, its direct application to the world which fails to meet those assumptions causes real problems.) In the banking world, if you finance using only equity and don't borrow, the shareholders hand over their pay-ments for shares and have few rights thereafter. They only have a right to a dividend to the extent there's cash available, the dividend is variable depen-dant on the profits made and the size of the dividend has to be voted on by both the board of directors and the shareholders themselves. As there's no right to demand repayment of the principal sum, a shareholder can't bank-rupt a company or (other than in a cumbersome shareholder vote) force it to take a particular action.

On the other hand, if you finance with effectively all debt, then you have entered into a totally different financial contract. The debt bank has the right to receive a fixed return plus full repayment; it will set covenants that limit your potential business operations and can force you into bank-ruptcy if the contractual terms aren't met. And all these payments rank ahead of returning money to the shareholders.

So, debt finance is riskier than equity finance from the company's view-point in the real world. (That's probably why PE investors rarely give a guarantee of the target's obligations and always have each deal done inde-pendently so that if one does fail, it doesn't contaminate the PE parent or the other companies in the portfolio.)

Notwithstanding Economics 1.01, the concept of leveraged finance took off in the 1980s (remember the saga of the takeover of RJR Nabisco, which literally took the biscuit and is one of the few financial stories to become a bestselling book and a film).

Of course, the acquisition of 'the target', its management and its funding are only the means to an end – the opportunity for the PE investor to make a handsome return on his original investment is his Exit Strategy. The way to get really, really rich was to be fortunate enough to float your company after three or five years (having given it a good wash and brush up or at least a nice lick of paint to cover the scratches) back onto the stockmarket (preferably in a boom year!) or you could make very good money by selling out to a larger competitor in your market or another company which wanted to add your complimentary products to its range – an outcome called the Trade Sale.

Latterly, at the top of the boom a third way out appeared. The Secondary Buy Out – where another PE investor would buy the company from you with the profit you made being financed by a borrowing facility based on an even higher EBITDA multiple (this being a version of 'the Bigger Fool Theory'). Some secondaries were even sold on to tertiaries… can you smell the bubble?

The market was booming. As the PE concept became better known, the big firms realised that they needn't use their own resources for all the equity investment. They formed large Buy Out funds where they were the 'general partner' and manager but the great majority of the investments came from other investors (pension funds, other equity houses, rich families, etc.). This improved the return on equity by a multiple for the PE house (as it was another form of leverage). This was a highly lucrative business as the management fee payable out of the fund to the PE House which was typically of order of 2 + 20 (two per cent annually on the total investment value plus 20 per cent of the annual profit made within the fund). Like the hedge funds, it was difficult for an investor to get out ahead of the fund's maturity date so the arranger held all the cards, and was getting well paid for doing so.

So we have a huge growth in equity, that 'wall of money' had to find a home, so the buy-out market grew aplenty. Naturally the debt market grew at a multiple of that and in chasing that dragon, lenders allowed rates, terms and conditions to weaken (ending up in the preposterous 'cov lite' structures – brain lite more like – that reduced the bank's ability to intervene in these highly leveraged companies). At the peak, it was even possible for PE firms to refinance the original deal in a 'dividend recap' where the loan outstanding was increased to finance payment of a dividend to the PE house effectively repaying the original cash equity.

Banks, bond holders and hedge funds competed to buy tranches of the debt either directly or bundled up into CLOs (Collaterlised Loan Obligations – a variant on CDOs) and so many were caught short when the financing music stopped in 2008. Much of the debt is held by banks and institutions as toxic or at least stressed assets maybe now valued at 80 per cent of face value if you could find a buyer anywhere. Some enterprising PE kings have bought their own company's distressed debt at say 85 cents on the dollar which is a bargain compared with spending the 100 cents you would do in repaying the loan or bond! Many bankers think this stinks. (I can't imagine your credit card company being happy if you called up to say that financial markets were weak, so here's £85 to pay off my £100 balance).

Whatever you think, there's over US$400bn in leveraged loans which fall due for repayment over the next five years – while the amounts due in 2010 look challenging but not impossible, what next my friend?

Who has most to lose? Keep watching and find out.

> A man in debt is so far a slave; and Wall Street thinks it easy
> for a millionaire to be a man of his word, a man of honor, but
> that in failing circumstances, no man can be relied on to keep
> his integrity.
>
> Ralph Waldo Emerson, Wealth, 1860

THE TWO MOST IMPORTANT FINANCIAL FACTORS ARE COMPOUND INTEREST AND SELF INTEREST –

If you don't know what's happening then it's probably happening to you and mounting up fast

No banking system can be invented which will suspend the economical laws under which improvident trading leads to ruin.

Bertram W Currie, Partner, Glyn Mills & Co., 1891

In a boardroom high up in one of the City's few skyscrapers, the directors of London's oldest merchant bank, Baring Brothers, met to approve the 1994 accounts. The investment banking world had a poor 1994, with further Latin American bad news leading all the major banks into profit declines. The old chaps were happy, for Barings would be reporting a modest increase in its results – which would mark them out as fine financiers with safe hands in choppy markets. There were a few questions asked, for while the mainstream bank had followed its peer group, the ace in the hole was a small futures operation in Singapore which, for the second year running, had more than punched above its weight and had delivered incredible profits from a very low-risk business. The bright young lad in charge well deserved the proposed £1 million bonus for his hard work.

How unfortunate that none of the men round that table knew that the head of that far away but profitable operation had left his desk earlier that day and was trying to run away before the truth came out. Nick Leeson was a rogue trader: the profits were fiction. Barings' ace was just a big hole. The risks were overwhelming. But they wouldn't know that for a further 48 hours.

Barings has always been one of the smaller of the primary group of merchant banks in London. Its history – whilst it was proud to have been described in 1818 as the sixth great power in Europe (after Britain, Prussia, France, Austria and Russia) – was not without major blemishes. At the peak of its Victorian power, the firm had an important market niche in bringing South American companies onto the London markets to raise capital. An unfortunate (and ironic) underwriting of the Buenos Aires sewerage company had absorbed all of Barings' capital and a secret 'lifeboat' was coordinated by the Bank of England where, to preserve the integrity of the London market, the leading banks would guarantee the obligations of a new Baring Brothers Limited (to be majority owned not by family, but by a charitable foundation with small shares to be held by the salaried managers of the new enterprise), while the 'toxic assets' as we would now call them remained in the old partnership, causing the Baring family and partners to sell up their personal estates to make good any losses.

That was generations ago, but there were other warning signs in the 1980s after 'Big Bang', when a division called Baring Securities Limited was founded as a Barings subsidiary under the charismatic banker Christopher Heath who became the leading foreign trader in Japanese shares and derivatives. Heath built a team that made two-thirds of Barings' total profits in 1989 (the year he was reported to have been the highest paid person in the whole of the UK). It took two goes of replacing management to try and curb the red-blooded proprietary trading in Baring Securities that swung madly from huge profits to huge losses. Peter Baring and his colleagues had built a new management structure in the Far East that was taking a little time sort out as part of the ambition to integrate the securities business with the core investment banking franchise to acheive a balance of risk and reward.

History, as Faulkner says, isn't the past and it has not yet finished, so when Peter Baring took the phone call on that Friday morning, the realisation that the family faced disaster once again must have hit hard. Leeson was missing and the numbers he left just did not add up. There was a huge potential hole on Barings' balance sheet and teams from treasury were trying through the night to work out what was going on.

What the Baring management believed Leeson did was quite simple. The futures contract on the main Japanese stock exchange (The Nikkei 225) was traded both on the Osaka Stock Exchange and offshore in Singapore on their SIMEX exchange. He was supposed to be performing closed arbitrage – finding tiny anomalies between the two exchanges and pouncing on them – using his electronic trading screens to buy on one exchange and simultaneously sell on the other (or vice versa) crystallising a small profit on every trade without having a risk on the volatile shares underpinning the contract. At the end of the day there was supposed to be an exact balance between the total futures sold and the total futures bought. The treasury boffins doing the audit found otherwise. The books were long US$7bn of contracts on the Nikkei and there was an unexpected short book on Japanese interest rate futures. Leeson had bet the bank that (a) Japanese equities would rise (they had in fact been falling for weeks following a major earthquake in Kobe) and (b) that Japanese interest rates would move in his favour.

Facing growing losses, Leeson carried on doggedly at this strategy, buying more and more contracts, hoping that the larger volume would allow him to close out his unauthorised losses on the back of a modest rise in market prices which must, as every gambler hopes, be round the corner. He was able to cover his tracks because the old Baring Securities structure – in the process of change but the dull janitorial parts are often the last to have anything done – allowed Leeson as an operational manager to undertake the administration of the trades executed by himself in his trading capacity. He siphoned off losses into a suspense account – now famous as Error Account 88888 (as the character 8 is extremely lucky in feng shui... is this a disproof of the system?) – and explained that the large cash payments and bank guarantees needed to support the futures business (which should have been effectively zero if the approved strategy was being followed) were due to errors, timing delays or deals done for clients which would be settled shortly. By using these smokescreens Leeson kept his back office and his London masters happy (the management was fragmented and not very team spirited) and in any case, he was making such a lot of money for apparently such little risk, he should be encouraged, not shouted at, for forgetting a few bits of paper here and there. That certainly was the practical response to an internal audit report on the unit the year before which highlighted the risk of Leeson's dual responsibility to the matrix of managers who shared in Leeson's reflected glory and bonuses.

As the sombre senior team sat round Barings' offices digesting the shock of what was looking like a US$400m hit, they pulled together as much information as possible and called the Bank of England (in these happy days responsible for the regulation of both money markets and the banks), who pulled together a group of the largest and most prestigious UK banks that afternoon. When the markets had closed and the latest mark-to-market loss (if the base assumptions were correct, and the numbers were still being worked on) was now US$650m. This was an important level, for Barings' entire capital base that would support losses was about US$790m (£541m). The numbers were looking tight. The assembled bankers quickly came to the conclusion that the bank had to be recapitalised before the London markets opened on Monday. One thing was clear – the Bank of England (and HM Government) would not inject funds into Barings as they felt that this was a localised catastrophe rather than a systemic problem. If Barings collapsed, it would not imperil any other banks, so there were only

48 hours to find a commercial solution. The other point which niggled was how a regulated bank such as Baring Bros could effectively lend so much money to its subsidiary Baring Securities (which was not even a regulated bank, merely a brokerage) – unfortunately in Thread Street, the bank regulators seemed to have had a naive assumption that 'it was all in the family' so the bank's biggest exposure by far was never truly questioned, in the way it would have been if that much money was lent to an independent customer.

There seemed to be a number of options, albeit constrained by the markets' timetable. The Barings name and reputation would be a good acquisition for a major universal bank – certainly four or five when approached flew in due diligence teams – but that presupposed that the fraud didn't wipe out the whole bank leaving nothing to acquire. The other option was to follow the Baring great-grandfathers and have their London banking brothers launch a second lifeboat, but for that to float everyone had to know exactly what the losses were on Lesson's book. More dodgy trades were uncovered, this time in the options market (again totally unauthorised) and by now the estimated losses were well over Barings' capital reserves.

With bankers whizzing round the world, and unexpected activity in Barings international offices, it wasn't a surprise that market rumours started. Or at least intensified. For what was not plain to the senior Barings management had been discussed in the bars and lap dance clubs of the PacRim for ages – what was Leeson doing in the markets (in fact what was he doing in bars – he had recently been fined for disorderly conduct after 'mooning' a girl in a breach – pun intended – of Singapore's strict code of conduct; maybe that just made the wunderkind seem more human to his bosses?). The papers ran stories and the markets braced themselves for impact on Monday when it was anticipated there would be a 10 per cent fall in the Nikkei that would take Leeson's losses to more than a billion Sterling, with yet more downside as the drama unwound unless there was a way to cap that derivatives liability – everyone felt they had a handle on what contracts were in the portfolio – but this felt like uncharted waters. If the banks round the table agreed to the lifeboat and it wasn't enough to staunch Leeson's losses then they would be dragged into the debacle alongside Peter Baring. Informal reports suggest that the chairman of Barclays, Andrew Buxton (himself a scion of one of the founding Barclays families but perhaps on the side of the family tree that the banking gene has passed down), cajoled his fellows into a bridging loan for three months to allow potential purchasers time to audit the books. Subject to working out a cap, Buxton got his fellows to agree £600m in aid which, with Barings own resources (though there were some liquidity issues   but that's another story), would just balance the books if there were no further fall in the markets.

Coincidentally the world's richest man, the Sultan of Brunei, approached the Governor with the offer to cap the derivatives liability, and inject funds into the lifeboat in return for a fee.

Alas, it all turned out to be a false hope and terms could not be reached. The Governor told the Chancellor that all bets were off, who then had an unpleasant night drafting a statement for Parliament in the morning. The formalities began in front of a High Court judge to bury the Baring family's bank. Again.

The oddest part of the spectacle wasn't the pictures of the German police intercepting Leeson off a commercial flight in Frankfurt a few days later, nor his trial, disgrace and reappearance as a celebrity speaker, but it was the sheer detachment of the management of the failed bank. Firstly Peter Baring went on record saying that he believed there was an underlying conspiracy, then as the government inquiry progressed all the senior mangers just couldn't believe it could have happened.

The Dutch banking and insurance group ING bought the core of Barings for £1 so the name lives on. Or at least the memories. Nick Leeson, after nearly five years in a Singapore jail, a serious illness, a divorce, a psychology degree and a remarriage, now gets paid to lecture on fraud. Ironic is too kind a word.

> The recovery in profitability has been amazing following the
> reorganisation, leaving Barings to conclude that it was
> actually not all that terribly difficult to make money in the
> securities business.
>
> Peter Baring, 1993

Shagloads.

> Remark attributed to Nick Leeson on the size of the bonus
> paid to him by Barings Singapore, 1993

Part IV
Epilogue (Or Is It An Epitaph...)

Naturam expellas furca, tamen usque revenit.

(You can drive nature out with a pitchfork, but she will come back.)

Horace, Epistles x. 24, 20BC

In the aftermath of this, the greatest financial debacle in history, as individuals we all look for sympathy as the innocent victims of the crunch, and as victims we naturally call for someone in authority to identify the proximate cause of our pain and punish it.

Who is at fault?

Who can we blame?

There are some common themes when it comes to identifying the scapegoats.

- CASINO BANKING: there is a popular nostalgia that if we could only return to the good old days of separate boring High Street banks and racy Wall Street investment firms, surely that reform would make us safe? These fond memories are false. As we've seen, it's not just casino banks that fail – dull commercial banks have been going bust for centuries too. Why? Because lending money is inherently difficult and dangerous. It is only once you understand that the bank is the biggest borrower in the market that you realise that. Rebuilding the financial Berlin Wall will not alter that fundamental truth. The primary way a boring bank makes money is the net interest margin (especially now that as consumers we all said we did not want to pay charges to our banks for simple banking products like opening accounts or exceeding our overdraft limit). The narrow bank's profits come from borrowing money that needs repaying in the short term and lending it out for longer periods. Even boring banks face credit risks and above all liquidity risks every minute of the working day. Even boring banks need credit and credibility to stay in business. The plain fact is that banking is a risky business, that's why it makes money. That's why some will fail.

- TOO BIG TO FAIL: should we blame those financial institutions that have grown so large (or at least are so interconnected in the market) that governments have to step in using taxpayers money to avert the catastrophe the giant vampire squid firms have recklessly created? This shouldn't be a new question: since the Second World War at least, the largest bank in the world by assets has usually run aground in one fashion or another (Midland, Bank of America, Citibank, Mitsubishi and Citibank again all come to mind). These are not too big to fail, but in the past they seem to have been too big to be either managed or regulated effectively (either in life or at the point of death).

- TOXIC ASSETS: is it simply that innovation went too far? That these new sliced-and-diced, pumped-and-dumped investments were impossible to understand? Certainly, the final holders of these notes probably think so. Yet we've crashed and burned with other asset classes many times – it's not the asset that creates the bubble, it's us. At both ends of the product: every toxic asset has a defaulted consumer at one end and a poor taxpayer at the other. Bubbles are a cycle of human misery independent of the underlying investment.

- BANKERS' BONUSES: these are a very popular target (especially for tarnished politicians) but the bonus culture is not the root of the problem. Certainly, having traditional 'partnership' type bonus calculations grafted onto banks which are public companies is far from optimal (particularly if rescued by taxpayers). This gives the banker the rewards of being a principal but without the risk of having his capital invested in the firm. Aligning that risk and reward is a good idea, but not a panacea: both Lehman Brothers and Bear Stearns rewarded staff heavily in shares which were only released to bankers after an agreed period. That longer term approach didn't stop them falling over. Legislation on large pay packets has been attempted before. The US tried to regulate CEO compensation in

1992/93 by setting reporting requirements and capping the amount of pay that was tax deductable – yet pay and perks continue to escalate such that by some measures the average head of a large quoted company will take home about 400 times what his average employee receives today.

For every problem we face there is an answer that is neat, concise, simple – and generally wrong.

This crisis involved all of us: consumers piling on credit to maintain lifestyles and consumption, the banks leveraging up to hold assets they didn't understand, governments gorging on the tax bills from bank profits and bankers' bonuses, shareholders happily cashing their dividends and watching the share price skyrocket, economists who believed in their philosophies not the reality of the world, rating agencies who unwittingly created a parallel and less effective rating system for toxic structures, central bankers who ignored asset inflation believing they could mop up the aftermath of any bubble, regulators out of touch with the big picture, journalists and politicians who were silent. That's a lot of actors on the stage of this tragedy: not just a soliloquy from the guilty banker.

It's easy then to blame the banks. But everyone involved, not just banks and bankers, forgets the horrible things that happen in down markets. Each interest group in its own time comes to agree that a particular market has become a one way bet; each then voluntarily leverages up in its own way to its maximum capacity; each eats up its own reserves until there are insufficient liquid resources left to compensate for the inevitable change in price, sentiment and availability of credit. The mist of Collective Amnesia descends on one and all guaranteeing that the phrase 'never again' will be proved wrong as these errors will happen again. In fact, I am certain that as we keep watch for the green shoots of the next boom, we will be ignoring the brown seeds of the next bust that are being sown around us even now.

Have I a solution? I would like to think that we could all make some new mistakes rather than play beggar my grandfather, but the debate about this economic meltdown rarely reaches that philosophical height. The world looks at how human nature responds to a particular environment and hopes that by passing new laws or tighter regulations then the world will change. Believing that you can legislate to outlaw greed and fear is a proposition akin to passing laws against sloth, envy, lust, vanity, gluttony and anger. The process will make the politicians look busy and will give us a cosy feeling but it will not change human nature and its desire to forget unpleasant truths in the face of a booming market, with the promise of ever rising prices and richer lifestyles.

Bubbles, manias and panics happen because we all share in them. We all want to join in, and we all do. Banks provide the credit that allows us to participate and make a lot of money out of doing so but they are not solely blameworthy. The banks' assets are our follies – houses, tulips, subprime mortgages or whatever will be the next flavour of the month. The banks' liabilities are the limited amounts deposited by us and a vast wall of money borrowed from rival banks across the global markets. Every penny needs to be repaid one day. Our Collective Amnesia insulates us from that cold and eventually cruel truth. The obligation to repay never goes away.

We've looked together at case studies of folly in the past and at recent events in the markets, we've looked at the underlying principles of finance and how simple they are to follow and how easy they are to break, we will even parse the jargon in the next section– but why did we have to do this now? Why haven't we learned from the repeated cycle of boom and bust? Because of that pair of conflicting motivations – carrot and stick, yin and yang, Tom and Jerry, black and white, heads and tails – that pair of inextricably linked drivers which definitely underpin all finance (and probably most human endeavour); the trade off between

Fear and Greed

I am inclined to agree with Dickens, who didn't think there was an easy way to break this cycle which is rooted in the overwhelming human desire to believe that these markets are essentially different to the markets where we previously lost a fortune. By this standard, the vision of human progress is always a regression. There is this exchange at the end of *Little Dorrit*:

> The next man who has as large a capacity and as genuine a taste for swindling, will succeed as well. Pardon me, but I really do think you have no idea how the human bees will swarm to the beating of any old tin kettle; in that fact lies the complete manual of governing them. When they can be got to believe that the kettle is made of the precious metals, in that fact lies the whole power of men like our late lamented [Merdle].

If you still don't believe me, or if novels aren't your thing, how about a nice textbook in the field of economics, as JK Galbraith said:

> The controlling fact is not the tendency to brilliant invention;
> the controlling fact is the shortness of public memory,
> especially when it contends with a euphoric desire to forget.

That sums up what I have called 'Collective Amnesia' pretty succinctly.

This book is not about predicting the form of the next crash – my colleagues have accused me of forecasting nineteen out of the last three recessions in the past. In the old days of the City you'd sometimes find a chap wearing cufflinks representing the four fastest ways for a banker to lose money: with enamelled pictures of Horses, Cards, Drinks and Women. But everyone knew that the quickest and most certain way to lose money is by making firm predictions.

The thesis I present is, therefore, not a forecast or a prediction – how, when and where the next boom, bubble and crash will appear is beyond my ken, but I know as night follows day that there will be another. For we will make these mistakes – or very similar ones – again, rest assured of that.

Perhaps by thinking about what has hurt us in the past we can at least give ourselves the opportunity to recognise that this has all happened before – many times before – and hopefully that understanding will mitigate the worst effects of the next Bull Run.

However, the prognosis for successful change is not looking too good. At least the next onset of Collective Amnesia will perhaps keep this volume in print for a few generations – keep it close by you to be ready for the next crunch.

See you next time!

> The thing that hath been, it is that which shall be;
>
> and that which is done is that which shall be done:
>
> **and there is no new thing under the sun.**

Ecclesiastes i: 9

Part V
Glossary: New Meanings for Old Words
(or your Money Back)

Words are wise men's counters, they do but reckon with them, but they are the money of fools.

Thomas Hobbes, *Leviathan*, 1651

Every club, cabal, guild, mystery, lodge, conspiracy, secret society, monopoly, or team uses language as a weapon. Finance is no different.

There's a lot of jargon involved in the world of finance so I thought it would help to shine a light on the lexicon of Wall Street and the Square Mile. So here is a glossary, even though the gloss is well off the financial world and the thesaurus is empty of golden treasure. I suppose it might have been called a 'Lossary' since the word paints a picture of many ways to lose a thousand dollars. So here's a list of commonly used terms on the financial pages and what they mean today.

AAA (Triple A) Used to stand for something like 'Absolutely Accurate Assessment', now tarnished a tad as the

A		A		A	
verage		nalytical		bilities of the	
lmighty		merican		gencies	
re		ll		ttacked	

There are conflicts in everything, but many look at the business model which gets the borrower/issuer to pay the agency's fees for the task of classifying the risk on his own obligations and see one of the seeds of disaster. The market for Alphabet Soup Bonds couldn't have grown without the quality stamp from the 'Nationally Recognised Statistical Organisations' (as the SEC defines the firms 'qualified' to give assessments) who, as private companies, sought to maximise their revenue stream with gay abandon. Structurers established warm relationships with the independent (!) analysts and played the ratings firms against each other in a race to the bottom.

One famous instant message conversation used in evidence goes like this:

> *Official #1: Btw ['by the way' for our older readers] that deal is ridiculous.*
> *Official #2: I know right... model def does not capture half the risk.*
> *Official #1: We should not be rating it.*
> *Official #2: We rate every deal. It could be structured by cows and we would rate it.*

Related concepts include: Conflict of Interest, Equity Analysts, Reputational Risk, Being Dumb.

ABS (Asset Backed Securities) It seemed like a good idea at the time... At the most simple, a bond is a promise by a company to repay the amount borrowed (with interest) over an agreed period out of the cash flows of the company. An ABS is similar – but instead of having an industrial or trading company behind the bond producing cash to pay, an ABS is backed by a pool of limited and specifically identified assets. At first credit cards and mortgages were used, then gradually any sort of 'securitised' structures. It is the cashflow out of these investments alone that repay the bondholder, with no call (or 'recourse') to the arranger of the ABS. They are usually longer term with a maturity greater than one year. There is a short-term variant, Asset Backed Commercial Paper, which was a popular alternative to bank deposits for short-dated investments where the investor would buy an IOU from the vehicle holding the assets.

Investors were comforted by the diversification in the underlying assets (as you've heard again and again) but also by the reputational risk the sponsor bank had and the liquidity support that was provided to ensure an orderly exit (*or that was the plan*). Long-term ABS bonds are a key part of the toxic assets that pong out the vaults of the financial system. An investor knows what the risks are in owning a government or investment-grade corporate bond: the credit risk can be assessed, the structure and terms of the bond will be fairly standard and the market is widespread and liquid. Everyone assumed that the markets would look at ABS in the same way (partly through relying on the credit ratings given them) – but when doubt crept in, no one was sure what was underlying the ABS – and didn't have the time or inclination to strip it down to its constituent bits or examine the complex legal documents. So people just stopped buying them and the values collapsed.

Annual General Meeting (or AGM) The opportunity for every investor to have tea and biscuits once a year (in the good years; no biscuits = recession) with their board to discuss the Agency Problem (what's in it for the company managers to run your company to maximise the benefit to you rather than maximising the benefit to them!) and to ask questions with 20/20 hindsight (not that it matters as all the votes are decided by the board and the big institutional investors, but you'll get in the newspapers asking questions about the expenses policy of the CEO). There are great cultural differences in AGM etiquette. In the UK many small shareholders love coming to AGMs primarily to get free food and drink and samples of the company's produce,

but it is relatively easy in Britain for significant shareholders to raise questions, to vote for (and very occasionally against) directors and approve the
accounts. In the USA the proxy (as the agenda is called) is much more tightly
controlled by the company's directors. The oddest AGMs are in Japan
where most large companies are targeted by sokai gangsters who spent
decades from the 1960s disrupting the meeting unless paid off. Many large
Japanese corporations hold their AGMs simultaneously to make it difficult
for the gangsters to attend more than one or two nowadays. Even family
companies have to hold them. The Miller Group is a Scottish contracting
and house building firm created by Sir James Miller (the only man to be
both Lord Provost of Edinburgh and Lord Mayor of London) – one year
a young cousin came to the AGM (which Sir James, as company chairman,
was wont to conduct in slightly under five minutes in total) and the lad
tried to ask a question as he had the right to do as a shareholder Sir James
disagreed. 'One more word from you and I'll tell your mother.' (Proving
that not all Shareholder Activism is effective.)

Companies have to make various reports to shareholders and regulators
ahead of this meeting so that the company's true owners are well informed to
take the important decisions. Often these reports are published as volumes
which are too heavy to be carried by postmen under health and safety regulations. But by the time the lawyers, accountants and PR spinmeisters get
through it, you need a sixth sense to understand where the issues lie. An
odd few glimpses of openness occur, such as this brief report from the Savings
and Loans crisis:

> To our shareholders,
>
> The good news is that I am able to write my second letter
> to the Shareholders. The bad news is that we lost US$87.3
> million in the first six months of the year. You undoubtedly
> thought that things could not get worse and that nobody
> could lose that amount of money in such a short period of
> time. The excuse is that I am new to the banking business and,
> having read about the major losses being incurred by the large
> money centre banks [the big US commercial banks], I became
> confused. I realise that US$87.3 million is a pittance compared
> to the dollars the big boys are losing, but we all have to start
> somewhere.

This was, I think, the first (and probably the last) official pronouncement of
the chairman of a small Alaskan bank in the 1980s whose assets were

literally frozen shortly after. I lost the reference just as they lost the share-holders' reserves.

Asset Strippers Relatively outdated insult (made famous in England by Slater Walker in the '70s) about private equity investors who buy compa-nies using huge loans and repay the loans by selling off the key properties of the target company, then squeeze costs out to leave a smaller and (hope-fully) profitable business. Compare downsizing and its proponents like Albert – aka Chainsaw Al – J Dunlap, who was the personification of the slash and burn approach to corporate reconstruction, closing factories in swathes and firing workers in droves. Eventually his management tech-niques resulted in his being fired by Sunbeam, agreeing to pay a US$15m settlement and receiving a lifetime's inverse achievement award from the SEC – banning him from ever serving as a director again.

Auctions Nowadays, this refers to the firesales arranged by the ailing and failing of the banking sector. Lehman's art collection is under the hammer to offset the huge pile of debts. The proceeds don't look as if they'll be more than a drop in a very big bucket with the collection of 400 odd mod-ern paintings expected to make just over US$1m – on the other hand ex CEO Dick Fuld sold his personal collection last year for US$13.5m. The auctions that really hurt though were a financial invention called the Auction Rate Security (or ARS). Here, a cash rich investor is looking to invest his money safely, in a short term instrument, at a better rate than the bank pays on deposits. On the other side is an issuer of long term bonds to finance long term loans (typically student loans were a big part of this market). How can you marry these two? This is how: issue the long term bond, but rather than setting an interest rate coupon in stone at the begin-ning why not get the cash rich investors to bid periodically (say monthly or up to three monthly) on the interest rate they would seek. This reverse auction means that the issuer resets his interest rate at the most competi-tive pricing in the market. If the short term investor wanted out, then he simply did not bid and the deep liquid market meant some other investor would bid and buy the long term bond off him to hold for another short timescale. In February 2008, people stopped bidding. The game of pass the parcel stopped. There were no musical chairs left. The holders looking to get out were in fact locked in. As the ancient Romans knew, ARS *longa, vita brevis*.

That was the risk they took to get the higher yield, but as often happens, the downside was disregarded. The market simply could not freeze – it really could never happen. Well, guess what? It did – so welcome to the Ice Age.

Bad And Doubtful Debts You might have noticed that banks can lose money. A lot of money in fact, often due to Bad Debts: amounts lent which may not be repaid (or at least not repaid in full). Those credit losses have to be paid for out of the bank's capital and reserves (if there is insufficient capital to cover these shortfalls, then the bank won't have enough cash to give the depositors their money back in full). Banks operate a prudent policy of looking forward (based on past experience) to estimate what percentage of loans might be pressured (or which specific transactions are riskier than initially thought) and then set aside a 'provision' out of this year's profit to create a reserve which can be called upon on a rainy day for these doubtful transactions. When those black clouds appear, the bank writes off the actual bad loan against the provision; if, on the other hand, the problem loan improves then the provision can be released back to profit. In the old days, many banks used this as a way to smooth their taxable income – provision heavily in the profitable years, and release the excess provisions in weak years. The opposite strategy could also be seen – where a bank with weak profitability would understate the need to build reserves. A fine balancing act (as is so much of banking). To address that, international accounting standards tightened up the definition of what could be provided for, linking provisions directly to losses which the bank had actually incurred (or which it could specifically identify in whole or part), stopping the ability to add a pot of general provisions. Just think how helpful those general provisions would have been today.

Bad Bank Most of them, I hear you say, or hear you sing a wistful song 'where have all the good banks gone?' Specifically, however, this is a regulated bank entity created to acquire 'toxic' assets from commercial banks with a view to liquidating them over time, thus cleaning up the commercial banks' balance sheets and potentially maximising returns on the toxic items. The two big questions are – which assets are transferred in and at what price? If the market and its participants are in shock (let alone freefall) – how do you get a really objective price that someone's prepared to close on?

Banker In current society either (a) a component of the unemployment statistics or (b) a subject of obloquy in the popular press and at dinner parties (see also Estate Agents, Military Dictators, Politicians). The trade of banking is directly condemned by the Bible, (Leviticus xxv:37 'Thou shalt not give him thy money upon usury, nor lend him thy victuals for increase.' Or Deuteronomy xxiii:19 'Thou shalt not lend upon usury to thy brother; usury of money, usury of victuals, usury of any thing that is lent upon usury:' Or, 'lend, expecting nothing in return' Luke vi:35. Transactions which generate interest payable or receivable are also substantially circumscribed in Islamic teaching. Interestingly, bankers were assigned a place in the 7th Circle of Hell (with the sodomites) by Dante in his Inferno. *Maybe this should have been a warning to us all.*

Barbarians Pejorative term for private equity firms when attacking corporations. From the famed days when the RJR Nabisco hostile takeover took the biscuit.

Basis Point The smallest financial percentage – 1/100 of 1 per cent. Used for pricing debt instruments but never for setting bonuses.

Basle II Accord (also known as 'a good idea at the time'). For many folk, the hardest thing about the international regulation of bank capital is that its committee sits in Switzerland in a city whose name no one can agree how to spell (Basel, Basle or Bâle). I find it disconcerting that the badge of the city is a pair of crooks... The first banking accord, Basle 1, was Daddy Bear – too simple (simplistically, every corporate loan from GE and its Triple A rating all the way down to Joe Schmo the bottom feeder had to have the same level of capital applied to it by a bank – there were special rules for governments and mortgages but it was a good first stab at international compromise). Basle 11 introduced capital requirements that varied according to the riskiness of each individual credit, with a reduced capital requirement for assets held by the bank within its trading operations. This is Mummy Bear – too smart. What wasn't focused on is that in a downturn almost all companies become riskier, so more capital has to be applied; thus reducing the amount the banks have to lend to stimulate the economy and pull everything up. This is the very real and unforseen danger called procyclicity. The capital rules unwittingly emphasise boom (as credit conditions are benign and companies are strong – less bank capital is required for each loan) allowing more lending into the crash, while the bust is similarly magnified (weaker company balance sheets create a demand to set aside incremental bank capital) denying critical loans to the real economy. Will we see Goldilocks or a brand new Baby Bear in a new Basle 111??

Bear Today, any guy saying 'I told you so!' *(present company included...)*. A Bear Market is a market that's declining and a Bear is an investor or speculator who is selling rather than buying. A good friend who was in New York with me says that he was told on a tour of the Financial District in New York in 1998 that the metaphor comes from the fact that bears lower their heads down to kill, while bulls raise their horns to achieve their aim. Again, there's no statutory definition (but it's a good rule of thumb that a 20 per cent decline in values over two months is a typical indication that the bear's teeth are flashing), it's more a combination of observation and sentiment. If you see women wearing longer skirts and redder lipstick, or sales of sweets overtake sales of chocolate, these are the water cooler moments that show a bear market in progress (allegedly). An easier way to recognise it is that you get poorer every day. Some think this is from the ursine habit of hibernation where Bear Investors would just leave the market until warmer conditions resumed, but it actually comes from an old English banking proverb – 'don't sell the bear skin till you've shot the bear'. Interestingly enough there is no statue to the Bear in New York but I'll happily take donations (see Section 419 scams below…)

Bid/Offer The price that you will buy (bid for) or (offer to) sell a particular security. It is dangerous and costly to confuse the two. As a market maker you make your profit on the differential between the two prices – called the spread. In the good old days spreads could be quite wide when prices were quoted in fractions but the creation of the basis point changed all that. The more liquid the market, the tighter (i.e. smaller) the spread. Of course a proportion of liquidity is provided by mugs who can't differentiate between a truly liquid and deep market (such as gold or Uncle Sam) and a narrow market with few real players. These guys come into markets as new entrants, showing tighter spreads on more structured/riskier product. At the point of turn, their offer price will be very attractive (as they haven't clocked that the buyers have gone home) and they will be as long as a wet Wednesday afternoon in Scotland.

Black Days Every day you lose money is a bad day, but there have been a lot of favourites in history – these often gain the accolade of Black Someday:

- **Black Monday** Monday 19 October 1987 – the largest set of one-day stockmarket falls ever. The Dow Jones shed over 22 per cent with FTSE and the Nikkei leeching red too. At the time economists warned that this would herald the worst downturn since the 1930s.

- **Black Tuesday** Tuesday 29 October 1929 – the peak of the Wall Street Crash – an avalanche of sellers kept driving the market down.

- **Black Wednesday** Wednesday 16 September 1992, when the UK government was forced (after trying to defend the pound against George Soros and a sceptical market) to exit the European Exchange Rate Mechanism.

- **Black Thursday** Thursday 24 October 1929 – Day One of the Great Wall Street Crash (followed as it happened by its own Black Friday, Black Monday and Black Tuesday...). At the time, economists had no idea they were creating the great depression of the 1930s.

- **Black Friday** is also the definition of the Friday after Thanksgiving in the USA where, for the first time in the year, the retailers expect customer sales to take them into profit 'into the black'. The real Black Fridays were:
  - Friday 5 December 1745 – as Bonnie Prince Charlie's rebels reached Derby in the '45 Rebellion, the price of UK Government bonds fell to its lowest ever price and a run even started on the Bank of England (who slowed down the outflow by paying out sixpences when depositors came to extract their cash).
  - Friday 11 May 1866 – the failure of Messrs Overend Gurney, a highly influential London discount bank, took down scores of little provincial lenders in what we would now call a systemic crisis. The Bank of England took on the Lender of Last Resort role after this.
  - Friday 24 September 1869 – the US gold panic as Gould and Fisk (robber barons par excellence) tried to corner the gold market. Gould sold gold and the world took a bath.

- Fortunately, there are no Black weekends – except for summer traffic on the Autoroute du Sud – but it's a good idea to sell out your long position on the way home on a Friday and buy on a Monday. The London stock exchange had a famous old saying: 'Sell in May and go away, Buy again St Leger Day (the famous flat horse race held annually in mid September).

Boiler Room Greed is Good! Every fraud needs a sucker and every sucker is motivated by greed. A group of high-pressure salesmen based in some dingy office with no connection to a bank save for a bank of phones, calls potential investors and sells them worthless paper (with fabulous promised returns). Police say that most of these scams go unreported as the victims are too embarrassed to admit their folly. Different to the almighty Section 419 scam (named after an oft-used clause in the Criminal Code of Nigeria, this wheeze goes something like: 'Please help me release US$10 million from my late mother's account with the Central Bank of Nigeria by sending your bank account details and a copy of your signature to…') or the Business Partner Fraud ('We have a secret invention but have used all our money in building the prototype. If you send us US$100,000 to cover legal expenses you will get 51 per cent of the patent rights for a bargain price') or the Advance Fee Fraud ('we can remortgage your house for a lower interest rate, longer term and greater amount, you have been pre-approved by our credit department, so if you send the arrangement fee of US$10,000 we can send the paperwork to you for your new loan'). It's a Newtonian law: for every greedy crook, there's an equal and oppositely greedy dupe.

Bonds (also known as fixed income securities or, in old UK usage, stocks) 'Gentlemen prefer bonds' – an agreement between a borrower (the issuer) and a creditor (the investor) to borrow a fixed amount over a fixed period (usually longer than one year) at an agreed interest rate (or coupon), which can be calculated on either a fixed or a variable rate of interest. Variants include Perpetual Bonds (which never expire) or Convertible Bonds (exchangeable at some point into equity shares in the company at an agreed 'strike' price).

Bonus The Newtonian force that holds the financial world together. (though that's a bit unfair to Sir Isaac Newton who famously lost money in the South Sea Bubble and was reported to have remarked: 'I can calculate the motions of the heavenly bodies but not the madness of people.')

The annual letter which defines your worth to the firm (and if you are that way inclined, to your friends, your family and image in the mirror each morning). Also used as a 'guaranteed bonus' which is one of those oxymoronic things. How can you guarantee that this guy is going to outperform sufficiently in future to receive a bonus out of profits that the firm doesn't know it's going to have? The initial (simple) idea was that if someone left a shop midway through the year, his new employer would guarantee the bonus accrued at the old place as a joining incentive (or 'Golden Hello'). Then it snowballed. It was called 'lumber money' as a trader might join on '4x2' (US$4m guaranteed for two years). This is now consigned by the wisdom of the G20 to 'never again' territory (or at least to the end of the next financial year). Except for the 'very few' cases reported by one UK bank recently and the existing contracts that were grandfathered (or the guys who got a pay rise instead – not that a pay rise is just a perpetually guaranteed bonus – it allows you to have a bigger pension too). Similar concepts include 'Golden Handcuffs' where the employees loyalty is guaranteed by purchase and 'Golden Parachutes' where senior guys get rewarded one last time if their company is acquired and they lose their jobs. Needs must when the Devil drives. It's the war for talent. It will be back soon, regardless of what legislation is proposed.

Of course, it is rather simplistic to believe that 'the bonus culture' is exclusively a problem in banking There are deep issues within banking about remuneration, but it's not the only trough in town. A considerable amount of political capital (and muscle) has been expended on this topic, without anyone mentioning that two of the most conservative bonus structures on Wall Street were Lehman and Bear!

It's an easy political football and while the extremes of the banking bonus are expensive and foolhardy, the same drivers have increased the pay packets of many CEOs and managers in businesses, of footballers and media personalities, even of legislators. There are more bishops in the church per communicant member in England than ever before and there are more junior ministers in the House of Commons. It's the same sort of inflation. So an industry is created of remuneration consultants, who add a bogus science to this Pareto effect (or is it Pay-reto) where the bulk of the money goes to a small elite.

Break the Buck (not to be confused with 'Passing the Buck') The ultimate sin for a Money Market Fund (or MMF). These investment schemes are designed to be ultra-cautious, investing in short-term government debt, bank deposits and very low-risk securities in a strategy that generates a bit more return than from stuffing the cash into a dull old bank account. Investors popularly believe that their capital is very, very safe, virtually (if not legally/explicitly) guaranteed in fact. Breaking the Buck is very rare and is when the fund returns less than the capital amount. This happened to Primary Reserve Fund – the oldest MMF in the US – when it had to write off a truckload of defaulted paper issued by Lehman.

Broker How you feel when you compare this year's tax return to last year's. A friend in the boom years and a bane in the bust. Brokers are the middlemen of the financial world, standing in between the buyer and the seller in the markets. In an ideal world, the broker will have no incentive in doing the deal except the commission you pay. Unfortunately, the seller may be incentivising him too (say with a bonus for selling that particular fund or product) or his firm may have a position in those securities, so his view is coloured by that. Of course there are regulations to counteract these human instincts. The old adage runs thus: 'The broker made money, the firm made money – two out of three isn't bad'.

Bubble Too many fools chasing too little wealth. For some bizarre reason many economists and central bankers refused to focus on house pricing, equities and commodity prices (see also Irrational Exuberance and Greenspan – he wasn't that smart after all) as they spiralled north largely on the back of increased leverage – you've guessed this by now. Economists say that it is impossible to define 'a bubble' (personally, I think they could try a little harder to be helpful here), but real-life experience suggests that the initial identification of an asset class yielding higher returns draws in initial capital where investors look to make above-average returns by selling the commodity to a third party in the future (see The Bigger Fool Theory). The investor base grows from the specialist who identified it, to the general public, and the only ways to maintain the return are (a) to pay for the asset with increasing amounts of leverage and (b) to weaken the core definition of the asset. As the amount of invested capital falls and borrowings increase, the price of the asset becomes a function not of fundamentals but of how much your bank will lend you to buy it. At some point an external shock (often called The Minsky Moment) arrests the growth of bank debt and there can be no more buyers at that price. The assets therefore fall in price, as the income earned (if any) is not enough to cover the payments to the bank (see Interest Cover and Margin Call) so sales occur at a distressed price which then becomes the market price for all holders of the asset, stressed or not. (At that point: Ruin Stares You In The Face).

Recent central banking philosophy focused on letting bubbles take their course while getting ready to 'mop up' the aftermath. While successful after the relatively modest aftermath of the dot com boom, this time was just too big. Some bucket. Some mop. Some mess.

Bull The quality of your broker's advice. *Up up and away in my beautiful balloon.* Bulls are buyers so a sustained period of rising prices/values in an investment class or stockmarket is a Bull Market. There's no strict definition of a Bull Market, but traditionally you know you are in it when the lift attendant and the shoeshine man give you stock tips. Maybe the fact that that there are virtually no shoeshiners and lift attendants now is why the last Bull Market went on so long? The metaphor is easier to understand than the Bear (qv) – picture a noisy herd of testosteroned prime rib charging down the Wall Street canyon (Wall Street was once defined as a canyon connecting a fish market and a graveyard). When these lads are rising, all is well and stocks grow apace. But just as the cattle get beefed up for the slaughter, all good bull markets meet their slaughterhouse. (In the USA sometimes the phrase used is a Bull Run – not sure if Pamplona's festival was the metaphor – a handful of two-legged participants get squashed on the way – or was it remembering the two US Civil War battles thus named – a pretty ghastly day for all parties with a lot of carnage in the end). But on balance, all the world loves a Bull Market – and there's even the iconic Charging Bull statue at Bowling Green Park in downtown New York. Never forget that *bullish* rhymes with *foolish*.

Capital The airbag of capitalism (compare with CNBC or other business TV channels which are the windbag of capitalism).

In boring terms, real capital is where you invest *equity* or ordinary/common shares in a bank (or any venture). This contract is simple. To the extent the business makes a profit the equity holders may receive a dividend – a share of that profit. To the extent that the business makes a loss, the equity is used to repay tradesmen, suppliers and creditors. Shareholders have no rights to be repaid their equity investment until in the final analysis of liquidating the company forever, after all the liabilities of the company are paid off and the assets all sold, the equity holders will share in the small pot left in proportion to the number of shares held. This is the highest risk investment and so is relatively costly to the company to raise (plus, the more common equity that's issued, the profit cake gets cut up for many more mouths – a process called 'dilution'). At the other end of the spectrum is *debt* – where an external lender provides long-term finance but has the right to a contractually agreed ongoing return and a repayment in instalments or in one 'bullet' at the end of the facility.

And in between? You should have worked out by now that the money in investment banking is usually made in the 'in-betweens'. In capital terms, hybrids, bastards then mutants were created. Preference shares promise a fixed dividend annually (payable before the common shareholders see a divi) with a repayment date fixed some years out. These could be 'cumulative' (if there's no profit to pay the coupon, it gets rolled up) or could be 'convertible' (named after the BMWs bought by the arranging investment banker from the resultant bonus) where there was an option to transform the prefs (or bonds) into ordinary shares at an agreed price. The mutants were PIKs – payment in kind bonds – when the company can't afford to pay its interest, it creates new IOUs to settle its interest bill, because things will only get better and later on there will be enough cash to pay everyone out.

Bank's capital structures had these nuances too as regulators permitted different kinds of capital to be used together to build what was supposed to be a robust structure.

- **Tier One** – the gold plate of bank capital consisting of ordinary shares plus all the profits the bank has not yet distributed (minus any losses). As the bank is under no contractual obligation to distribute these back to anyone, this part of the capital base is the bedrock of the bank's business.

- **Tier Two** – pure equity is costly, and the argument went, if a bank can borrow for a long time – say 25 years and the bond holder can't force early repayment (and may even have his interest payments subordinated) – surely that looks a bit like equity if you are the average maturity of the bank's own loans are under a year or so? It became accepted that these hybrids could count as capital. In a further innovation, these long dated bonds were structured increasingly such that the bank had the right – but no obligation – to redeem the bond 5 year into its 25 year life. The trick was that interest rate payable to the bond holder jumped by a horrible quantum at year five, so it was priced as a five year bond, as no bank in its right mind would pay that higher coupon but the regulators allowed it to remain in the capital base, (In the crisis, when LIBORS peaked, and the risk margin on banks ballooned it was cheaper not to exercise those options and the investors got stuck.) Other bones could be thrown into this capital pot – any revaluation reserve on real estate or other assets for example (so as a real estate boom carries on, your HQ rises in value generating more capital for you lend to property developers).

- There is also **Tier Three** capital, but it's hardly worth the effort to describe.

Every national regulator had discretion to interpret these rules, but the global agreement was that regulated banks would hold capital at least equal to eight per cent of their balance sheet, with a minimum of half that as Tier One.

There is no one on the planet today who believes that a Tier One ratio of four per cent is anywhere near prudent, safe or acceptable.

One worrying feature is the sudden rush to create new improved hybrids to meet new regulatory demands. Nicknamed CoCos (Contingent capital obligations) they are a kind of bond that will be automatically converted into ordinary shares if the Tier One ratio falls say below five per cent. After what we have just been through, it seems amazing that anyone has faith in anything other than good old fashioned shares. But then they are so expensive… and the crash will never happen because we are all so careful now we've learned our lesson.

Carry Trade Often said to be a favourite of Mrs Watanabe (the traditional small Japanese investor). The wizard scheme of borrowing in a low interest rate currency (often the Japanese Yen) and investing in a high interest rate currency, pocketing the differential in yield as profit. Proponents liken it to shooting fish in a barrel. Of course, if you miss the fish you shoot a hole in the barrel, a real liquidity problem then ensues. The obvious risk is that fluctuations in the foreign exchange rates open you to a capital loss when you look to sell your investment to repay the loan. Of course, you could just find a Japanese bank happy to roll the loan *sine die* and keep on rolling the dice. There have been a fair few calamities over the years.

Casino Banking Pejorative term (beloved of legislators) for investment banking. It's a nice newspaper headline – images of betting the depositor's money down in New Jersey (or Monaco if you are classier) and expecting the Treasury to sign off on the credit card bill at the end of the session. The other way to look at it is that running a casino is a great business – the House always wins – a bit like the utility banks who provide payment services, earning bid/offer spread on FX, making use of your money while it's travelling round the systems slowly (the float) and charging fees for this and fees for that.

The key question is – should trading and investment banking activities be permitted by financial institutions whose deposits are guaranteed by government, effectively (in case you hadn't been paying attention recently) saddling the taxpayer with the resultant loss? Many commentators are calling for the re-repeal of the classic Glass-Steagall Act of 1933 which defined an institutional gulf between retail and investment banks until in 1999 it fell to the power of the Wall Street lobbyists and all bets were on. There is a call from a credible group of commentators to create 'narrow' banks severely constrained in a utility function. Every complex problem has a solution that is clear, simple, quick and totally wrong. It's hard – probably impossible – to create a 'narrow bank' that's substantially risk free. Banking is a risky business full stop.

CDO/CLO (Collateralised Debt or Loan Obligations) Welcome to the world of alphabetti spaghetti. By analogy with the Mortgage Backed Security (which is created out of hundreds of individual mortgages), the Collateralised Debt Obligation was created to handle corporate bonds in the same process and then developed into the Collateralised Loan Obligation, where banks bundled together slices of their term loans to compete. As we've discussed, diversification is in theory a good thing, but as many CDOs and CLOs invested in exactly the same underlying obligations, or at least a series of loans and bonds that shared fundamental traits and characteristics, that meant they would respond to economic stress in similar or correlated ways. Naturally the derivatives boys built even more highly leveraged versions called synthetic CLOs and CDOs. The investor who bought five different CLOs and saw them all under stress had the same names in each instrument – so it wasn't as diverse as expected – and when the whole market turned, there was a great correlation between all kinds of debt – so the theory of diversification was pretty illusory.

CDO²/CLO² (CDO squared and CLO squared) As a general rule if you see anything marked to a power in the financial markets, run for the hills as this is an exponential way to drop a packet of money. Making a CDO out of other CDOs (rather than bonds or loans) was a great way to make fees, but it did not help diversify portfolios as the same names kept coming up in all sorts of places. Add in the sheer volume of due diligence you'd need to analyse each constituent part – so just rely on the Agency Rating and you'll be OK². Didn't work out that way alas.

CDS (Credit Default Swap) Like rats in London or roaches in NY, you're never more than three feet away from a CDS... which is now a US$30 trillion odd market. This is a relatively new development in the derivative market. It started as a simple contract between two counterparties: one paid a premium to the other in return for a promise that if a particular bond defaulted then the face value of the bond would be repaid when the buyer of the CDS delivers the bust bond to the seller. The papers (and even some market professionals who should know better) often call this 'insurance', but it's not in the real sense (counterparties are not necessarily regulated as insurers are, for example, and unlike an insurance policy, it can be used to bet on price rises as well as to cover a potential risk as the buyer does not need to have 'an insurable interest' and can be a mere speculator).

In parallel with real risk hedging, there are 'naked' CDS investors – speculators who don't own the underlying bonds, looking to make a profit as a firm goes under. These instruments can influence the real economy in quite malign ways – imagine a lender who has taken out a CDS on an industrial company to hedge its lending. When the borrower gets into trouble, the lender has a sharp dilemma – if he supports the company to give it a long-term future by agreeing a debt-to-equity swap, he will lose money on his loan, but if he allows the company to go under, he can claim the whole amount owed under the CDS. We have started to see lenders and investors deliberately send companies and jobs to the wall because of the economic effect of the CDS.

The numbers are huge, albeit there's a great netting potential and as with almost all financial subjects, the larger the numbers the less rational the debate. Are they a symptom or a cause? They are opaque enough to be a great bogey-man though!

Chapter 11 The penultimate chapter in a horror story. This is the chapter in the US bankruptcy code which has the sensible theory of trying to save as much of the defaulting company's business and jobs as possible. As with everything in the meeting of the law and money, there are huge opportunities to win or lose. There are several famous entrepreneurs who are habitués of this process such that one's ghosted biography is made up entirely of Chapter 11s.

Club Fed Once the description of the open prison regime used for financial scapegoats. No more! Public opinion has hardened since the dot com Crash, and we have stopped seeing financial crimes as 'victimless' (just look at your investment statement and tell me that there were no victims – and there are people worse off than you) to the extent that major white collar criminals now wear their orange jumpsuits for a long time in rather nasty venues.

The disgraced financier Bernie Madoff was sent down for 150 years (at the time he swapped his pinstriped suit for the day-glo jumpsuit he was 70 years old), as investigators looked for the US$64bn missing funds. He was comparatively lucky (he'll get free bed, board and medical assistance for the rest of his life, which is rather more than many of his elderly victims can look forward to) but his isn't the longest financial fraud sentence. One was handed down to two Persian con-men who, in 1969, got 7,109 years each. (The good news is that, with time off for good behaviour they only expected to serve half of that.)

As the excoriating judgement from Judge Chin put it:

> Here, the message must be sent that Mr. Madoff's crimes
> were extraordinarily evil and that this kind of irresponsible
> manipulation of the system is not merely a bloodless financial
> crime that takes place just on paper, but it is instead ... one
> that takes a staggering human toll.

So Bernie (now known as inmate #61727–054 in Butner NC) joins the big
leaguers. In fact his prison sentence is longer than most of the other business criminals put together:

- Bernard Ebbers, CEO, WorldCom (inmate #56022–054):
  25 years in prison

- Scott Sullivan, CFO, WorldCom (inmate #54011–054):
  5 years in prison (after helping prosecutors)

- Jeff Skilling, CEO Enron (inmate #29296–179): 24 years 3
  months in prison

- Andrew Fastow, CFO, Enron (inmate #14343–179):
  6 years in prison, plus 2 years' community service
  (after helping prosecutors and his wife – she took a year's
  sentence for falsifying her tax return)

- Dennis Kozlowski, CEO, Tyco (inmate #05A4820): 8 1/3
  to 25 years in prison

- Mark Swartz, CFO, Tyco (inmate #05A4823): 8 1/3 to 25
  years in prison

- John Rigas, Founder, Adelphia (inmate #53983–054)
  15 years in prison (reduced because of poor health)

- Timothy Rigas, CFO, Adelphia (inmate #53982–054):
  20 years in prison

Commodities Basic raw materials needed for industry or which can be
used as an investment asset class. Subsets include Precious Metals: led by
Gold (the classic 'safe haven trade'), PGM (platinum group metals), Silver
etc; Base Metals (like iron, copper, aluminium); Softs (e.g. sugar, spices,
pork bellies) and Oil. Typically the preserve of specialist traders given
volatility and physical issues (if you buy 50,000 bushels of wheat you have
to put it somewhere, insure it, etc.) and traded across specialised exchanges.
The physical commodity markets have, with a good deal of justification,
been considered a sight more risky than the financial markets. The mystery is
maintained today where in the London Metal Exchange ancient astrological

symbols are used for the metals traded. They have been curiously absent in the financial debacle currently, though there have been some good bust-ups in the past:

- SILVER: the Bunker Hunt Brothers and a bunch of oil-wealthy investors 'cornered' half the world's silver supply between 1973 and 1980. When that bubble burst the Brothers owed US$2.5bn borrowed to buy silver worth a mere US$1.5bn at the new depressed price. End result: the Bunker Hunts were hunted out of their bunkers into bankruptcy. Every silver scam has a cloudy lining...

- COPPER: Hamanaka-san was Sumitomo's chief trader in copper from 1986 for 10 years – his influence in the market being so great that the papers called him 'Mr Copper'. His goal was to corner the market for copper and draw huge profits from the growing number of new and inexperienced financial institutions who had started to trade in the metal. When his bubble burst it cost his employers about US$2bn – they called the coppers pretty quickly. Mr Copper came a cropper as the headline reported it. Cu in court one day...

- SALAD OIL (I am not making this up...) Tino De Angelis 'The Salad Oil King', started as a butcher from the Bronx, created a new business: Allied Crude Vegetable Oil, to capitalise on America's growing fashion for salad dressings. By 1963 most of the big commodities banks were supporting about US$200m of Tino's oil investments – secured on warehouse receipts. These gave the holder the right to arrive at the warehouse (in this case huge tanks in NJ) and demand delivery of the oil therein. Or they could if there was salad oil and not just swimming pools of water with a skim of oil on the top. Never work with slick operators.

Conduit A key part of the shadowy world of Shadow Banking (take a minute and look at that entry below). There was no light at the end of these tunnels, unless it was the lights of the oncoming train.

Credit Risk The fundamental building block of finance. The very simple risk that the guy you give money to cannot/will not repay it in full on its due date and until that day he will pay you your periodic interest. The old saying is that anyone can be a lender; it takes a banker's skill to get repaid.

Crisis 'Crisis, what crisis' (James Callaghan – he didn't actually say this, but everyone thinks he did, so the phrase has stuck and until recently he was regarded as the least effective UK Prime Minister in the last 50 years) 'Gentlemen, between the crisis and the catastrophe there is always time for a glass of champagne' (Paul Claudel). A rather sharper world view than: 'Events, dear boy, events'. Related thoughts include Crunch, Nuclear Winter, Poverty, Redundancy, Inevitability, Predictability.

Dead Cat Bounce An upward but short-term 'blip' in a falling market. Typically this tempts fools back into buying just as the price collapses again. (Even a dead cat will bounce if thrown hard enough). The only way to predict it however remains hindsight. Investors should beware of trying to catch a falling knife in these circumstances (and similar clichés). Don't get shot by the green shoots.

Default A failure to make payment or to fulfil the obligations of a financial contract. There is also a Limited Default (or Limited Recourse), where the default language means that particular loan, and only it, is in trouble and the bank has no right to attack the wealth of the sponsors outside that specific project. One of the important cultural changes over the years has been to recognise that there are 'honest' defaults – typically entrepreneurs taking on new ventures or products – where the principal backer should perhaps have another chance (or chances) to fulfil this socially important role. On the other hand, there are many deals done on a 'limited recourse' basis (as a trend in the bubble to weaken the security taken by lenders). Here, the money is lent to a company or special purpose vehicle with no direct connection to the principal backer. If this goes bust he loses his equity investment (which may be modest) but can carry on in his other ventures. There are a number of well-known businessmen who have a history of default and dispute with banks and bond-holders. At the personal level, the US mortgage market saw 'Jingle Mail' where borrowers (who having borrowed virtually all of the cost of their home – and significantly more than its current market value) mailed back the keys to the house to the bank and walked away from the mortgage free and clear. That's the end of a beautiful friendship.

Deposit Protection A governmental scheme which guarantees the return of amounts (up to a defined limit and/or percentage) to depositors in regulated banks. The logic is to assure the ordinary folk with money in the bank that there's no need to run out and start a run at times of trouble. But, as with all schemes involving folly, it's not foolproof (as we found out with the Northern Rock).

Derivative Derivatives take the place of handguns in financial debate – derivatives don't lose money, people lose money. A derivative is a contract between two counterparties who agree to make periodic payments over an agreed period based on the value of an underlying commodity or index.

Directors Who are the directors and what are they for? The UK has seen tonnes of paper wasted on good corporate governance and independence of directors. Are they a special breed of grey-suited WASP 50-year-old university males destined to receive a fee for four days a month's meetings (from eight different companies) or are they the masterful business minds of all races and genders who pilot the company around the ego of the CEO?

Due Diligence In the arena of high finance, DD is the process whereby vast teams of bankers, accountants, lawyers and valuers descend on a company to check on every part of its business preparatory to a takeover, or to a large loan being advanced. Every assumption has to be questioned, tested and ultimately verified in a 'drains up' approach. Its intensity causes those who have gone through it to call it as much fun as gargling with razor blades. It is often said that every company has three sets of accounts: the ones to show the taxman; the ones to show the bankers and the one that shows the real profits that only the owner sees. DD seeks to establish where the truth lies. It's a commonsense approach: always squeeze the melon before you buy it.

In the old days, it was more like 'kicking the tyres' – having the manager check and see that there really was a car to be financed, or a house to be purchased. Banking mythology tells many tales, including the City banker lending money to two sheep farmers in a distant village. The bank made a loan to each farmer based on each having a flock of 200 sheep. He visited the first farm in the morning counted his 200 animals and was taken for a liquid lunch in the pub, thus allowing the second farmer time to move the flock round the back lanes to his farm (you've guessed it – each of them only had a hundred sheep) so that the banker, suitably refreshed, could count the same 200 sheep on the other farm that afternoon reporting back to the bank that all was hunky dory.

DD is hard to complete on very complex deals (or at least very expensive and time consuming to complete) which is why the rating agencies became so important. Failure to carry it out effectively allowed rogues like Leeson and Madoff a free rein, so there is bound to be a backlash – in the personal market, for example, mortgage applicants will have to show more detail on income and expenditure to allow mortgage officials to assess spending patterns and, hence, serviceability. The cautionary tale of Lloyds Bank buying

HBOS after a chat at a cocktail party followed up by what management admits was three to five times less DD than was required is a hard lesson for management and for us taxpayers, too. Certainly it was the most expensive plate of canapés ever eaten. Black Horse d'oeuvres.

Efficient Market Theory The triumph of academic economics over common sense. This believes that, in a liquid market, every element that can affect a security's price will be in the valuation (including stupidity, mishearing, mistyping, etc.). The folly of this groupthink is exemplified in the old joke about the three economists walking down the street and finding a £20 note on the sidewalk. They walked on, ignoring it, for any sensible economist knows that in an efficient market the cash would have been picked up by now...

This is part of a real philosophical problem which underpins this crisis. Let's look at the laws of physics. Take Boyle's Law:

$$P \text{ (pressure)} \times V \text{ (volume)} = k \text{ (constant)}$$

Wherever you go in the world, at any time and place, if you increase the pressure exerted on a gas, its volume decreases. And vice versa. You can observe this and measure it to tiny levels of accuracy. That is science.

Compare that with one from economics about the law of demand: when the price of a good falls, the quantity demanded rises. This is a different category of 'law' and its irreducibility to mathematics means that as these laws of economics become more complex, they move further away from the world-linked algebra needed in financial analysis. We act as if the law of demand and Boyle's Law are equally helpful for predicting what will happen tomorrow. We act as if the economic laws were hard and fast, then build models around them (assuming the assumptions are constant) bet trillions on the outcome and lose it because it is not a universal and scientific law.

Emerging Markets Take your savings on holiday to exotic places and watch them catch Delhi Belly. Come back lighter, and hopefully wiser. Repeated forays into Latin/South America are common whether by fraudsters such as our friend Gregor MacGregor or in the centuries of cross border trade and investment where we have flirted with country risk. Partly this is because of the mad search for yield at any price, partly by real trading ambition to open new markets for goods and services but also psychologically, partly by a love for the exotic – including in the latest boom the BRICs (an artificial grouping of Brazil, Russia, India and China – one-way exponential growth prospects) were a popular investment grouping;

although calling Portugal, Ireland, Greece and Spain the PIGS met with some hostility from those national governments. 'Countries Don't Go Bust' is the mantra of the country risk banker – while that might be true in a legal sense, it still takes a lot of time and effort to get a recalcitrant country to cough up. Why, even the state of Mississippi has a defaulted bond, and it looks very pretty when framed (which costs more than the bond's value). Usually these cases come round as the cycle turns and the countries need to seek access to the external financial world (which needs the fees and margins).

Fallen Angels Companies who have fallen below the investment grade threshold (see Junk – sorry – High Yield Bonds), or sometimes equities which have fallen out of the index. Optimists want to buy them in their sorrows to watch them rise to their former glory. Pessimists don't.

Firm The old investment banks were partnerships, so the people who provided the risk capital were the same people who took the risks. Naturally they divided the spoils at the end of the year (or shared the pain). Then they became limited companies and bank subsidiaries (or banks themselves) and should share the incremental rewards with the depositors and the shareholders (who are the folk providing the oxygen to breathe). So when you find any manager, director or employee of a bank talking about his employer and calling it 'the firm' rest assured, he's proposing to take out a higher return than the other stakeholders.

Flagpoles When a company's new global headquarters is unveiled and it has (a) more than one flagpole (b) a corporate helicopter and (c) a fish tank (some commentators say an atrium with a commissioned artwork) then the combination of all three is a certain sign that the company is heading for financial collapse. Building huge new dealing rooms in investment banks is a similar sign – to be able to afford the vast expense of building a new mega trading floor inherently implies that the business is making so much profit it must be near the peak of the market.

Flight to Quality Or once bitten, twice shy. When markets are volatile, or assets are hard to assess and evaluate, canny investors flock to safe houses: US Government Bonds, overnight deposits with the highest rated banks, and pure gold. Better safe than sorry in terms of ensuring capital security albeit at the expense of income.

Fractional Reserves The world changed when Cosimo our goldsmith changed from being simply the custodian of gold – a glorified coat check clerk – into a banker who combined his money and his clients' into larger loans. As you remember (but the Ayr Bank and a few recent institutions forgot to their immense cost) those clients will want their money back one day. While your reputation is intact it is unlikely that everyone will want their deposits back in a hurry so you only need to keep sufficient cash in reserve to meet those demands. Some countries set that ratio in law or by central banking regulation. Others rely on the overall prudent approach. Regardless of that, every time money is deposited in the banking system a small fraction is kept as a cash reserve and the larger portion is lent – that amount being deposited in another bank which carries out the same process, multiplying the amount of money in the world. As a Victorian poet said, 'Great fleas have little fleas upon their backs to bite 'em, And little fleas have lesser fleas, and so ad infinitum', so too with bank deposits.

Futures In career terms, bleak for many, but Futures also refers to the standardised contracts traded on formal exchanges which allow participants to buy and/or sell round amounts of standardised quality of an underlying physical commodity (such as oil, pork bellies, rice) or a financial instrument (like FX, government bonds or interest rates) at a fixed future date. They can either be physically settled (you will deliver 1,000 lbs of potatoes to an agreed warehouse) or cash settled where one of the parties will owe the other the cash difference between the agreed futures price and the actual market price on the day.

FX Trading foreign exchange (or FX) is the biggest trading market in the world. It's a classic Over the Counter/OTC game which means there's virtually no cap on what can happen. It's largely speculation – about US$4 trillion is traded every day of which less than a third is linked to the movement of international trade or to your purchase of Baht for the Thai resorts... All over the world, all round the clock, every day (save Christmas Day and New Year) participants in the FX market sit hunched over screens (or occasionally smashing telephones) buying and selling foreign currency. Once this activity was tied to the flow of goods and services across boundaries, but now the bulk of activity is a profit centre in its own right, buying and selling for the bank itself. A colourful market with loads of slang: the major currencies are Cable (UK Sterling when measured against the US Dollar); The Buck (US Dollar); Euro and Japanese Yen (so boring it doesn't have a nickname) along with The Swissie, The Aussie, The Kiwi and The Loonie (in case you didn't guess the last is Canada where the Canuck dollar has a picture of a Loon on it).

There are markets in many minor currencies too, giving rise to ribald humour around the currencies of El Salvador (The Colon) and Vietnam (The Dong).

There's also a huge industry in forecasting future exchange rates (which Greenspan dismissed with 'There may be more forecasting of exchange rates with less success than almost any other economic variable') based on all sorts of theories – from macro economics on one hand to charting on the other. (This is a theory that the markets follow recognisable patterns if you make a graph of the FX rate. Many, many people believe this. Why, I just don't know).

Gambler's Curse Common to all asset classes, the trader/investor's reluctance to realise winning bets and 'keep the money on the table', this is particularly true at the end of bubbles. 'All gamblers die broke' (aka Runyon's Law). As Fred Schwed put it – when a trader makes his second million dollar profit, should we praise him for being a great trader or think him a fool for endangering his first million? Hmmm. And it's not just traders – when Enron and the dot coms went down, the pension plans were full of the company's own stock and the employees had piled in too. All those eggs in one basket case. But that could never happen to us – or could it?

Game (Skin In The) If the banker, structure, or advisor has no risk of losing money after selling this damn thing to you then he'll take less care than if he had an ownership interest and could lose money. This is SITG and by any definition is a *good thing*.

Greeks When you make a return on your investment, the theory goes that it's actually made up of a number of stripes. To add verisimilitude to the theory, these elements have been given Greek names so they look even more scientific. *Alpha* is the return attributable to the company's performance in excess of *beta* which is the overall market return. *Options* add all sorts of other levels to this. However described and calculated it remains all Greek to me.

Greenmail An out of fashion technique whereby an 'active investor' (corporate raider) takes a sizeable stake in a company and becomes such a pain to the management that they buy off the raider with cash or business assets. We will no doubt see a resurgence as part of the inevitable corporate restructurings ahead of us.

Haircut (see also Importance of creating a good professional impression). When lending against collateral, the prudent banker (see Characters in fairy tales) will discount the value of the security taken to allow for volatility in its price and the costs of selling it quickly. This discount is known as the haircut. A super-safe and liquid Gilt or T Bill will attract a tiny haircut, while equities will demand much higher discounts. The bigger the haircut the less you can borrow (decreasing leverage).

Hedge Fund Two years ago it was the Hedge Funds that were top of the list of likely dangers to the world's financial system. If you believed the papers and the politicians, these secretive powerful and unregulated pots of money were the spawn of the Devil waiting to wreck havoc on the markets. As it happened, most of the damage was done by the mainstream, highly regulated banking sector. Makes you think.

At the simplest level a hedge fund is an unregulated (or at least very very lightly regulated) mutual fund/unit trust with three important characteristics: (i) it can go short (sell shares it does not own), (ii) investors must be institutions or highly wealthy individuals and (iii) the investment strategy can involve a lot of leverage (although successful commentators inside the industry would suggest that this is usually considerably less than your average highly regulated conventional bank staffed with prudent bankers and an independent board of directors comprising titles and respected captains of industry!) Other typical characteristics are that withdrawals from the fund may only be made on specific dates (after giving notice) which can be suspended by the manager, and the investment manager's remuneration is mainly tied to performance (though in the boom many managers started a fixed fee arrangement too).

Critics suggest that the success in hedge fund strategies is often because high leverage combined with low intelligence still generates a positive return.

In the earliest days, Alfred Winslow Jones (a name missing from the Financial Hall of Fame – undeservedly) came up with a strategy involving a combination of choosing specific equity investments (long positions) while simultaneously taking short positions in the overall market index – this (if correct) would create income performance of the specific stock but with the overall gain or loss in the market netted off. To make a greater dollar return, Jones started to leverage up – to borrow against the security of the long position to reinvest in the strategy.

Roughly speaking, he invests in Amsmoke common stock and sells a short position on the Bobby Jones Index (of which Amsmoke is a constituent). Assuming the market rises and Amsmoke rises proportionately higher, then the cost of settling the short position rises and eliminates the market risk component of the long position. Jones is left with a value representing Amsmoke's outperformance of the Bobby Jones.

Conversely, if the market drops, but Amsmoke holds up better than its fellow constituents on the index, the losses on the long position are cancelled out by the gain on the short, leaving the residual return.

This hedging of the market risk is where the name came from. So it's wrong to assume that HFs are *ipso facto* very high risk – many in the industry would say that a conventional mutual fund 100 per cent exposed to a particular stockmarket and charging its investors two per cent per annum is not without its own set of risks. The difference, though, is threefold – the volume of leverage (both bank debt and derivatives) added to the risk of short selling (while your long position can only go down to zero, your short position in theory can cost you an infinite amount) and when it goes wrong, there's no authority figure to bail you out.

Widows and orphans should stop reading this now.

From 1949 through to the late 1960s, the hedge fund was a quirky alternative strategy on the sidelines of the investment world, partly owing to wanting to avoid publicity (and hence regulatory scrutiny) and partially because the opportunities to obtain leverage from conventional banks were limited.

In the 1970s and early 1980s more wealthy individuals (and family offices – private banks devoted to one specific family) and institutions got into this alternative investment strategy and out of this grew the golden age of the Towering Titans: George Soros (Quantum Fund) and Julian Robertson (Tiger). The public really noticed the HF in the 1990s – in two glorious and one inglorious chapters.

Soros made a public name in a currency strategy that targeted the British pound. For political rather than economic reasons, the British government at that time had a policy of pegging the pound against the basket of currencies called the ECU (the European Currency Unit – the forerunner of the Euro) where, effectively, each national currency has undertaken to maintain a value within an agreed band against the dominant German Deutschemark. Things went well until Germany's own problems (caused effectively when the Berlin Wall fell and the chancellor in a *grande geste* promised to unify East and West Germany but at 1 weak Ostmark for every 1 strong DM). This pushed the sister ECU currencies hard against their agreed bands. Speculators started aggressively selling the Pound Sterling (along with the Finnish Maarka, the Swedish Krone and the Italian Lire in particular) and buying DM, this pressuring the central banks of the 'sold' currencies to come into the market to buy their own currency to keep in synch with the permitted ranges.

16 September 1992 (or Black Wednesday as it was known ever after) saw the crisis burst – a hapless Chancellor of The Exchequer (Norman, now

Lord Lamont) stood on the floor of the House of Commons as everyone in the world (or so it seemed) was selling Sterling. When I say everyone, that was everyone except the Bank of England, who kept trying to bail out the titanic mess with two buckets – even more currency purchases, depleting our reserves and a nearly unprecedented double jump in interest rates to make Sterling a more attractive investment (in the morning Base Rate was raised from 10 per cent to 12 per cent and then in the afternoon another jump to 15 per cent – a Treasury official was asked when the last time interest rates had been increased twice in a day – '1914' he said – 'standard operating procedure when we go to war against Germany').

As night fell, and the UK with it (out of the European exchange mechanism anyway) Soros was widely believed to have made US$1bn by shorting the pound and many HFs (and the trading desks of international banks in London) had made a lot of money. HM Treasury estimated the trading loss on the day at £800m and the total cost (including opportunity cost) at about £3.4bn. That excludes the opportunity cost to the then ruling Conservative Party who saw their traditional role as a safe economic pair of hands squashed horribly in the gutter.

The negative consequence was in 1998 when Long Term Capital Management ('LTCM') exploded– a hedge fund whose board was the who's who of investment. It was founded by the Solomon's former star trader, John Meriwether and had two Nobel Laureates on the board – this was a rare mix of testosterone and grey matter that was designed to rule the world. It was a trophy investment at first – with over US$1 trillion from investors on Day One in February 1994 – four years later, its equity base had risen nearly fivefold and the leverage even faster to 25 times (and one of the biggest derivatives positions on the Street, which increased that effective leverage by 10 times). The crunch came when Russia defaulted on its bonds and investors panicked, selling international securities and fleeing to the safe haven of Uncle Sam and the Treasury bill.

The convergence on which LTCM had bet had become a divergence. The firm started haemorrhaging losses but worse than that, the lenders needed more collateral to be posted (or the debt reduced), so the firm was obliged to sell its profitable trades faster and faster to try and plug the hole caused by the declining Russian positions.

The real worry, though, was that everyone in the financial world had dealt with LTCM, so if it failed suddenly the system generally would take a blow which could force other banks and firms to fail and then that would affect the real economy. So the Federal Reserve of New York invited some of the most affected players for a not so cosy chat in the faux-medieval grandeur of its Downtown fortress. The hat (a rather large Stetson was needed) was passed round Wall Street and raised US$3.65bn from a syndicate of banks in return for a 90 per cent share stake in the firm. With that underpinned, some form of confidence returned to the markets who proceeded to unwind the positions without panic.

Once it was all done and dusted, LTCM lost just a bit more than the UK in the ERM. Meriwether went on to found a new fund, JWM. It announced its closure, due to losses, in mid 2009. Fortunately, no hats were needed this time round.

The effect of LTCM saw the macro hedge funds scale back over the next few years, but also saw a raft of smaller funds opening (and spectacularly closing) such that real estate in Greenwich CT and Mayfair in London has been pretty hot indeed.

Every fund is based on a management team and a strategy. The most talked about families of investment are:

- MARKET NEUTRAL (aka RELATIVE VALUE) – the classic Jonesian model focusing on Alpha and isolating Beta. In a sane world this could actually be quite a conservative strategy for a large investor.

- EVENT DRIVEN – look for the outcomes of mergers, bank-ruptcies or spin offs that will cause the price to rise or fall – the risk is, of course, that it doesn't happen or at least not in time. This approach is much riskier as it depends on the scenario playing out to your advantage – for example that a merger gets blocked by the regulators.

- LONG/SHORT – a twist on market neutral particularly in equity markets where there is a net long exposure (e.g. invest US$130 in the US stockmarket financed by US$25 of equity, US$75 of debt and US$30 generated by short selling).

- TACTICAL TRADERS – who speculate directly on market movements in any/all categories either using complex financial models (systemic managers) or by traditional stock picking (discretionary).

In the years preceding the crunch, there were hundreds of commentators who predicted the collapse of the world because of the evils of the unbridled, unregulated, unrestrained model of the hedge funds. While several did implode or explode (or some just plodded alone), the greatest of ironies in this debacle is that the worst offenders were the regulated banks. Now some specialist hedge funds are buying distressed bank assets – and even distressed banks.

Like an Agatha Christie story, we all expected the scapegrace second-hand car dealer brother to have committed the murder, and blow me it was the Vicar (when the Village Bobby wasn't looking!).

Herstatt Risk One lunchtime in June 1974, a little German bank called Herstatt Bank closed its doors in Cologne and raised a huge stink in the foreign exchange market. It was a well known counterparty in the new world of FX dealing. The problem that no one had envisaged was many banks had paid out the Deutschemarks they owed Herstatt but were now short of the pay out of the reciprocal currency because Herstatt was no more. This was particularly acute for the USA because of the time differences – they weren't open to receive payments yet but had instructed their German correspondents to release the DM during the German working day. It was as if you'd sold a man your car, delivered it against a bank cheque only to find it bounce at the counter when presented. Welcome to the world of settlement risk.

House Prices When the price goes up is it *an increase in asset values or just inflation?*

Property valuation is the recreational drug of choice for the middle classes.

The simple equation is that if you have no mortgage (lucky devil) or a steady job and certain to pay off your mortgage, then if you've bought a home rather than an investment, falling markets should mean you just live at home, pay your bills monthly and not worry too much about the capital value.

If you are so minded though, you can monitor your investment against one of the indices – but what a difference – try calculating it in the UK for example (from the respective websites) and you have a choice of conflicting methodologies.

Lets compare the data for the end of the Second Quarter in 2009.

Index	Year-on-year change in house prices (Average house price)	Positive Features	Negative Features
Nationwide	-11.7% £154,066	Creates a 'typical' house sale averaged over the country.	Based on the amount of the mortgage approvals on this one bank's books, not final sale price – in weak markets there are fewer mortgage applications. Nationwide has a c.10% market share.
Halifax	-15.0% £156,944	Largest UK mortgage lender – so very deep data from 1984.	As above – so last minute changes such as gazundering (where a nasty potential purchaser drops the price at the last minute in a declining market) aren't caught.
Land Registry	-14.0% £153,046	The official government ownership register based on final sale price.	England and Wales only (hence higher average after taking out Scotland and Northern Ireland). Solicitors can be slow in filing (surely not) so there is a lag of up to three months.
FT	-13.1% £197,802	Covers every transaction in England and Wales.	Mixes data from the three indices above Combines the problems of all three.
Rightmove	-5.5% £226,436	Online data, includes transactions without a mortgage.	Based on asking prices from sellers via estate agents, so hardly a robust sample. Can be very volatile.

It's not as easy as measuring temperature or speed, or someone's height. You get what you pay for.

Indices (Indexes) Keeping up with the Dow Joneses. There's an index for everything now. Of course, rising stockmarket indices are a very good thing. Rising cost-of-living indices are a very bad thing.

Inflation no one likes inflation unless it's in their investment valuation when it's called capital appreciation.

Don't get me wrong – inflation is a bad thing. Today people in Zimbabwe are dying because of its effects and not that long ago pensioners in the UK and US were struggling in poverty as inflation eroded the regular fixed pension annuity. Ronald Reagan captured it in his usual folksy style – inflation, he said was 'as violent as a mugger, as frightening as an armed robber and as deadly as a hit-man' while even the more sober *Economist* magazine in May 2008 called it an 'economic serial killer'.

There are some funny anomalies, though, in how we measure it. On the one hand, as economists are wont to say, 'we can manage what we can measure' (quoting the mantra of Jack Welch) while on the other 'any observed statistical regularity will tend to collapse once pressure is placed upon it for control purposes' (following the shrewd observation of Charles Goodhart).

Firstly, the focus is on consumer price inflation – the rise in living costs to you and me. But every family is different – young families need extra electricity for washing, nappies, buggies, package holidays. Ordinary bankers need commuter rail tickets, rolled umbrellas, pin striped suits, designer frocks and whisky. Pensioners focus on basic foodstuffs and heating. So the national economists build a notional basket of goods and services for the notional household and that is the measure of inflation that affects us all in terms of wage rises or indexation. By definition your household will see costs increase faster or slower than that depending on your pattern of consumption.

(It's also an interesting insight to the mind of the residents of the national statistics office who check the basket every year – this is a favourite quotation from 2008:

> Lager stubbies are not as popular as they were 10 years ago
> and although single bottles of regular sized lager are already
> in the basket, the inclusion of crates (20 bottles) reflects
> changing spending patterns.

Which encapsulates my worries about both inflation and liquidity.)

So there is a fundamental difference between your 'Cost of Living' and official 'Inflation'.

Using the UK as an example, for many years the official or 'headline' inflation rate was the Retail Price Index and this remains enshrined in many pensions, bonds and contracts as 'inflation'. It covers both consumer spending and housing costs, and takes account of taxation effects too, so it is calculated on a UK-specific formula.

It has two babies: RPI-X (excluding housing), which was the Bank of England's targeting benchmark until quite recently, and the more obscure RPI-Y, which takes out both housing and tax.

These indices were changed to follow a Harmonised Consumer Price Index within Europe (it was launched under that title but dealers began to call it Hiccup which annoyed the officials, so CPI it is). This is now the official target of the Bank of England and has a number of technical differences in the model (far too tedious to understand) that means it's almost always going to be a lower percentage number than RPI.

Dropping housing costs out of inflation seems counterintuitive to many – certainly my mortgage payment, insurance premium and ever-rising property tax takes a big bite out of my income, and that of most families I think. But when we are worrying about too much money chasing too many goods, don't forget that the official index of inflation won't tell you that your money is going faster when you spend on:

- Houses (homes, investments or speculation)
- Financial investments
- Yachts and speedboats
- Art
- Commodities
- Private jets and helicopters
- Recreational drugs and *belles du jour*

Insider Dealing For centuries, the sign of a good stockbroker was his ability to get friends and family 'in on the ground floor' of a new security issue before the public had a chance. Insider Dealing – the buying or selling of securities knowing a piece of material non-public information – is now quite rightly a crime in most jurisdictions and has claimed some high-profile scalps (Martha Stewart and in another infamous case the poor CEO who couldn't help but unburden himself to his prostitute girlfriend about the day's affairs, for example). There's even a new version, Outsider Dealing, which is where your broker implies that he has inside knowledge (but hasn't) to encourage you to buy. Only one case to date, but it's only a matter of time (not that I know anything specific, you know...)

Investment Bank A concept hard to define and therefore harder to regulate.

Junk Bonds Also known as NIG (non-investment grade) or High Yield (so as not to hurt the CFO's feelings). Invented by the investment bank Drexel Burnham Lambert that went famously bust.

Keynes There are relatively few jargon words beginning with 'K' – so I stick JMK in as does every newspaper columnist that has gone on a crash course in Keynesian economics. Unfortunately, so have a couple of governments. Mind you, the great man did predict in 1927 'We will not have any more crashes in our time.' But I'm sure that's out of context. In the long run we are all misquoted. Or penniless, or dead.

Lender of Last Resort A job no one wants to volunteer for. The Bank of England (aka The Old Lady of Threadneedle Street) for years fulfilled this role in the UK markets and the Federal Reserve across the pond and their sister central banks round the world's capitals– the LOLR's function is to provide significant lending at a penalty rate of interest against appropriate but not immediately saleable assets to allow an institution time to realise its assets in an orderly fashion. It involves two keen assessments: is the troubled bank merely illiquid – a question of getting the timing mismatch inherent in banking wrong – or is it insolvent? Nowadays, there is another element in the equation – is the failing bank 'systemic', which is to say, would its collapse affect the orderly operation of the markets (either practically in terms of being a near-omnipresent counterparty) or in terms of market sentiment ('If x has gone down then we are all ****ed). If you haven't worked this out yet, you and I as taxpayer have inherited this role. Enjoy.

Leverage What bankers apparently had over Capitol Hill. Even now the financial sector has spent about US$105m in lobbying fees in Washington for the first nine months of 2009 – down eight per cent on the previous year but still quite a chunk of change. Financial Leverage became the be-all and end-all of financial strategy. Simply put: if you have £100 to invest and buy £100 worth of shares which appreciate in value over a year by five per cent and also pay a 10 per cent dividend then your investment has grown to be worth £115. If you have that same £100 and a cheerful banker, you can persuade him to lend you £900 and when you buy £1,000 worth of shares, you'll deposit them all as security for the loan (see Non-Recourse for an important personal financial warning!). At the end of the year you'll receive a cash dividend of £100 and your shareholding will be worth a handsome £1,050. To repay the banker his loan plus three per cent interest you need £927, leaving you more than doubling your money with £223 in cash and shares. Sign me up for another year of this! You see how seductive a bubble can be! The investment guru Ben Graham (who is Warren Buffett's hero) always maintained that 'you can't go broke taking a profit' but it's hard to take your money off the roulette table when red has come up ten times in a row. And the way down hurts – if you are an investment bank levered up 35 times, then the value of your assets only needs to fall by three per cent to clean out every cent of equity. Does it still seem like a good idea?

LIBOR (London Inter Bank Offered Rate) The rate that banks don't actually lend to each other in the market. After Great Britain had spent all its pounds in saving the free world, the USA took over as the great financial powerhouse and the US (or 'Almighty') dollar became the world's favourite (or 'reserve' currency). The combination of banks holding US dollars in accounts outwith the continental USA and some ill-advised federal taxes for onshore transactions in the USA led London to create the Euro market – an offshore financing forum for the US dollar and eventually all sorts of currencies. In consequence, the British Bankers Association developed an interest rate setting methodology for these Euro currencies (including confusingly the Euro after its creation in 2000). The quirk in calculating LIBOR (and its sister LIBID, the index used to base deposit prices) is that it's not defined by actual trades: a panel of pre-agreed banks gives its individual opinion as to the rate at which it could borrow in the wholesale market at about 11 am London time. So you can imagine that any bank under stress as Lehman was about to fail felt honour bound to confirm that they would need to pay twice the previous month's rate to borrow. Or not. The calculation knocks off the top and bottom quotes, so there's some protection if a bank or two is out of kilter (as in the mid '90s when Japanese banks in London suffered heavily when it came to raising wholesale money to meet corporate loans based on LIBOR + margin totalling less than their cost of funds!), but when most of the banks are under pressure, that's a question that still needs to be answered.

There are other ways that interest rates are calculated:

- Discount (or official rates): each central bank announces at regular intervals the official rate at which it will lend short term money to recognised regulated banks. (There are usually other rates for banks borrowing 'from the window' to help with more pressing funding). The theory is that this official rate sets the market benchmark, so by reducing it the cost of borrowing in the wider economy falls, meaning more lending and spending to build the economy) or by increasing it, those costs go up (slowing down the economy). It has no direct or mathematical link to LIBOR, so when you hear comments that banks aren't passing on all the interest rate cuts, it's not always fair as the bank will be borrowing at LIBOR, has had to increase capital and potentially needs to increase margins to cover the worsening economic outlook.

- Base Rate or Prime Rate: commercial banks publish this rate which changes in line with official rates, but again has no link with LIBOR. In the olden days, the UK banks' Base Rate would be equal to the official rate +1 per cent and the minimum margin added to that would also be one per cent. This became known as the prime rate in the US (the rate that the best corporations would borrow at). These will soon be historical concepts, as the real cost of liquidity is both much more volatile and often more expensive.

Lipstick Index There are many long-held beliefs about how you can tell if we are in recession without looking at the economic data. I leave them to your judgement: In a recession

- Sales of red lipstick rise
- Sales of mints increase/sales of chocolate decline
- Skirt lengths fall
- Coffee shops close, supermarket sales of alcohol increase

Another example of 'voodoo' economics, but it does fill up long hours of speculation that could otherwise be used in even more unproductive endeavour within economics departments.

Living Will Just as ordinary folk fear facing their own mortality and thus often fail to write a will, the mega financial institutions believe in their own immortality and have no Plan B following corporate demise. When a bank fails, it's an awful mess, particularly if it has international branches or operations and can take years, if not decades, to sort out. The current proposal is that every institution should have a set of binding agreements with its regulator that would permit the complex group to be disaggregated in a crisis – critics say that doing this is akin to unscrambling eggs. Certainly it would imply a less efficient use of capital and liquidity while the bank was alive and functioning as individual subsidiaries or operations would have to hold their own buffers of both, rather than relying on balancing the books with Head Office by drawing down support, or by sweeping all excesses back to the mother ship each night. There will be a lot of discussion of this topic going forward.

Locusts A disparaging term coined by a German legislator to describe private equity firms. Herr Muenterfering (pronounced as in interfering) denounced these investors in 2004 as '*die Hauschreke*' – all severe insults sound more fun in a foreign language. (As GW Bush said, the French have no word for 'entrepreneur').

Mark-to-Market (Either the 'best idea in financial history' or the 'accountancy fetish which brought down the banks') For centuries only bankers knew how much their assets were really worth, for they were the only people with the information to do a complete analysis. On the other hand, a trading house or investment bank typically traded in things that were bought and sold on markets so you could see exactly how much those were worth. MTM works well in big liquid markets with many participants buying and selling. That's not always going to work today, alas. So you have Mark-to-Market in a few cases (e.g. Government bonds) where there is still a two-way market ('Level One' assets); Mark-to-Model, where no one's buying but there is an Excel spreadsheet that allows you to work out how much cash will be repaid ('Level Two' assets); and lastly, in the slop bucket, Mark-to-Myth, the toxic stuff that must be worth something to someone someday but you've just no idea how/who/when ('Level Three' if you can still believe these to be assets).

Masters of the Universe Initially a childish cartoon hero, subsequently (after Tom Wolfe's *Bonfire of the Vanities*) a leading investment banker. Neither is rooted in the real world but both share the characteristics of highly paid brands.

Merchant Bank An old fashioned English description of a kind of investment bank. These highly traditional firms either engaged in financing trade and commerce (the Accepting Houses) or advising companies and raising capital through shares and bonds (the Issuing Houses). Often based on a core of family members through generations, they combined financial innovation with an innate conservatism (dress standards being a famous example – a man wearing brown slip on shoes could not expect to progress his career). As blue blood hates red ink, they tended to be very cautious in committing the partnership to risk. Now these activities will be departments inside integrated investment banks or the universal banking behemoths.

Modelling Just as catwalk supermodels are an approximation of the human female, financial models are essentially unreal. The late great President Reagan was fond of a tale about the end of the Soviet Union. There in Red Square atop Lenin's tomb Mr Gorbachev is reviewing the military might of his Empire. Rank upon rank of tanks, missiles, bombs. Phalanx upon phalanx of stiff-legged soldiers, commandoes, marines and sailors, then at the end of the parade a disorganised bunch of guys in ill fitting civilian suits with yellow pads and pencils. When asked why this rag bag was involved, Gorby replied 'these are my economists – you have no idea how much more damage they do with their models'.

As all models have a degree of inefficiency, the more volume you force through them, the more apparent the difference. It's as if you were trying to fill your bath with bottled water – if you just needed to wash your hands, maybe one bottle would be enough – but by the time you've filled the whole bath – you can't get in because the bathroom is full of empty bottles. The danger is that the daily reliance on the model blinds its users to the real world outside.

'If the barometer is high and the clouds are black,' said JM Keynes, 'don't waste time on a debate on whether to take an umbrella.' One of the problems recently was that everyone was focused on his own electric barometer – no time to look out the window to see if the clouds were actually gathering. And it's the real world, not the measuring machine, that wins in the end.

The ultimate extension of the mantra 'you can only manage what you can measure' led to trading off the model regardless, bringing to fruition the old timer's prophecy from the '80s about what a trading room would look like in the future: each trading position of the desk will have a proprietary computer-driven trading model, an experienced trader and a large dog. The model makes all the trading decisions and automatically inputs them, the trader switches on the model on Monday and off on Friday. The dog bites the trader if he touches the model at any other time.

Moral Hazard If a regulator is unskilful, banks can run a high level of risk knowing that they will keep all the profits when they are lucky, but the regulator will have to rescue them if the bet goes against them. Not that any group of professionals would be that cynical. Sometimes called 'the privatisation of profit and the socialisation of losses'.

Narrow Bank In the simple world of politics there is a demand to find 'utility' banking services and to ring fence them from the risky 'casino' speculation of the tarnished investment banking world. This ignores the key point that all banking is risky. Unless you create the ultimate narrow bank – which would be like a safe deposit box, keeping all its deposits in cash or maybe government bonds and charging clients for the privilege – even a narrow bank will be involved in maturity transformation, taking in deposits and lending them out. Yes, you could restrict 'NB Limited' to customer deposits in amounts no greater than the government's deposit guarantee, with no dependence on the wholesale market but we also want NB Limited to lend to help stimulate its local economy – thus taking on liquidity risk and credit risk. That should mean that lending should be for no longer than the period that deposits are placed for – effectively a return to the old 'overdraft on demand' product which leaves small businesses vulnerable to losing funding overnight. Even narrow banks fail if they call those risks wrong. Is a narrow bank specialising in mortgage lending less risky than a well capitalised casino bank which only trades in government bonds? Of course, the real problem for narrow banks is how can they make money? Profit margins on the simplest products would be low, and the consumer will probably refuse to accept paying charges on current account services so who is going to provide the equity capital? Quite a big, and as yet, unanswered, question.

Nationalisation An outcome of bank stress – where the Government steps in and takes the institution into legal control. Politicians see this very much as a last step, though it's hard to see why if you think that informal or partial nationalisation is endemic, but it's one of those things it's rude to ask about. Given that the UK banks' total assets come to over 400 per cent of annual GDP (for France and Germany it's about 300 per cent, Spain a tad less, Japan and Canada round about 200 per cent and the US 100 per cent of an awfully big number), wholesale nationalisation does look to have its own problems. How can smaller countries with large financial crises survive without great pain. We watch Iceland and Ireland with interest.

Negative Equity That sinking feeling when the total amount outstanding on your mortgage is higher than the value of your house. In a logical world, where you buy a house as a home to live in and raise a family, Negative Equity isn't a real cashflow problem for you unless you suddenly need to sell your house – by moving to a new job in a new town, getting divorced and having to sell up, or becoming unemployed and unable to make repayments at the old level. It is of course irksome that you have to pay 'too much' money to the bank in repayments, but that's the contract you signed up to and if your income remains unchanged you can sit tight and not notice a difference. Unless interest rates start to rise and whittle away your monthly budget... Or if you come off your sweet tracker or fixed rate interest deal and the bank won't offer a new sweetheart rate because you've insufficient equity left in the house.

It can arise in one of two ways: you can either start off in Negative Equity by taking out one of the mortgage products that lends over 100 per cent of the value of the house (by rolling up fees or to help 'get a foot on the property ladder') which is basically both you and the financier taking a bet that house prices will rise, or you can get into Negative Equity by seeing a decline in the value of the house subsequent to buying it. The 1990s in the UK saw over 1.5 million households affected this time round, nearly a million families to date in the UK and in Ireland it is estimated that one in every four mortgages are under water. Looking forward, we can expect the same sort of bad tidings as a result of lax underwriting – with NINJA mortgagees (No Income No Job or Assets), self-certification (who needs a payslip when you have a good story) or buy-to-let (rhymes with one-way-bet), which is one of the main policy reasons for maintaining low interest rate environments. There is certainly more bad news to come, probably in a street near you.

Non-Recourse In the US a high proportion of mortgages were 'non-recourse' (ie you can hand your house keys back to the lender and walk away with no 'recourse'), whereas this is not the case in the UK. The prevalence of non-recourse home lending was one of the contributary factors in our current troubles. If you sell your house or car and there's not enough money to pay off the mortgage or loan, you have to pay the balance back out of your other savings (you do have other savings don't you?). This is the principle of recourse. If you take on an obligation you are responsible for meeting it in full and on time. Now there are ways around this. Some are shady: the old favourite is putting all your savings in the wife's name and all the debts in the husband's business (unless there is a formal guarantee in place from Mrs Money then the bank can go whistle when Mr Money can't pay up). Some are longstanding legal principles, the limited liability company being the most obvious: as shareholders we are not responsible for the debts contracted by the companies we own. That's why bankers traditionally took personal guarantees from the directors of businesses (and their wives) to keep that effective recourse. Sometimes, in fact increasingly over the boom, bankers agreed to structures that insulated the real borrower from his full recourse. Typically, the project or real estate development or leased asset or private equity investment would now be held in its own limited liability company (or 'Single Purpose Vehicle', the (in)famous SPV). The sponsor would inject a defined amount of cash as equity into the SPV and the bank would lend directly to the SPV. If things went awry, the bank could bankrupt the SPV and sell its assets, but the maximum loss to the sponsor was the amount of cash equity. He was not formally or contractually liable for any subsequent losses. The bank gets paid a higher margin on the loan and the sponsor limits his downside. Like all good ideas, it is capable of abuse and while there is a reputational risk in walking away, there are entrepreneurs who have built up personal wealth on a succession of failed non-recourse ventures without strictly breaking a single law or any contracts.

Operational Risk 'What can go wrong will go wrong'. As well as running credit risk and trading risk/market risk there are a bundle of things (rather prosaic things usually) that can go pear shaped. Fraud, of course, but more often cock-up and stupidity cost the money. There was a great case where one investment bank had an Excel spreadsheet to calculate its exposures in London, but the exchange rate cell referred to in the model was calculating the number using a totally different – and very wrong – cell. That cost a good fortune. This extra buffer of capital is needed to cover all these whoopsies.

Options A contract which gives the right but not the obligation to buy or sell a given agreed amount of an instrument or commodity on (or sometimes up to) a specified date at an agreed price.

OTC (Over The Counter) Any contract traded bilaterally – where two parties agree all the terms to suit themselves (compare Options, Futures). While the flexibility is undisputed, many commentators fear 'the devil is in the detail' and there are underlying conditions which one (or both) counterparties will not have evaluated in its risk calculation.

Pawnbroking A banking term for arranging a deal that looks unlikely to succeed in the long term, but where there's enough security to be sold to get the bank out of trouble. A well-structured deal should analyse the counterparty, the asset and the structure to reach a balanced opinion. But then if you know someone will buy it off you come what may then you might just take a short cut.

PIK 'Payment in Kind' Notes, derisively called 'Pay if You Can Notes'. A part of leveraged finance that means that rather than paying interest to lenders, the borrower (because there is no cash) issues a new bond which compounds interest at a furious rate to be redeemed at some future date when the business has turned the corner (bankers, therefore, hope it's not stuck on a roundabout).

Politicians The people who were happy to spend the vast corporation tax receipts from the banks in the boom years, to take donations from all financial groupings, to give out honours and titles, and to lift nearly half of the personal income (including the bonuses that they will later come to criticise) of the financial industry in tax, not to mention the VAT on the banker's Porsche and the stamp duty on his second home. Now they are the vociferous opponents of all that went before. It's a bit like the Chief of Police in the film *Casablanca*, (you must remember this) when Captain Renault closes Rick's café to please the Germans, ostensibly on the grounds of the illegal (but tolerated) casino in the back room. On the way out Renault is given his winnings by the croupier!

Ponzi A challenger for the most overused word in the Credit Crunch... But you have to be a class act to have a whole family of frauds named after you. Step into the limelight, Charles Ponzi. He followed the American dream, emigrating from Italy in the first years of last century and, recognising that fortune favoured the brave, tried to cheat his way to the top. His initial little scams were unsuccessful and he spent some time in the pen in Montreal and Atlanta.

But he hit the lode in Boston in 1919. That conservative, matronly city of finance woke up to find Mr Ponzi and The Securities And Exchange Co Inc offering remarkable rates for depositors. Who wouldn't want a 50 per cent gain every 45 days! There wasn't too much explanation (don't want the big guys muscling in) but the gist was whiz kid with a non-traditional background, nimble decision making and low-cost overheads – so all that lovely profit flows home to you and your Granny.

It was a much simpler scheme, though. The cost of investing was very low, because there were no investments. Maturing deposits were paid out of new incoming deposits. This pyramid scheme (as we call it in England – but still also a Ponzi scheme) depended on consistent drive for ever increasing investment from the public. The poor immigrant financed his share of the American dream by dipping into the flow of greenbacks. Silk suits, flash cars and a huge mansion underscored his success – the very sight of him walking down State Street with a solid gold handled cane had encouraged more people to come to his door to share in the largesse.

His only mistake was not to get out – and he was rumbled. Total collapse. Losses everywhere and a 10-year stretch for Ponzi.

And Charles's last thought on the subject?

'The public deserves exactly what it gets. No more. No less.'

Prime Broker For a long time the bankers who provided custody services (physically looking after the stock and shares in the days when they existed in the form of real paper certificates) and 'settlements' (shifting them back and forward to the registrars and exchanges) were regarded as the Cinderellas of the financial world. As hedge funds grew, someone had the bright idea of bundling up these two effectively risk-free businesses (plus reporting and account keeping) with banking services like keeping deposits and also real risk activities such as margin lending and stock lending. This was a great product for hedge funds because, in theory, the prime broker could see all the financial position at any time and so was the best person to lend to the hedgie. So this Prime Brokerage product became a way to capture the cash, trading and financing of big funds. Of course, if the whole market is going to Hell in a Handcart, then the Prime Broker is having as much fun as any other banker. Maybe a bit less. Maybe a great deal less.

Private Equity A methodology for obtaining vast sums of debt to buy and restructure companies. Lauded by supporters as a business model which perfectly aligns the interests of owners and managers; or decried by others as a scheme to use bank money to acquire companies in a tax efficient way before inflicting financial pain on the workforce and flogging off all the assets.

Procyclical Not merely in favour of wider use of the bicycle in modern transportation. (There was an elderly member of the Kleinwort's banking family who lived on a hill in North London and boasted that he still cycled to work – he did each morning, but getting the Daimler home in the afternoon, and using another bike the following morning down the hill with a van delivering five bikes home each Saturday to renew the cycle in both senses.) Many bankers are tempted to follow a similar philosophy in their lending. Downhill as fast as you can, but when the hill rises in front of you, get off the bike. This means that too many banks tend to lend too much going into the end of a boom (larger amounts, lower graded counterparties, weaker structures, longer tenors and cheaper prices) then when the economic cycle turns, overcompensation happens – firstly, to rebuild the bank's battered capital; secondly, as stronger counterparties defer capex and borrowing needs; and finally, as the loan officers who made the bad decisions are now scared to make new decisions. Nowadays, this is magnified by Basle II, which makes banks set aside greater capital in downturns, reducing the volume that can be lent (see Politicians).

Pro-Forma Numbers The financial results you had hoped to make rather than what the accountants believe can be reported fairly. Pro-forma adjustments are usually adding profit to a company by flagging onetime items (the cost of closing a division, the bills involved in settling a lawsuit or strike – that sort of one-off incident that you could say actually obscures an investor's ability to analyse the company's performance.) On the other hand, all life (in business or at home) is a mass of one offs, so critics of pro-formas ('bad stuff adjustment') often see it as putting a shine on the issues.

Quantitative Easing There comes a point in every crisis when the central bank is lowering interest rates to stimulate the economy but realises that it can't go below zero. As the theory is that more people will borrow money if rates are low (or at least, some people will borrow more) then QE is a scheme where the Bank offers to buy government or corporate bonds, thus directly releasing cash into the seller's hands, to increase demand and stimulate a bit of well-controlled inflation. Critics call this 'printing money' and compare the process to countries like Zimbabwe (where inflation is virtually impossible to calculate – with serious estimates at 100,000,000,000,000,000,000,000,000,000,000,000,000,000,000,000,000,000,000,000,000,000,000,000,000,000,000,000,000,000,000,000,000,000,000,000,000,000,000,000,000,000,000,000,000,000,000,000,000,000,000,000,000,000,000,000,000,000,000,000,000,000,000,000,000,000,000,000,000,000,000,000,000,000,000,000,000,000 per cent per annum – a public toilet on the Zambian border exhorts visitors to use the loo roll provided as Zim dollars clog up the drains). Of course our Western banks create the money electronically, so that's a good thing.

Quants Extraordinarily highly paid bank analysts (or at least they were), as they used university maths to create real world profits. Famously described as fabulously clever but colour-blind artists doing painting by numbers by algorithm assuming that the numbers on the paint pots and the paper were 100 per cent aligned. Nice Monet if you can get it.

Queer Street The old term for being broke on Lombard Street and Wall Street. There are relatively few financial companies with a real presence on the physical thoroughfares of Lombard Street and Wall Street, yet they remain in the rhetoric of finance as our financial arenas. Oddly enough, Lombard Street, San Francisco, is famously twisty and is called the second crookedest street the USA (after Wall Street in Manhattan of course!).

Recession An unpopular word. Myth maintains that the word 'banana' has to be used within the White House as its use of the R world would knock the economic parrot off his perch. The technical definition (which is pretty impractical) is that a recession starts after two consecutive quarters of negative GDP growth (obvious temptation is to quote your GDP statistics annually...) but many commentators feel that there are overlays of pessimism and consumer feeling which add colour to that. President Reagan said in his first presidential campaign: 'It's a recession when your neighbour loses his job; it's a depression when you lose your job; it's a recovery when President Carter loses his.'

Red Ink If this were a commodity it would have rocketed in value as demand grew to write up the write-offs.

Reputational Risk Don't ever do a deal (or when you think of it, any human or inhuman endeavour) if you'd be ashamed to have your Mum read about it on the front page of the local paper. Reputational risk is very real: the risk that what seems to be a great transaction will make you money but lose you friends, colleagues, regulatory goodwill and ultimately a pay packet.

This time round, it all got so complex that the local papers wouldn't print it as no one could understand it – it only came home when the bricks started to fly.

Rights Issue When things are going wrong, it's time to come up with the rights. Many jurisdictions insist that a company should offer any new equity being raised to the existing shareholders on the register first (pre-emption), otherwise their holding in the company would be reduced (diluted) by the entrance of new capital. For many bank shareholders, this was their chance to launch good money after bad... One of the big worries if you own shares in a company is that you will be diluted. If you own 10 per cent of the issued shares you will receive 10 per cent of the announced dividend. If the company issues more shares to other people then your percentage drops, and all things being equal, your income too. There are other problems it can cause, so in many markets there is a concept of 'pre-emption' – the right of existing shareholders to have first dibs on any new shares – that right is offered through a mechanism called a Rights Issue. (If you ever owned bank equity, you'll know to your cost what this means.) The shares are often offered at a discount (a 'deep discount' if the cash is needed quickly) and is usually underwritten by a major bank (or in very dangerous times even Governments in the form of part-nationalisation we have just seen.) Not saving but drowning...

Rogue Traders An officer of a bank (or other company) in the dealing room who undertakes trades outwith his authority or mandate. Always use this term in reference to those who do so and make losses. Rarely seen are the rogue traders who make a profit being canned. Like most things, this scenario can only occur if others in the system willingly (albeit unwittingly) assist. From counterparty traders who perhaps see unusual volumes or odd strategies but trade anyway (he's in a loss, so you will make a profit as he goes down), to the failure of the internal controls and processes or the joy of management who see the profit flowing. At this stage in the cycle every trader is regarded by the papers as a near criminal, so it's been a while since anyone has broken the rules.

We've talked about the iconic Leeson – the poster child of Rogue Trading – but like all our amnesias, rogue traders come round and round. The investigations currently include some former traders at Soc Gen (where the numbers involved top US$7bn lost on stock index futures) and Caisse d'Epergne who lost only about a tenth of that. They have the potential to enter the history books alongside John Rusnak (ex AIB) who plea-bargained a sentence of seven and a half years for a US$691m loss. In terms the ratio of sentence of years/hundred million lost, he appears as bad a plea-bargainer as a trader – the greatest rogue (thus far discovered) was Toshihide Iguchi, who was so good at Daiwa that he was only caught on his own confession when it got too much for him. The staggering story of over 30,000 dodgy trades in a rogue career of 11 years in the US bond market seems unsurpassable. The result? The regulators shut Daiwa's operation in the US (hear the noise of the stable door) and Iguchi-san got four years and a fine of US$2.6m. Cheap at the price.

Run The fear that if you don't get your money out of the bank first, someone else will and there won't be enough for you. Commentators had believed that this could not happen in developed economies any more, but that just goes to show that human fear is deeper rooted than a classical education in economics. The concept is quite sweet in *Mary Poppins* when the Banks children refuse to deposit their tuppences in the Dawes, Tomes, Mousely, Grubbs Fidelity Fiduciary Bank but rather starker for the grown-ups at Northern Rock. And, unlike Jimmy Stewart in *It's a Wonderful Life*, there's no happy ending in sight yet!

Securitisation A good tool put to odd uses. If you were a chicken farmer (and if you were with Lehman you might just be one now) imagine the simplest way to do business. Take a basket of chickens to market and sell them live. Every happy customer gets the fun of wringing its neck, plucking it and eating it all. But the consumer certainly doesn't like that. So we have a model that someone grows the chickens, delivers them to a processing centre where they are dispatched neatly and carved up into different cuts. If we have thousands of chickens then we can package the meat up, ranging from top grade breast meat only, or brown meat thighs, to a bucket of legs, we can sell the wings to bars in Buffalo, the bones for soup and the feathers for pillows. Everything else goes into chicken nuggets, and of course there are many more nuggets than breasts. That's how securitisation works, but using financial instruments, not chickens. They still come home to roost, alas.

Shadow Banking Or, if you are in a bad mood, you can call it regulatory arbitrage. Legal structures such as Conduits and Structured Investment Funds that are lightly capitalised and depend on wholesale funding to buy tracts of assets from banks which otherwise would have to apportion a lot of capital to keep those loans on the parent balance sheet – did I say 'parent', that's the wrong word – as the bank and the shadow are completely independent (at least in strict legal and accounting terms). However, of the 29 SIVs in existence in July 2009, 13 of them were taken over and reconsolidated with the original sponsor bank to avoid the fate of those who totally collapsed where investors are reported to have lost between 50 per cent and 85 per cent of their investment. It's a bit like reducing your risk at home by storing dynamite, not in the attic, but in the garage. OK – it's not 'at home' any more, but when it goes off, it's going to annoy your neighbours, increase your insurance and give you a big headache even if you try to walk away. The term is not unrelated to the concept in law of a Shadow Director: a person (often a banker) who exercises effective control over a company without being a legally appointed director.

Shorting The act of selling stock or shares that you don't own in the hope of buying them cheaper to make a profit. The New York market has a rhyme:

> He who sells what isn't his 'n
>
> Must buy it back or go to prison.

Usually regarded in the press as a satanic act and usually very strictly regulated (and, in fact, was banned in many jurisdictions as an exceptional step when bank shares were falling rapidly in the crisis). Supporters say that it is just a strategy like any other – without ethical implications – which in fact helps liquidity, creating sellers to match with buyers (opponents point out that when you are shorting there are often dam' few mugs out there buying – so it is a one-way trade) and that a short seller has relatively little upside compared with the long investor – the short's profit potential is limited by the share reaching zero. The truth is probably somewhere in between, but it is hard not to see professional shorters as the people pointing out the way to the cliff for the lemmings having sold them life cover a few minutes before.

Sorry 'Sorry Seems To Be The Hardest Word', in the lyrics of the Elton John/Bernie Taupin hit. This is a sentiment apparently shared by many of the world's banking leaders (with some very honourable exceptions). The overall lack of contrition and some of the 'business as usual' attitudes around remuneration in particular have gathered strong words in opposition from leading commentators and particularly church leaders. The Archbishop of Canterbury marked the anniversary of the financial collapse in a BBC interview with these stinging words: 'There hasn't been what I would, as a Christian, call repentance. We haven't heard people saying 'well actually, no, we got it wrong and the whole fundamental principle on which we worked was unreal, was empty'.' Or the UK's Chief Rabbi in *The Times* in March 2009: 'The continuing disclosures about excessive pensions and payoffs, salaries and bonuses for people at the top stir in us feelings for the oldest of human blood sports: the search for a scapegoat. But they ought to lead us to think more deeply about the values of our culture as a whole... the gradual disappearance of the cluster of principles that went by the name of morality.' From The Vatican, Pope Benedict issued an Encyclical warning: 'Once profit becomes the exclusive goal, if it is produced by improper means and without the common good as its ultimate end, it risks destroying wealth and creating poverty.' It's rare to find a paragraph that starts citing Elton John and ends up quoting the Pontiff, which proves how widespread the genuine concern is.

Sovereign Wealth Fund (SWF) Just as Clausewitz propounded that 'war is nothing but a continuation of politics by other means', so is the SWF is the continuation of politics by the use of a wall of money. SWFs represent a huge pool of money amassed by a government and generally gained from oil or commodities sold and making profits in US dollars. The UK rather unwisely spent the largesse of the North Sea with little if anything to show for the ride. Initially institutions like KIA (Kuwaiti Investment Authority) were created as 'fund managers' in the London market to place deposits and invest in bonds and equities. Now their immense holdings can be used globally and geopolitically resulting in a range of protectionist measures from investee nations to 'safeguard' strategic or systemic assets from overseas investors. Of course, it doesn't always run smoothly. The Finance Minister of Brunei (who was the ruling Sultan's brother) was alleged to have overseen an 'investment strategy' that resulted in personal lawsuits to recover US$8bn from him which was spent under his watch (a diamond and gold Rolex Oyster I'd bet) by the Brunei SWF. While Brunei and BIA managed to build a portfolio of prestige assets – the Sultan's favourite Dorchester Hotel in London was joined by investments in Asprey's the Bond Street jeweller and a raft of prime real estate in London, New York, and internationally. Additionally, however, investments which looked more like lifestyle purchases abounded: nearly two thousand cars from top marques, a small fleet of jets and helicopters, a collection of Modigliani paintings and one of the world's most tasteless superyachts. The Sultan was not a happy investor when all this came to light. It's hard getting the right management for your SWF!

Spivs Not a kind of investment vehicle (Special Purpose Investment Vehicles) but a popular term of abuse for bank traders, using an old term coined for the profiteers and opportunists who traded black market luxuries in the Second World War such as Walker in *Dad's Army* or Flash Harry at St Trinians. On the other hand, a SPV (**Single Purpose Vehicle**) is a legal company usually in a tax friendly (i.e. low/no taxes payable) jurisdiction (BVI, Grand Cayman, Aruba, etc.) which is created to hold one transaction to insulate its sponsors from the risk of failure. If the transaction goes bad, then the bank loses only the tiny share capital of the SPV. Sometimes they are known as 'brass plate' companies, because the only physical existence they have is a shiny name plate on a foreign attorney's door. One building in Bermuda is reputed to be the headquarters for 60,000 different corporations. Must be quite busy if they all hold their Christmas party on the same night.

Subprime If you haven't worked this out by now, it's too late – go back to page 1. If you can afford to buy the book, that is.

Swap The most common OTC derivative. They haven't yet developed one for Toxic Assets, or Broken Hopes.

Swindle JK Galbraith maintained that there was a calculable amount of money siphoned out of the financial system at any time, which he called the Bezzle in the boom. The bezzle actually adds (albeit briefly) to the economy's growth but then in the bust it not only reduces but creates a climate of distrust. Until the good times roll again.

Teenage scribblers A popular insult for bank economists and forecasters.

Terrorist: An emotive term: I am a freedom fighter; you are a guerilla; he/she/it is a terrorist. Just as the government of Iceland thought things couldn't get worse after the collapse of its banking sector where the three biggest groups had borrowed €50bn in the international interbank market that needed repaying out of local currency where the kronur was plunging against the Euro effectively multiplying the banks' repayment. All the banks went bust, the currency fell to a quarter of its average value in euro terms, the stockmarket dived over 90% and the repayment of deposits to account holders in foreign branches including the UK looked challenging. And this looked as if it was only the tip of the iceberg. To protect British residents, HM Government extended the UK deposit guarantee scheme but in reprisal froze Icebank's accounts (too good a joke to miss) but in a rather odd way. Ministers invoked the provisions of part 2, article 4 of Anti-Terrorism Crime and Security Act 2001 which was enacted after 9/11 to 'freeze the assets of overseas governments or residents who have taken, or are likely to take, action to the detriment of the UK's economy'. So in one sweep of the pen, poor old Iceland (a fellow member of NATO after all) entered an exclusive club of about 7,000 odd people ranging from al-Qaeda all the way to the Government of Zimbabwe. Intergovernmental relationships remain strained.

Tobin Tax A mad belief that by adding a tax on every single financial transaction you can save the world by using that enormous stash of wealth to (a) reduce the amount paid to evil bankers and simultaneously (b) cure cancer, save donkeys from the knackers' yard or promote climate change. James Tobin of Yale came up with this idea to combat currency speculation after the US came off the Gold Standard in 1971. It ignored the experience learned when the US introduced Regulation Q (Reg-Q) which imposed official rates for one month US dollar deposits from 1957. As the East Bloc countries were increasingly scared of the political risk of depositing their dollars in New York banks during the Cold War, this saw the start of the Eurodollar market (where London became a rival – and a strong rival – to Wall Street in holding offshore deposits and recycling them into dollar-denominated loans). Arbitrary taxation of any industry leads either to ways of avoidance (as it's worth spending lots of fees to find the inevitable loopholes) or a wholesale move to another (untaxed) centre. Another great example demonstrating that economics is too important to be left in the hand of economists. Even Nobel laureates.

Too Big To Fail The biggest question of them all! And now applicable to other sectors such as auto manufacturers and airlines. It can only be time for airports, steelworks and rail franchises to follow. Once the phrase meant that the bank was so broad and balanced it could not fall over, its natural weight and capital would see it wobble but not fall down ('Weebles'

Law'). Now it refers to those institutions that trade with everyone, or have a particular market share in a complex trading field or whose failure would cause impossible shockwaves through 'the system'. The USA thought that it could drop Lehman and that was a bad idea, so now everyone with a big trading book and international counterparties is looked at in a different light.

Toxic Seemed like a good idea at the time. This is a wonderfully evocative and emotional term which is impossible to define, but you'd know it if you had it on your balance sheet. Fossilised ingenuity stuck to the sole of the financial shoe. Another way to look on it is that it was a deal which made its bank originator a huge bonus last year and which makes a great write-off this year, thus inviting the shareholder to pay twice. Or even three times.

Trading Book Regulators look at bank assets in a couple of ways – the Banking Book (simplistically) holds bank loans and the Trading Book holds securities in the course of being traded. The former holds the credit risk of the borrowers lent to while the latter is more 'market' risk – that the price would move negatively in between the trader buying and selling. In simple logic, a credit risk could wipe out the whole loan amount, while trading risks were unlikely to reach that catastrophic level. Once upon a time, when these were simple and liquid (corporate bonds, government securities) then the Trading Book 'turned' regularly and little capital was required. As traders dealt in more complex instruments, regulators did not think to ratchet up the amount of capital to be applied to assets that had come out of the Banking Book, for example (CDOs, CLOs). When the music stopped, the Trading Book was full of less liquid assets than some of the Banking Book. Not a good idea, for the capital levels held were far too low in general.

Underwriting Taking the risk on the deal by buying the shares or bonds and expecting to sell them off quickly for a profit. The greatest underwriting disaster was the privatisation of BP, which happened during the 1987 stockmarket crash. The four underwriters had agreed the price with HM Government but hadn't time to sell into the retail market, so the firms were significantly in trouble and the Bank of England had to offer help by repurchasing the shares, but even then the firms carried a US$300m+ loss on the trade. Don't worry, they are all still in business!

Usurers Naughty people. Make bankers look like Boy Scouts.

VaR Value at Risk, a mathematical tool which works very well for 95 per cent of the time, well enough for 99 per cent, and once in a while it is as much predictive use as a compass in an iron mine. It was nice to know how much the bank had lost on a daily basis historically. The problem was the outlier – the infamous fat tail – there would be one or two days a year where the sky could be the limit, and when all the variables went volatile in this market, ouch.

It's a bit like going to a clam shack on the beach at South Carolina and looking at the marks the owner has carved in the wall showing how high the tide came in during the various hurricane seasons. You get pretty comfy that four-foot high water has been the worst and the old shack survived. Then you go back a hundred yards landwards to the next one. It shows the highest tide at 22 feet – which of course had washed the predecessor of the first shack out to sea. We set all our models in that first shack. Splosh. Get your waterproofs on quickly. What do you mean you don't bring them on vacation? Collective Amnesia again!

Vultures A fund with the capital and financing to pick over the bones of failed businesses to extract the assets which will increase in value, leaving the bad debt and weaker assets in the hands of the previous hapless management or their bankers and administrators. Pejorative, but effective.

Wimbledonisation Just as England holds Wimbledon, the greatest Grand Slam event in the sport of tennis, but hasn't won the finals in donkey's years, (Men's 1938, Ladies' 1977) so the City of London is said to be the greatest financial and trading centre even though all the investment banks were bought out by the Americans (with a bit of help from the French, Dutch, Japanese and Germans).

Window The emergency funding facility offered by a central bank. The idea is that any bank (broadly speaking) should be able to deposit good-quality collateral (even if illiquid) and then receive funding in return.

Window Ledge Supposedly in 1929 a stockbroker tried to book a hotel room just off Wall Street in a high building. 'Is that for sleeping or jumping Sir?' asked the clerk. It's a myth I am afraid, but perhaps one which made the poverty stricken see that there was some justice in the world. (As in the old joke: 'What do you call one banker on a window ledge?' 'A good start!')

Wrap What a monoline or other insurer does to a complicated or risky deal so that the simplest minds in the market can buy a share of the transaction. Not without its own risks as the cover is only valuable if the wrapper has the capital strength to meet its obligations.

Exchange Traded (I couldn't think of anything interesting beginning with X – sorry). Whether ships or satsumas, swaps or Sterling, you can buy and sell anything but the age-old problem is that unless both parties meet together and hand over the goods and the cash simultaneously, there is counterparty risk – the risk of releasing your money and not getting the goods.

When I was a wee boy in Ayr I wanted a pet and there was a man at the harbour who had a big sign – pet seagulls £5 each. It sounded like a good idea, so I ran home to get my piggy bank savings (even then I was distrustful of banks) and ran all the way to the harbour. I handed over my life savings and asked for my new best friend. That's him up there he said, pointing to a grey one circling overhead...

The risks in these 'over-the-counter trades' can be mitigated by trading on a regulated exchange. The exchange offers a number of important protections:

- The products you can buy are standardised – you know exactly what you are getting.

- The exchange has rules governing how trading, settlement, etc. are conducted and it imposes a code of conduct and discipline on the members allowed to trade.

- The exchange is regulated by Government and the traders are in turn regulated by the exchange.

- When you buy or sell from a broker operating on the exchange, the trade you complete is split into two parts: a trade between you and the exchange, and a trade between the exchange and the broker. Your risk is now the exchange itself and not the financial institution – if your original trader goes bust your trade will still be settled.

- The exchange mitigates its risk by calling for margin – required payments as security in case of default.

Yard Banking slang for a billion. Some say it's an abbreviation of the old 'milliard'.

Yield The return an investor makes on an investment, or doesn't.

Yield Curve The relationship between interest rates and time. Normally interest rates are greater the longer the period, encouraging people to borrow short-dated money cheaply to invest in long-dated higher yielding paper. An inverted curve is where the opposite happens.

Zombie Companies or banks who have their capital destroyed, but by dint of not writing off bad assets or by government support manage to lumber on in the imitation of life. A real problem in the Japanese economy where banks failed to take real action in the 1990s. A key issue here and now.

> 'When I use a word,' Humpty Dumpty said, in rather a scornful tone, 'it means just what I choose it to mean – neither more nor less.'
>
> 'The question is,' said Alice, 'whether you can make words mean so many different things.'
>
> 'The question is,' said Humpty Dumpty, 'which is to be master – that's all.'
>
> Lewis Carroll, *Alice Through The Looking Glass,* 1896

Part VI
A Memorable Chronology of Collective Amnesia

3 1/3 silver sigloi, at interest of 1/6 sigloi and 6 grains per sigloi, has Amurritum, servant of Ikun-pi-Istar, received on loan from Ilum-nasir. In the third month she shall pay the silver owed. Witnesses: Salsalum, son of Uqa, Sissu-I, Nur-Ea, Daserum, su-Belitum, the scribe.

> Cuneiform tablet recording a loan, *c.*1800BC, Mesopotamia
> (Bank of Italy Collection)

Banking is as old as the devil

> Bert Heemskerk, 2009

How your
Early Ancestors lost their money

Other than losing your wealth through natural disasters such as fire, plague, war and death, there seem to have been ways to become poorer using banking and investment tools as early as 2000BC when King Hammurabi of Babylon cast the oldest existing code of laws which contained rules about loans, deposits and investments (including defaults).

These were themes taken up in the books of the law of Moses, then the Chinese, Egyptians and Greeks all developed the business which has started to get a bad name by the time Jesus chased the money changers out of the Temple.

Possibly the first big banking bust was the fall of the Knights Templar in 1307. The Templars had a very modern banking proposition – their backbone of castles across Europe and into the Holy Land provided impenetrable vaults for storing extraordinary wealth. Pilgrims and settlers found the perfect service – depositing their riches safely in the Temple in London or Paris and, armed with a Letter of Credit and a bodyguard of fighting monks, they could draw out enough gold for living expenses from the Temple when they arrived in Jerusalem. As a by-line the money in the home vaults could be lent to the King to finance the Crusades (and any peccadilloes at the Royal Court). The mistake the Order made as bankers was a big one – they lent far too much to a borrower who had no intention of repaying. The day came when it was easier for the King of France to denounce the Templars as heretics and devil worshippers – once all the bankers have been burned at the stake, there's no one left to ask him for the money back! Holey de Moley!

The next 300 years saw bankers/goldsmiths and kings/princes play a game of running up debts and then running them out of town. The real world of ordinary people losing money started about four centuries ago. The advent of modern financial markets allowed us all to share in the losses.

How your GREAT GREAT GREAT GREAT GREAT GREAT Grandparents lost their money		
1618	Holy Roman Empire	Debased the coinage (not surprising since the organisation was not particularly holy, certainly not Roman and arguably hardly an empire).
1634	Tulips	One of the greatest and daftest bubbles was one of the first. Bouquets all round! (see Case Studies).
1640	King Charles I	As one of many counterproductive ideas to keep the royal revenues healthy without calling parliament, the king disrupts the markets by buying two years production of pepper forcibly from the East India company and selling it at a loss, then he 'borrows' the goldsmiths' gold from the Mint and 'forgets' to give it back.
1672	King Charles II	Owes a truckload to the goldsmiths and bankers, and stops all state payments to them out of the exchequer, conveniently bankrupting his personal creditors. This would remain a sore memory, leading to the creation of an independent banking company, the Bank of England in 1694.

How your GREAT GREAT GREAT GREAT GREAT Grandparents lost their money		
1698 – 99	**The Darien Disaster**	William Paterson, who founded the Bank of England, next persuaded Scotland to launch a colony in Central America. Disaster ensued – a combination of unfriendly natives and even less friendly English politics cost Scotland over half its population's savings and the loss of the country's independence soon followed.
1719 – 20	**Mississippi Scheme**	France goes pop: the revolution in finance leads to the Revolution in France. (see Case Studies).
1720	**South Sea Bubble**	Parliament (with its nose in the trough) fails to control a crooked share bubble. (see Case Studies).
1772 – 73	**Ayr Bank Collapse**	A small but feisty Scottish bank takes on the big boys until the liquidity dries up. (see Case Studies).
1792 – 93	**English Canals**	Another lack of liquidity – an early tech boom (and an early bust). Life's a ditch.

How your GREAT GREAT GREAT GREAT Grandparents lost their money		
1825	**Latin American Bonds**	At least the pretty old bonds have a value framed on the wall, the paper from later crises has lower artistic qualities. 'Emerging Markets' (see Case Studies).
1825	**The Failure of Messrs. Pole Thornton**	A major London 'correspondent bank' is saved at the eleventh hour by a whisker, but the rumours wipe out many other banks from county towns. We don't have space to include all the banking crises. (UK, for example: 1809, 1816, 1836, 1837 aka the 'W Bank' crisis, 1847 aka suspension of the Bank Charter Act, 1857, 1873, 1890, 1906–07). (or in the USA: 1819, 1837, 1847, 1857, 1873, 1884, 1890 and 1896).
1836–38	**Cotton**	Supporting British industry but the financiers lost the thread.
1847–48	**UK Railways**	George Hudson's tech boom – limitless increases in productivity allow limitless growth in borrowing (with limited ability to repay). (see Case Studies).
1857	**US Railways**	The battles of Commodore Vanderbilt (like Hudson, his statue still stands in prominence) and the first Robber Baron fortunes.
1866	**Overend Gurney**	The banker's bank ends up on its own gurney. This was such a shocking blow, it was the last major bank run in England until now.

How your GREAT GREAT GREAT Grandparents lost their money		
1873	**US Railroads**	Once more with gusto – the *grand guignol* of Fiske and Gould – and the firework end of Jay Cooke. The era of the Robber Barons.
1878	**City of Glasgow Bank**	All the directors ended up in jail after fraudulent accounting and bad lending caused economic havoc in the second city of the Empire.
1890	**Barings**	Baring all for the first and not the last time – at least this time they did it themselves without a rogue trader. (see Case Studies).

How your GREAT GREAT Grandparents lost their money		
1907	New York Bank Panic	JP Morgan's nose is all that stands between the collapse of the Knickerbocker Trust and Doomsday on the New York Stock Exchange. A dry run for 1929.
1914 – 18	The Great War	The opening shots of war forced a one-month moratorium on the London market and signalled the beginning of the end of London's dominance of world finance.
1926 – 27	Florida Homes	Hot money seeking warmer climates starts a boomlet in waterside properties. The lucky investors cashed in early (to invest in Wall Street), the rest are probably still selling oranges beside the freeway. From Panhandle to panhandler.
1929	**The Great Crash**	Form an orderly queue along the window ledge, please, gentlemen. Followed of course by the Great Depression. 'I am convinced we have now passed through the worst ... and shall rapidly recover,' President Herbert Hoover 1 May, 1930. Hmm.

How your
GREAT
Grandparents lost their money

Actually, they were too busy coping with the Depression and the War to lose anything. After both they had precious little to lose.

Interestingly, David Kynaston in his magisterial history *The City of London* vol III (1915–45) has no banking crises in the index; compared with 14 in vol I (1815–90) and six in vol II (1891–1914).

Fortunately after a generation of hard work, they had sufficient funds to bequeath to the next generation to start to lose it again.

How your Grandparents lost their money		
1965 – 70	**Nifty Fifty**	These 50 large cap us stocks are only going one way – if you didn't go bust holding them 30 years ago they're probably a good core investment now.
1971	**Collapse of Bretton Woods System**	The us ends the convertibility of the greenback into gold. The world moves to a new paradigm of floating foreign exchange rates (and higher bonuses for FX dealers).
1973 – 75	**UK Secondary Bank Crisis**	Liberalisation of the Bank of England's rules in 1971 led to a boom in lending. Following the 73/74 bear market on Wall Street and London; with rising oil prices (another pair of crises) the smaller UK banks who had lent heavily on real estate were forced to the wall. The Old Lady coordinated a 'lifeboat' – it only sold its last shares in these institutions in the late '80s.
1973 – 80	**Inflation**	The loosening of interest rates in response to oil price rises by OPEC results in long-term persistent inflation until the Reagan/Thatcher years. (a gross simplification but all that I can fit in this box).
1973 – 89	**The LDC (Less Developed Country) Crisis**	Countries Don't Go Bust (Ha!), they just don't pay for years... Mexico, Brazil, Argentina and Venezuela led a group of 27 LDC nations in rescheduling us$240 bn of international debts.

How your Parents lost their money		
1982 – 91	**S&L Crisis**	Thrifts turn out to be less than thrifty, endangering the whole US banking system – about 750 banks fail at a cost of US$170bn. (see Case Studies).
1987	**October Crash**	First we had a hurricane in London which knocked down most of our trees, and then the stockmarket did it to our pockets.
1987 – whenever	**Japan's Banking System**	Bubble in the 80s, Minsky in 87 and then a feast of Zero interest rates, Zombies, and a lack of political will – when just a few years before people predicted that Japanese capital was about to buy California and New York. Now, stagnation for generations.
1990	**Nordic Banking Crisis**	Was it one crisis or three? All of the major Nordic institutions (except Iceland – its time would come) face unprecedented pressure and governmental control.
1990 – 91	**UK Corporate Accounting Scandals**	As the UK slipped into recession, several major UK corporates collapsed with questions over their accounting treatment (including Atlantic Computers – Maxwell again – and Polly Peck).
1991	**BCCI Closed**	BCCI goes from being the seventh biggest bank in the world to nothing in moments as regulators step in after uncovering rather enthusiastic banking practices.

1990 – 98	**Negative Equity**	The UK housing boom goes into reverse – many families (particularly in London and the South East) have mortgage debts in excess of the current market value of their house.
1994	**Mexican Peso Crisis**	After hard work in liberalising the economy, US dollar debt was sucked in to finance the real estate boom. A devaluation of the peso caught borrowers and lenders in a vice.
1997	**Asian Banking Crisis**	Booms in the tiger economies were financed by foreign denominated debts and borrowing. Thailand abandoned its currency link to the US dollar and the collapse engulfed Indonesia, S Korea and then other Asian nations.
1998	**Long Term Capital Management (LTCM)**	The cleverest minds make the cleverest models which make the dumbest mistakes in the real world losing US$5bn – the NY Fed holds a midnight party to defuse the time bomb successfully.
2000	**dot com Boom (and bust)**	Everyone owned tech stocks until the mammoth (and not very successful) Time Warner/AOL acquisition in January 2000. Then the events of 9/11 changes the mood from optimism to pessimism – with a consequent effect on stockmarket prices and a fair few jail sentences.
2001	**Enron**	Fast growth and faster accounting ballooned this energy company all the way up the stock charts into the courthouse.

How
YOU'VE just lost your money

At the practical level, you've just participated in an asset boom fuelled by virtually unlimited and relatively cheap borrowing (this goes for you whether you are an ordinary punter or one of the formerly biggest banks in the world) and guess what? It couldn't go onwards and upwards forever.

Philosophically, while there are arguments that say it's hard to set quantitative judgements about asset and bubbles, that's a total cop out. Look at the history of repeated failure. It has happened again and again and it will happen again and again.

This chronological approach shouldn't be a surprise: Charles Kindleberger taught this to us all. With thanks to him.

À la recherche de l'argent perdu...

How your
KIDS will lose their money

I've left this blank for you to fill in any of the above repetitive ways to lose money.

Whatever does happen will be a variant of one of the wheezes above. If or when we challenge Collective Amnesia – can we do it? From the long view it doesn't look like a good bet!

Reporter: 'Why do you rob banks?'

Willy Sutton: 'Because that's where the money is.'

Willy Sutton, Bank Robber, 1901–1980

What is robbing a bank compared with founding a bank?

Bertold Brecht, *Die Dreigroschenoper*, 1928

Book Group Discussion Topics

1   If a doctor had treated his patient the way financial regulators supervised their banks would s/he have been struck off for negligence?

2   What is the best solution to the 'agency problem'? Are bonuses the best way to align the interests of a bank's shareholders with those of its employees? What about those of customers and the wider population?

3   What is an asset bubble and can you see it as it happens? How come we all saw house prices rise faster than the cost of living but Messrs Greenspan and Bernanke didn't?

4   Would you borrow £50 from twenty friends which had to be paid back on Friday and then lend a thousand pounds to your partner to buy a second hand car which he needs to use to stay in a job?

5   To what extent is government policy influenced by the risk of losing corporation taxes from banks and income tax from bankers' pay and bonuses in the good years? Can anyone recall a financial minister cautioning the rate of growth in taxable profits from the banking sector?

6   Should there be statutory rules on how much a person can borrow to buy a house? Should equity withdrawal be banned again?

7   Is it safe to assume that economists live in the real world?

8   Should banks be supervised or regulated? Does it make a difference?

9   Should bank CEOs, politicians, central bank governors, analysts, financial economists, regulators or investors say 'sorry'?

10 Do you feel it's still 'business as usual' in the banking sector?

11 Will this happen again? Why will we let it happen again? What can be done to prevent Collective Amnesia?

Luath Press Limited
committed to publishing well written books worth reading

LUATH PRESS takes its name from Robert Burns, whose little collie Luath (Gael, swift or nimble) tripped up Jean Armour at a wedding and gave him the chance to speak to the woman who was to be his wife and the abiding love of his life. Burns called one of 'The Twa Dogs' Luath after Cuchullin's hunting dog in Ossian's *Fingal*. Luath Press was established in 1981 in the heart of Burns country, and is now based a few steps up the road from Burns' first lodgings on Edinburgh's Royal Mile.

Luath offers you distinctive writing with a hint of unexpected pleasures.

Most bookshops in the UK, the US, Canada, Australia, New Zealand and parts of Europe either carry our books in stock or can order them for you. To order direct from us, please send a £sterling cheque, postal order, international money order or your credit card details (number, address of cardholder and expiry date) to us at the address below. Please add post and packing as follows: UK – £1.00 per delivery address; overseas surface mail – £2.50 per delivery address; overseas airmail – £3.50 for the first book to each delivery address, plus £1.00 for each additional book by airmail to the same address. If your order is a gift, we will happily enclose your card or message at no extra charge.

Luath Press Limited
543/2 Castlehill
The Royal Mile
Edinburgh EH1 2ND
Scotland
Telephone: 0131 225 4326 (24 hours)
Fax: 0131 225 4324
email: sales@luath.co.uk
Website: www.luath.co.uk

Some other books published by **LUATH** PRESS

The Ultimate Guide to Being Scottish
Clark McGinn
ISBN 1 906307 81 4 PBK £8.99

A sweep of quite enormous cultural and historical dimensions... a bit like letting King Herod loose in the maternity ward... utterly engaging.
From the foreword by
Charles Kennedy, MP

Essential reading for Scots everywhere, and for non-Scots with Scottish spouses, lovers, colleagues, friends or foes.

Clark McGinn knows all about the pride that glints in the eyes of those with even a small percentage of tartan in the blood. But what exactly puts it there, and how do you know whether you're a true Scot at heart (if not under your kilt)? And above all, how do you get a share in the action even if you're not a Scot?

This lighthearted yet thoroughly researched book examines the great things about being Scottish: Hogmanay, Burns Night, Up Helly Aa, the Edinburgh Fringe Festival, Hallowe'en and (the only one not celebrated in Scotland) Tartan Day – and getting the most out of the big Scottish party occasions.

- Ceilidhs, Highland dancing and The Royal Caledonian Ball – how to put your best foot forward
- The National Spirit – the history of whisky
- Munros, monuments and midges – how to survive the great Scottish countryside
- ... and a great deal else, from a potted history of Scotia's monarchs to deep-fried Mars bars to the bits of Auld Lang Syne nobody can remember.

The Ultimate Burns Supper Book
Clark McGinn
ISBN 1 906817 50 2 PBK £7.99

Everything you need to enjoy or arrange a Burns Supper – whether as host, speaker or guest, this book is full of advice, anecdotes, poetry and wit – just add food, drink and friends.

Clark McGinn, one of the foremost Burns Supper speakers in the world, presents *The Ultimate Burns Supper Book* which includes:

- A complete run through of what to expect on the night, with a list of courses and speeches
- Advice on what to wear
- A section on how to prepare and present speeches
- A list of common Burns Supper questions (and their answers!)
- A selection of Burns's greatest poems, including a full English verse translation of the 'Address to a Haggis'
- Answers your concerns about eating haggis and extols the pleasures of drinking whisky

Details of these and other books published by Luath Press can be found at: **www.luath.co.uk**